Home
Buying & Selling
Manual

Published in February 2009

British Library Cataloguing in Publication Data:
A catalogue record for this book is available
from the British Library

ISBN 978 1 84425 535 1

Published by Haynes Publishing,
Sparkford, Yeovil, Somerset BA22 7JJ, UK
Tel: 01963 442030 Fax: 01963 440001
Int. tel: +44 1963 442030 Int. fax: +44 1963 440001
E-mail: sales@haynes.co.uk
Website: www.haynes.co.uk

Haynes North America Inc.
861 Lawrence Drive, Newbury Park, California 91320, USA

Printed and bound in Great Britain
by J. H. Haynes & Co. Ltd, Sparkford

Acknowledgements

SPECIAL THANKS TO
Bernard Braun of Browns Solicitors in Aylesbury,
Graeme McCormick, Solicitor and Managing
Partner of Conveyancing Direct in Glasgow,
Jonathan Mortimer and all the staff at
Mortimers Estate Agents in Aylesbury,
John Ovens of Lightfoots Solicitors in Thame.

PHOTOGRAPHY
The author, except where credited

THANKS ALSO TO
Ian MacMillan FRICS
David Hodges Partner, Browns Solicitors
Richard Palmer MRICS
Darrell C Litchfield at JNP Estate Agents
Lyndsey Daykin at Pickfords Removals

Home
Buying & Selling
Manual

Ian Alistair Rock MRICS

CONTENTS

INTRODUCTION

When was the last time someone told you 'We moved house and it went like dream'?

The fact is, you have more consumer protection buying a Mars bar than a house. And with one in every three transactions likely to end in failure, it's essential to take control, both of your sale and purchase, to be sure of success.

It is often claimed that buying and selling property brings out the worst in people; if true, this is hardly surprising. One of life's rich ironies is that our property-mad nation is afflicted with one of the most frustrating and cumbersome home-buying systems ever devised. Even the widely acclaimed Scottish system has its drawbacks.

Today the UK property market is rapidly changing. The 'credit crunch' has made it more important than ever for home-owners to reap the benefits of new technology. Internet listings, online estate agents, HIPs and e-conveyancing are all starting to revolutionise the way houses are bought and sold.

The good news is that market downturns have always presented big opportunities, and there are rich pickings for those who know how to steer a course through the home-buying jungle.

Whether you're buying, selling or both, this Haynes step-by-step guide shows how to successfully manage each stage – just like a building project. It is divided into three clear sections: Part 1 explains how the housing market works, and shows how to get started by picking the right solicitor, Part 2 focuses exclusively on your sale, and Part 3 on your purchase, making it easy for you to look up each step of the process and check what should be happening. At each stage we list the problems that can arise and provide tried and tested solutions. Part 3 also explores the logistical challenges of moving house and, having reached the winning post, how to make money by refurbishing and investing for the future. Throughout the book, professional tips and unbiased advice show how you can save money, and avoid the many nasty traps that await the unwary.

On average, people in Britain move house 3.4 times during their lifetime. But whether you're a first-time buyer or have dealt in property over many years, each transaction has the potential

to blow up in your face and collapse in failure. So this manual aims to explain the whole process in plain English – for example, the word 'seller' is used rather than 'vendor'. Even so, the home buying and selling system is a bit like a gearbox – until you take it apart and realisé how many complex moving parts there are that can all potentially go wrong, you may blissfully assume that everything will invariably run smoothly! But by understanding how it all works you can take control and successfully manage

your sale and purchase; and by staying focused you can get the property you really want with the minimum of stress.

WEBSITE
For further information and
useful links visit
www.home-moving.co.uk

SOLICITORS & CONVEYANCING
MORTGAGE LENDERS

SURVEYOR
ESTATE AG

PART 1

GETTING STARTED

VALUERS

ITS

1 | THE PROPERTY MARKET

If you plan to buy or sell a property, you have no choice but to navigate some highly treacherous waters. Although there are plenty of 'property experts' out there willing to help you, most are primarily focused on lining their own pockets. So to achieve a successful transaction you either have to be lucky, or know exactly what you are doing. Preferably both.

Above: Fashionable rental properties in Georgian Bath

Left: Warding off ill-fortune – not all estate agents offer this service

Getting to know the system

As everyone knows, the home-buying system in England and Wales is horribly inefficient and stressful. The big problem is that either party can pull out for any reason, and at any time, until contracts have been exchanged. Even in reasonably buoyant conditions, most properties sit around on the market for a month or two before a buyer is found. It can then take three or four further months on average between an offer being accepted and safely reaching exchange of contracts. This is twice as long as in many other Western countries. But the really scary statistic is this: *more than a third of all agreed sales fall through*, never making it as far as exchange, leaving buyers nursing ruinous bills for abortive legal work, mortgages and surveys. Of course, the longer the process drags on the more chance there is of someone changing their mind or something going wrong. But by understanding the process you can solve problems before they cause trouble, thereby speeding things up and giving yourself the best chance of success. So before getting started it's worth taking a look at the big picture – is the market with you or against you?

Bricks and mortar

If you travelled back in time to Victorian Britain you would find very few people who owned their own homes. Renting was very much the order of the day for the vast majority, be they rich or poor. The British love affair with home ownership only really kicked off in the 1930s when a major building boom, combined for the first time with plentiful Building Society mortgages, allowed mass home ownership.

Today, renting is still very popular in much of mainland Europe. In Germany owner-occupation remains below 50 per cent, and there's a vibrant private rented sector. The great attraction is that renting doesn't pin you down and cramp your lifestyle. Signing a tenancy agreement allows you flexibility, with the freedom to move house easily and cheaply. Plus you can actually have a life, without becoming a penniless slave to a lifetime of crippling mortgage repayments.

However, there is one overriding argument in favour of home ownership. If you choose to rent for 25 years you will end up with precisely nothing at the end of it. But by purchasing the same property and paying off the mortgage you will own a sizeable chunk of real estate, a tax-free capital gain. You will also have more control, without a landlord able to boot you out with only a couple of months' notice. And not least, you have complete freedom to decorate and furnish your home entirely to your own taste, keep smelly pets, or smoke yourself silly without anyone objecting.

UK home ownership now exceeds 75 per cent – higher than any other European country. Even with the downturn in the market, you don't have to look far to explain the huge appeal of bricks and mortar. Property prices tripled between 1996 and 2007 and, despite the subsequent crash, are likely to show substantial increases again in the future. But there's more to it than making tax-free big bucks. Dabbling in property affords an opportunity to express creativity and design flair, modifying decor and room layouts to your heart's content. It can also act as your piggy bank for old age, providing control over a self-invested personal pension.

The media

The ongoing state of the property market has become something of a national media obsession. If we're to believe what we read in the papers, at any one time the property market is either spinning crazily into orbit propelled by the mother of all booms, or else house prices are plunging suicidally off a precipice. You rarely see a headline announcing 'Property Market Steady'. In an upturn the media pronounce an 'affordability' crisis, and in a downturn a 'negative equity' crisis. Neither is actually a crisis, but both involve winners and losers. In an upturn, rising house prices allow home-owners to remortgage and use some of the increased value of their homes for spending and investing, keeping the economy going. In a downturn, falling values should allow more first-time buyers to take a step onto the housing ladder.

Such sensationalist reporting only perpetuates the tendency amongst buyers to all plunge in together when the market's buoyant, thereby boosting demand further and causing prices to rise ever higher. Conversely, if potential buyers hold back at the first hint of prices dropping, it can only encourage market prices to fall further.

There are two main ingredients to a stable or growing market: buyer confidence and availability of funding. In recent years cheap and easy credit has fed booming demand. Media tales of fabulous and easy profits encouraged many to speculate indiscriminately. But, like a perilous jungle rope-bridge, held up by City bonuses at the top end and buy-to-let investors at the bottom, it couldn't last.

The market

Markets exert a strange psychological power. In the good times we somehow kid ourselves that booming prices will continue unabated forever, and our investments are as safe as 'bricks and mortar'. Conversely during the long years of a downturn, trying to stay afloat amidst a sea of repossessions, it seems plain that investing in property is a mug's game.

Markets run in cycles. They always have, and always will, despite the Canute-like boasts of egocentric politicians foolishly claiming to have vanquished the tides of boom and bust. Even within the space of a typical year demand is subject to mini cycles, with the market busiest in the spring or autumn when the largest number of buyers are active. The housing market constantly fluctuates and the ups and downs present opportunities. The easiest way to make money in any market is to buy and sell at the right time. Sounds easy doesn't it? But even the experts consistently fail to spot the peaks and troughs, so what chance do the rest of us have of pinpointing the 'right time'? Professional investors accept this imperfection, reconciled to the virtual inevitability of 'selling too soon and buying too late'. But by keeping an ear to the ground it should still be possible to reap most of the rewards of an upswing and dodge the worst of a downturn. History has a tendency to repeat itself, so to get a feel for future trends; it's worth taking a glance back in time.

The good times, 1996–2007

One of the great mysteries posed by TV property shows in recent years was how some of the people featured carrying out property development could make all the mistakes in the book and yet still walk away clutching several years' salary in profit. The answer, of course, was that most if not all of the profit was actually down to soaring house prices.

From 1996 to 2007 the average house price tripled, massively outstripping incomes (wages only grew by 63 per cent). Although this caused affordability to slump, lower mortgage rates softened the blow. Of course, hindsight is a wonderful thing. Being wise after the event, it always seems horribly clear how unsustainable the boom really was, whether you're looking back in time from the post-peak years of 1979, 1990 or 2008.

Year	Average house price	Yearly increase
1996	£66,094	7.4%
1997	£69,657	5.4%
1998	£73,286	5.2%
1999	£81,595	11.3%
2000	£86,095	5.5%
2001	£96,337	11.9%
2002	£121,137	25.7%
2003	£140,687	16.1%
2004	£161,742	15.0%
2005	£170,043	5.1%
2006	£187,250	10.1%
2007	£196,792	5.1%

Source: Halifax house price index

The bad times 1989–96

History repeats itself, so we may be able to learn something valuable from the last lot of 'bad times'. Prices peaked in early 1989. It then took until the first quarter of 1998 for the average house price to reach its former peak (plus at least another three years if you allow for inflation).

House prices will eventually return to their long-term average, but as in all markets, they tend to first overshoot and fall below this level. That is the 'right time' to buy.

Downturns are buyers' markets, with bargains galore. Sellers struggle as 'the best sells and the rest sticks'. Sellers of poorly maintained homes or those in scruffy neighbourhoods have to slash their prices if they want to find a buyer. Of course life goes on, and career moves and growing families mean people still have to sell, although

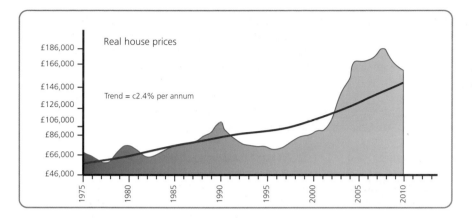

Real house prices

Trend = c2.4% per annum

£186,000
£166,000
£146,000
£126,000
£106,000
£86,000
£66,000
£46,000

1975 1980 1985 1990 1995 2000 2005 2010

Peaks and troughs – red line shows long term market trend

Source: extrapolated from Nationwide house price guide 2008

extensions and loft conversions become a popular alternative. But in the main, only those who are desperate will attempt to sell, perhaps because of one of the 'three Ds' – divorce, death or debt. Meanwhile buyers are thin on the ground, leaving predatory bargain hunters circling overhead.

Market recovery

The good news is that markets recover. As everyone knows, supply and demand ultimately dictate prices, and Britain is a small country with severe planning restrictions that hold back the supply of housing. This supply shortage contrasts with a growing population and high levels of immigration. And although house prices appear to be expensive in relation to incomes, interest rates are much lower than they were 20 years ago, making mortgage payments more affordable.

Property market recovery depends on a number of factors:

Rents increasing – In a depressed sales market, demand for property rental tends to increase, causing rents to rise. Investment returns therefore rise, especially if house prices also fall. Cuts in interest rates help property become more attractive for investors to start buying.

Wages catching up – In the long run, house prices rise in relation to incomes. Over time, increased wages and lower house prices mean improved affordability, leading to higher demand.

A growing economy with high employment – Low interest rates combined with acceptable levels of inflation should encourage a strong economy with high levels of employment, and money in people's pockets.

Confidence recovering – As prices stabilise or start to rise, profit-hungry banks regain the confidence to lend. Buyer confidence returns as the overall economy picks up, fuelled by the media reporting price rises and spotting 'up and coming' areas.

For those who've overindulged beyond their credit limit, a period of higher price inflation can work wonders by helping reduce such debts. As prices, wages and property values increase, mortgages and other debts stay at the same level, shrinking in relation to higher asset values. The snag is, higher inflation tends to mean higher interest rates and dearer mortgages.

2 | SELL FIRST OR BUY FIRST?

Having decided that you want to move house, the first question is where to begin. Should you start by going house hunting? Or should you first put your existing property on the market? Logically, it would make sense to take all the time you need to track down that perfect new home; then once you've found the place of your dreams, you can get down to disposing of the old one. After all, you wouldn't normally sell your old car before buying a new one, to ensure you're not marooned without transport.

Unfortunately, however, dealing in property isn't quite as simple as swapping motors. The problem with buying first is that as soon as you've found your fabulous new home, you have to very quickly sell your present house in order to release the money to pay for the new place, otherwise someone else could snap it up. And achieving a quick sale can mean having to slash your price – otherwise you could be stuck with two properties and two cripplingly expensive mortgages.

Estate agents know the risks of such a strategy and will not take you seriously as a buyer if you haven't already sold and are not 'in a position to proceed'. Even if the seller of the property you want to buy will accept your offer, they may insist on keeping it on the market so as not to miss out on a better offer from someone else who *is* capable of proceeding. With the best will in the world, it could take you ages to find a buyer for your house, and even if it's already under offer, the sale could drag on interminably or it could later fall through, causing you to lose the house you want to buy. In which case you'd be back to Square One, and all that time and effort house hunting would have been wasted.

But what about in a booming market with prices rising rapidly and even the grottiest properties being eagerly snapped up by dozens of competing buyers? When selling is so easy, surely it would make sense to buy first? Unfortunately, the problem then is that with stiff competition to buy the house you want, the person you're buying from, or their agent, will normally favour potential buyers who've already sold.

For these reasons, selling first is nearly always the better option. Indeed, more than 80 per cent of buyers sell their existing home (*ie* have it under offer) before attempting to buy the next one. But inevitably there's a downside to selling first. As soon as you've sold, you're immediately put under immense pressure to find a new property in a very short time. This means you risk paying over the odds, or buying a house that you don't really like out of sheer desperation – which rather defeats the point of moving in the first place.

Most people start by doing a fair amount of background research – getting a feel for different locations, and sounding out what's available, before they start viewing seriously. While your house is on the market waiting for a buyer, property listings and ads can be usefully investigated to refine the picture of what types of houses are within your price range. This can also be a good time to double-check your finances, bearing in mind that the average cost of selling a home won't leave much change from £5,000, while the average buyer pays nearly four times this amount.

So to get a clear run at your purchase, there's no doubt that selling first is the best strategy. But suppose you've already fallen in love with the home of your dreams and haven't begun to put your existing place on the market. What can you do?

Chains come in all shapes and sizes, but a full 'top to bottom' chain of five transactions might look something like this:

Chains

Unless you're a first-time buyer or a cash purchaser, one of the major challenges of moving house is trying to simultaneously co-ordinate the sale of your existing property with the purchase of another. This can be a tall order at the best of times, and is rather like trying to juggle balls in the air whilst riding a bicycle. As if that wasn't hard enough, the people you're selling to, as well as the people you're buying from, may also be struggling to balance their own sales and purchases. The net result is a highly unstable 'chain' of transactions, where one small slip anywhere along the line can bring the whole house of cards tumbling down. Your meticulously choreographed house move can be sabotaged because of a complete stranger's problems a million miles away. As one gob-smacked purchaser recently observed 'everything was set up for exchange of contracts, but then we were told that the person at the bottom of the chain didn't have funds to pay their deposit…'

Chains are the curse of estate agents and everyone else involved in the house buying process. At the bottom of the chain will normally be a first-time buyer or investor without a property to sell. At the top will be a seller who doesn't plan to buy another property, at least not immediately – perhaps someone of a ripe old age moving into a care home. Thankfully, most chains don't extend all the way from first-time buyers to 'last-time sellers' and may only involve two or three transactions, where the person at the top is either planning to rent for a while or perhaps buying a newly constructed property from a developer.

Alternatives – breaking the chain

In an ideal world, you'd be free to focus exclusively on one task at a time – your sale or your purchase. Trying to process two major transactions at the same time, one dependent on the other, massively increases the chances of failure, because if one hits the rocks it will normally drag the other one down with it (along with everyone else in the chain). It therefore makes sense to try and break this vicious cycle.

There are two main ways you can do this – either by going into rented accommodation for a short time between homes, or by taking out a 'bridging loan'. Both options involve extra expense, but will put you into a far better bargaining position, allowing you to hold out for a better price. Without the baggage of having a property to sell, you can really score as a buyer.

Let's rent
In the short-term, renting can be a very useful card to play to make the home-buying system work for you. At a stroke it can allow you to jump queues and negotiate big savings.

So even if you're allergic to the very concept of renting, a temporary arrangement may be worth a closer look.

Renting has other strategic uses. Before rushing into buying, renting locally can be a useful way of getting to know an area. Surveyors are often amazed at high prices paid by 'out-of-towners' buying new properties in parts of town known to locals as having a 'sub prime' reputation. The estate agent acting for the seller sure as hell isn't going to bend over backwards to point out the marauding nocturnal drug gangs and peak-hour gridlock!

Although renting is normally dearer than owning, if you plan to stay at a property for less than a couple of years it's usually cheaper to rent. This is because of the massive amounts of tax and fees you have to pay when moving house, typically totalling £10,000 to £20,000 in hard cash that may as well be flushed down the drain. One snag is that many rented properties are only available for fixed terms of six or twelve months at a time. To avoid the disruption of having to make any unnecessary further moves, you need to agree a long enough term at the outset. On the other hand, if you sign a contract for twelve months or longer, and need to move out after only three months, you'll still be liable for paying the rent for the full term, although it may be possible to negotiate a more flexible lease with the help of a solicitor.

'Moving into rented' can therefore be a handy solution if you want to exchange on your sale before committing to your purchase. But what if you want to do the exact opposite – to go ahead and buy your new house before having sold your existing home?

Bridging finance

If you're desperate to move, but the old place just isn't selling, or if your buyer suddenly announces they're pulling

out at the critical moment, arranging a bridging loan could save the day. It could also free you to negotiate a better price on the property you're buying, perhaps offsetting some of the costs of raising the extra funding. However, bridging normally involves owning two properties for a while, which may not be a bad thing in a rising market or if you can rent out one of them for a good price.

There are three types of bridging loan:

■ Closed loans

Theses are loans for a fixed but relatively short period of time. For example, having exchanged contracts on both your purchase and sale you would normally co-ordinate the completion dates so that the money from the sale of your old house is transferred to pay for the new one. But suppose that in order to prevent the chain from collapsing you have no option but to complete on your purchase a couple of weeks in advance of completing on your sale? Here, a short term bridging loan will provide the money to literally bridge the gap until you can complete the purchase. Banks regard this as a low risk loan and although they don't stand to make a huge profit, it should be fairly easy to arrange. It's often best to organise this via your mortgage lender (new or existing). The main drawback is the cost of arranging it, probably at an uncompetitive interest rate with all manner of nasty fees thrown in.

■ Open loans

As the name suggests, these are for an open-ended period of time. This can be useful in a boom market, where you may need to push hard to secure your new 'dream home' but haven't yet exchanged on your sale. There is clearly a certain amount of risk. Grave voices will be heard cautioning against such a foolhardy venture because you can't be certain how quickly your old house will sell, or whether you'll actually get as much as you expect for it.

Such a loan may be OK for a few months, but what if you're unlucky and your buyers pull out, causing the sale to fall through? Before you know it a couple of years might have flown by, during which time you will have to pay your new mortgage as well as a ruinously expensive loan. To cover themselves for such risks, banks tend to charge fairly exorbitant interest rates. Not surprisingly, open loans are also harder to arrange than the more predictable closed variety, although a number of lenders specialise in this part of the market. You might want to instead consider a buy-to-let mortgage as a more competitive alternative.

■ Buy-to-let (BTL)

If it looks like you're going to be in for the long haul, why not bite the bullet and become a landlord? One of the drawbacks with conventional bridging finance is that the bank may require you to pay off the current mortgage on your existing house before arranging any new loans. But

buying the new property with a BTL mortgage should allow you to keep your existing home and mortgage intact. Of course, this assumes you can raise at least 25 per cent of the purchase price in cash to meet the stricter BTL lending criteria. You could then rent out the new place (or perhaps the old house) until market conditions permitted an easier sale. Most BTL lenders will advance a maximum of 75 per cent of a property's value, and will also want to see projected rental income that more than covers the monthly interest payments, exceeding them by around 130 per cent. Of course, you'd need to factor in the costs and hassle of being a landlord or using a letting agent, and it's essential to first do your sums very carefully. Both open loans and BTLs are best avoided if the property market is likely to drop in the short term. (See Chapter 24.)

Auctions

There is a more direct way of getting around the problem of lengthy, slow-moving chains – selling at auction is quick and relatively easy. When the auctioneer's gavel falls, the deal is done, and buyers are legally committed to proceed. Of course, buyers at auctions are often in search of amazing bargains, but they sometimes forget that sellers are equally convinced they will achieve a great result, hoping that punters with more optimism than experience will succumb to 'auction fever' and wildly overbid. Properties are marketed with 'guide prices', supposedly an indication of the price the seller is hoping to achieve. In reality they are often pitched significantly below the likely final sale price to entice wide-eyed buyers. There will also

be a secret 'reserve price' which is the minimum the seller will accept. Although reserves are never disclosed, once the bidding exceeds this figure, the seller is then legally obliged to sell the property to the highest bidder. If it doesn't sell, buyers often make 'side-offers' afterwards.

However, in a weak market, achievable sale prices are likely to be low. (See 'Selling at auction', Chapter 9.)

Chain-breakers

One of the signs of a buoyant market is when firms with names like 'Chain-breakers' pop up offering to buy your property for cash, thereby freeing you to get on with your purchase. The downside is that the price they are prepared to pay will be at a significant discount to the property's true market value. Nevertheless, in some circumstances this may be worth exploring, for example if you've spotted an amazing bargain yourself, or to secure a unique once-in-a-lifetime property that you've set your heart set on. Achieving a lower price for your sale is OK if you make a similar or greater saving on your purchase. It's just rather galling when you see your old home being advertised a few weeks later at a far higher price than you've just sold it for.

Part-exchange

One attraction of buying a newbuild property is that developers may take your existing house in part-exchange – as long as you're trading up and buying a new property worth at least 25 per cent more. But check whether they pay 'market value', and how this is decided (*eg* the average of three surveyors' valuations).

Moving house in a market downturn

When the housing market weather is stormy, there's a lot that sellers can do to give their homes the best chance of selling. By making the right moves, you can leapfrog rival sellers, most of whom will be stunned into inaction and do nothing. In a slow market, where purchasers have the upper hand, there are still buyers around looking to spend money and properties are still being sold, but at a lower level than we've been used to in recent years.

Not so long ago, in periods of very strong demand, houses would virtually 'sell themselves', making easy money for estate agents, but perhaps also making us all a little lazy when it came to the two most important factors when selling a house – presentation and pricing. When selling was simple, we got used to focusing on the difficult part of the moving process – purchasing the next property. Now, in a slow market, the exact opposite holds true. Today it's the sale that demands special care and attention. Once that's all done, you should be able to look forward to a relatively easy purchase.

In Part 2 of this book we look in depth at how to manage your sale. In the meantime, here are some top tips for selling in a market downturn (each point is fully explored later in the book):

■ Focus only on your sale

Normally it's possible to synchronise your sale and purchase, so that you can step straight out of your old property into your new home. But in a downturn you need to grab every advantage you can. So for the time being, put your purchase on the back-burner. You now need to focus exclusively on your sale. This is likely to mean going into rented accommodation for a few months between selling and buying.

By taking this step, at a stroke you will boost the chances of a successful sale, because you can fit in with your buyer's agenda. It also means that if buyers muck you about, you won't be stressed-out about losing the place you're buying. By keeping it simple and doing one thing at a time, when it later comes to buying you should have the advantage of being able to negotiate an excellent deal without a chain.

■ Sell privately

In a quiet market there are fewer buyers out there, so you need to try harder to reach them. By all means appoint an estate agent, or more than one. But be wise to private selling opportunities. A lot of sellers don't realise that it is

perfectly legitimate to sell privately whilst your home is being simultaneously marketed by an estate agent. This means listing your home on the best private sellers' websites (see www.sellersnet.co.uk) as well as devising your own local marketing strategy. (See Chapter 9.)

■ Preparation and presentation

First impressions are vital because most buyers respond emotionally to a house within the first thirty seconds of arriving. It costs nothing to tidy up, so start with the front garden and the drive and give the front door a fresh lick of paint. Kitchens and bathrooms sell houses, so get cleaning and polishing. It needn't cost much to replace any obviously shabby stuff, perhaps just some new floor coverings and door handles. It's essential to clear out all the clutter, remove excessive numbers of ornaments, and be sure to clean the windows to make rooms look lighter and brighter. After clearing, cleaning and tidying, decoration is the next most cost-effective thing to do. It's true that tricking out rooms in neutral colours can make them

feel brighter and larger, which all helps add value. (See Chapter 10.)

■ Price it keenly

You need to attract the maximum number of buyers. A high price is not going to get people through the door. Buyers will still want to negotiate a chunk off the asking price, which itself needs to be competitive. The key thing to remember is that what you lose on your sale you should gain on your purchase. If you're trading up to a more expensive house,

negotiating the same percentage discount that you're accepting on your sale will be worth even more. So bite the bullet and price it keenly. If it still doesn't sell, it's probably too expensive. Take the house off the market for a couple of weeks before launching it with a new agent at a price at least five per cent lower. By dropping the price substantially you can suddenly appeal to a whole new level of buyers. To really grab the bull by the horns, instead of setting a conventional 'asking price', try putting it on at a 'guide price' pitched at the bottom end of your expectations. This technique is used at auctions to encourage competing bidders to push the price up. (See Chapter 9.)

■ Pick the best

When it comes to appointing an agent, make sure you select the best one for your type of property. A lot of the 'easy money' brigade who set up in the boom years don't know how to work a tough market to secure a sale. Look in their window to see if houses similar to yours are being advertised and ask yourself how impressive the overall presentation looks. It's also a good idea to check their local reputation, perhaps by contacting some of their other seller clients with the agent's boards up. (See 'Selecting the right agent', Chapter 8.)

These are some top tips, but there are many other things you can do to achieve a successful sale – see Part 2.

3 | THE ROLES OF THE MAIN PLAYERS

The estate agent, the mortgage lender, the surveyor and the solicitor

A lot of disputes in the house-buying process arise from misunderstandings about what the main players are actually supposed to do. Even experienced property people aren't always totally clear about this. So at this stage it's worth reminding ourselves what exactly, as paying customers, we should expect.

Estate agents

Surveys in the media routinely remind us that estate agents are about as popular as wheel-clampers, traffic wardens and MPs. But if it's really true that these are the people we love to hate, how come their opinions are so eagerly sought? And if estate agents are so reviled, how is it that in some branches, greetings cards from grateful customers adorn the walls? Rather than being some form of elaborate self-promotion, this may explain one of the key misunderstandings of the estate agent's role. As buyers, we often forget that agents are acting for the other side, with a duty to negotiate the best deal for their seller client, not the purchaser.

However, for a lot of folk one of the great mysteries of life is what exactly estate agents do for their money. Conventional wisdom has it that they stick a photo of your house in their shop window and make a couple of phone calls before proceeding to relieve you of several thousand quid. Certainly in a boom market, selling houses can be extremely lucrative and doesn't require huge skill or effort. But in today's market conditions, it can be a real slog. The 'no sale no fee' business model can mean a lot of effort for precious little reward. For junior negotiators earning commission-based salaries, this can be a poorly paid job that demands long hours. So to answer the question, let's take a brief look at the estate agent's main duties:

- To advise sellers on setting an asking price that will achieve a realistic sale price.
- Where necessary to order the Home Information Pack * (sellers may prefer to instruct this privately).
- To take professional photographs and write sales particulars, verifying them with the seller for accuracy.
- To arrange online listings on appropriate 'trade' websites.
- To post and email sales particulars to potential buyers, and follow up with phone calls.
- To vet potential buyers and assess whether they are genuinely in a position to proceed.
- To arrange and conduct accompanied viewings, and encourage viewers to make an offer.
- To provide feedback to clients.
- Where necessary to assist buyers with mortgage finance.*
- To negotiate on behalf of the seller to achieve the optimum sale price.
- To liaise with the buyer, seller, solicitors, surveyors, mortgage lenders and other parties in the chain to steer a successful course towards exchange of contracts and then completion.

*Fees or commission will normally be charged for these services.

Buckell & Ballard

RESIDENTIAL SALES + LETTINGS

TELEPHONE:
01844 213115

Contrary to popular opinion, in reality the job isn't without its frustrations. Agents need to tactfully dampen unrealistic price expectations harboured by owners of flea-infested hovels, and yet still win their business. They have to deal with a cross-section of the general public, including self-proclaimed 'cash buyers' who turn out not to have two pennies to rub together. Part of the job involves developing a sixth sense to filter out nosy, time-wasting viewers who have not the slightest intention of buying. Then there's the 'marriage-guidance' role, acting as peacekeepers desperately trying to hold together fragile chains as disgruntled buyers and sellers set about tearing each other's throats out. Add to the mix pedantic solicitors, 'Doctor Death' surveyors and the world's slowest home-buying system and, frankly, it's a wonder any sales ever get as far as completion.

Mortgage lenders

A mortgage is by far the biggest financial commitment most of us ever make. For banks and building societies charging interest on large sums of money over many years, safely secured against a valuable asset, can be a hugely profitable business. Better still, they know that home buyers can be very susceptible to being sold (or in some cases miss-sold) insurance and other lucrative financial products.

Traditionally, banks and building societies would recycle their customers' savings, lending them out in the form of mortgages and charging a higher interest rate than they paid; but since the late 1980s mortgage funds have increasingly been sourced from the international money markets, releasing a huge upsurge of finance to fuel demand for property. As everyone knows, excessive and irresponsible lending ultimately ended in tears. The ensuing sudden withdrawal of mortgage funding provoked a sharp downturn in the housing market, risking a downward spiral of defaulting and repossession. As a result, banks have since tightened up their lending procedures, albeit a little too late.

Before handing over the money, lenders now need to be sure that you are a good credit-risk, unlikely to vanish into thin air with shed-loads of their dosh. They need to be satisfied that you can afford the monthly repayments, and that if it came to the worst, your property could be repossessed and sold to get their money back, extracting some juicy fees along the way as compensation for their trouble in having to evict you.

Delays and problems with mortgage applications are one of the main causes of property deals collapsing. Tempting though it is to blame the banks, this is not always their fault. Job references, credit references and even wayward property valuations can all throw a spanner in the works. And of course, it helps greatly if applicants aren't tempted to be economical with the truth when completing the mortgage application form.

Surveyors

The role of the chartered surveyor is sometimes misunderstood. One major point of confusion relates to mortgage valuations. These are often mistakenly referred to as 'surveys', something buyers interpret to mean a cast-iron guarantee that nothing will ever go wrong with their property unless the surveyor has pointed it out on the form.

In actual fact, the purpose of a mortgage valuation is simply to advise the lender whether the property is suitable security for the loan, so should you later default and the property need to be repossessed, they know their money could be recouped. Many lenders deliberately restrict what the surveyor can say in such reports, so unless the property is visibly collapsing it's unlikely that even quite serious defects would be pointed out.

This misunderstanding may account for the fact that as many as 80 per cent of buyers traditionally haven't bothered to instruct a survey, instead relying on a second-hand 'courtesy copy' of the lender's mortgage valuation report.

However, things are now changing. Even these brief inspections are increasingly being ditched as lenders save money by relying on superficial 'drive-by' valuations or computer generated 'desktop valuations' which are simply educated guesses as to a property's market value.

For a true assessment on the condition of a property, it's necessary to instruct a proper survey – either a Homebuyer or a Building Survey. (See Chapters 11 and 21.)

Further scope for confusion arose with recent government attempts to introduce Home Condition Reports – short 'tick box' surveys paid for by the seller – as part of the Home Information Pack (HIP). Rather than being carried out by qualified chartered surveyors these reports could be produced by a new breed of 'home inspectors'. But the idea of a survey commissioned by sellers on their own properties was widely greeted with derision and mistrust and the requirement was later dropped, although sellers can still opt to pay for one if they wish.

Another recent arrival on the property inspection scene is the Energy Performance Certificate, which is the key part of the Home Information Pack. This is carried out by a 'Domestic Energy Assessor' when the property is put on the market and is paid for by the seller (as part of the HIP). This involves an inspection of the house to determine how thermally efficient it is, ultimately issuing an energy rating labelling the house somewhere between A (good) and G (could do better).

Domestic Energy Assessors are not usually qualified surveyors, but have an appropriate energy-related qualification. They record key information about the house, such as the thickness of the walls, and type of heating system, which then enables the 'SAP' software to churn out a suitable energy rating. It will also offer advice on how this can be improved, for example by insulating the loft. Despite grandiose government claims to the contrary, for most home buyers a property's energy performance comes somewhere near the bottom of the list.

Solicitors

If it's perfectly possible to sell a car in an afternoon, how come selling a house can take several months? The simple answer is that it's the sheer complexity of the commodity being bought and sold – land and property – that's so often to blame for the delays that bedevil the home-buying process. What appears to be a bog standard house can potentially mask all manner of legal horrors. And because buying property is very much a case of *caveat emptor*, or 'buyer beware', rushing headlong into a purchase can leave buyers badly stung in all kinds of embarrassing places. As a result, extreme caution is warranted.

Much of the delay often comes from the buyer's side whilst extensive searches and enquiries are carried out to prove that all is genuinely as it seems. Then there is the problem of the 'chain' of linked transactions when

several people all try to complete their sales and purchases on the same day. The result is that, like a wartime shipping convoy, the chain can only move at the pace of its slowest member. Despite such complexities, it's perfectly possible for this same system to be given a kick up the backside and made considerably quicker. At auctions, when sellers really get their act together and where buyers are motivated to make a swift commitment, deals can be struck in the space of a few hours (albeit after a couple of weeks' preparation).

The legal process of transferring ownership of property, known as 'conveyancing', is at the heart of every sale or purchase. This is normally handled by solicitors or licensed conveyancers, although it's possible to do your own conveyancing (except this is not always advisable – see next chapter).

In most cases your solicitor will be handling your sale as well as your purchase, whilst simultaneously acting for your mortgage lender. The job of the buyer's solicitor is essentially to safeguard their client's interests, for example by checking that no one else has legal rights over the property, such as footpaths across the garden or former spouses with a lawful right to remain in occupation. They will also check there are no outstanding loans secured against it, and that the local

council have no plans to turn the quiet residential street into a super casino or dual carriageway. Title documents are checked to confirm that the owner really is the genuine owner, and the property's planning history is investigated by carrying out searches to check that any extensions weren't built illegally. For leasehold properties, assessing the terms of the lease adds a whole extra dimension of complexity. Ultimately, once the terms of the draft contract are agreed, contracts can be exchanged and the purchase completed shortly afterwards.

The job of the seller's solicitor is more straightforward, but is pivotal to a smooth and successful sale. Their role is essentially to draw up and refine the draft contract and assist in providing the buyer's solicitor with the necessary information to facilitate the sale, answer various questions about the property, and ultimately to obtain the purchase money.

We look at the role of your legal adviser in detail in the next chapter. Then each stage is further explained in Part 2 *Selling* and Part 3 *Buying*.

Below is an outline of the traditional legal process. Modern practice and the advent of the Home Information Pack has tended to condense these steps so that they can be dealt with as early as possible in the transaction:

Seller's solicitor	Buyer's solicitor
■ Orders 'office copy entries' or obtains the title deeds for the property being sold, to prove ownership ■ Prepares draft contract, and sends to buyer's solicitor ■ Answers 'preliminary enquiries' ■ Prepares final 'engrossed' contract ■ Arranges for seller to sign contract ■ Receives deposit money	■ Receives and checks the draft contract prepared by the seller's solicitor ■ Sends 'preliminary enquiries' to seller's solicitor ■ Sends a local search to the Council and submits other relevant searches ■ Checks the title with the Land Registry ■ Checks the mortgage offer received from the lender ■ Arranges for buyer to sign the contracts
Exchanges contracts	**Exchanges contracts**
■ Sends evidence of title to buyer's solicitor ■ Arranges for seller to sign the final conveyance document ■ Completion: receives balance of purchase price and hands over the title deeds ■ Pays off seller's old mortgage	■ Checks seller's title ■ Arranges bankruptcy search and land charges or Land Registry search ■ Prepares mortgage deed ■ Prepares draft conveyance/transfer document ■ Arranges for buyer to sign the mortgage deed and the final conveyance/transfer document ■ Collects stamp duty tax, other fees and mortgage funds ■ Completion: pays the balance of the purchase price to the seller's solicitor ■ Applies to the Land Registry to register the transfer and the new mortgage

4 | SELECTING YOUR SOLICITOR

There are many reasons why property sales and purchases fall apart. But amidst the wreckage of collapsed transactions two particular complaints are frequently overheard. The first regards over-optimistic buyers not getting the mortgage that they'd assumed was possible. The second allegation relates to solicitors employing painfully slow Dickensian working practices.

As a profession, solicitors have traditionally enjoyed something of a reputation in the popular imagination for being cobweb-encrusted fogies whose main skill lies in knowing how to charge. Of course, this is grossly unfair to the many who pride themselves on providing an efficient service. But although solicitors may no longer write with quill pens on parchment there remains a popular perception that some

have been reluctant to embrace the benefits of modern technology. Fortunately times are now rapidly changing.

In a normal property market, it commonly takes around 12 weeks between an offer being accepted and exchange of contracts. One common cause of delay is buyers and sellers being slow to return documents. Nonetheless, picking the right person to do your conveyancing will be a major factor in ensuring success. In most cases it makes sense to use the same solicitor for your sale and purchase, so before looking at what's specifically involved in selling your existing property and buying a new home (covered in Parts 2 and 3), let's take a look at one of the first big decisions that needs to be made.

Solicitor, property lawyer or licensed conveyancer?

Conveyancing is the legal process of transferring the ownership of property, but a number of different words are bandied about to describe the people who perform this service. You don't want to end up with some unqualified numbskull in charge of your most important asset, so let's see who exactly is the best person to undertake this key task.

Until 1987 you could only appoint a solicitor to handle the legal side of a property sale or purchase. Today, the main alternative is a *licensed conveyancer*, a lawyer specifically trained in property law (but not qualified as a solicitor or barrister). Regulated by the Council for Licensed Conveyancers, these guys are legally authorised to carry out property transactions in England and Wales, and tend to offer fairly competitive prices. But in terms of numbers, licensed conveyancers are relatively thin on the ground, with less than 1,000 in the UK compared to more than 38,000 lawyers.

Just to confuse matters, another term you sometimes encounter is *property lawyer*. The word 'lawyer' is a general term for any qualified law professional. *Solicitors* are one type of lawyer, but not all solicitors specialise in property law or can do conveyancing, so the term *property lawyer* describes anyone who specialises in, and is qualified to practise, property law. Perhaps because it sounds more impressive than 'licensed conveyancer', firms offering online conveyancing services on the Internet tend to use this term.

Finally, *legal adviser* is a catch-all term for anyone dispensing legal advice. However, to keep it simple, for the purposes of this book we stick mainly to the words 'solicitor' or 'conveyancer'.

In reality much of the actual administrative work involved in the transfer of property may be undertaken by someone working in the office without a licence, under the supervision of a solicitor or licensed conveyancer.

Choosing the right firm

It's a good idea to choose your conveyancer as early as possible, before you put your house on the market or start viewing new houses.

A good solicitor will make your sale and purchase quicker and less stressful and will minimise the chances of collapse. They will also do you the courtesy of communicating, so if your move does ultimately go pear-shaped at least you will have the consolation of knowing why.

Conversely, by unnecessarily dragging out the process for months on end an inefficient conveyancer can invite disaster. Or if they miss something important there could be a hidden legal time bomb that only detonates when you eventually decide to sell.

Appointing someone who specialises in conveyancing is always going to be a better option than instructing an eminent QC who may be able to pontificate with supreme eloquence in court, but has little experience of residential property. Lack of experience and overwork are often the cause of costly legal mistakes, such as failing to check documentation, which can in turn lead to last-minute crises and deals collapsing.

Should problems arise, someone who does conveyancing all the time should have the right experience to work around them, having handled similar issues in the past. Critically, they will also be able to apply sound judgement, knowing when not to jeopardise your deal by pedantically delaying the process due to some very minor discrepancy in ancient documentation.

So who exactly should you choose? The days of going straight to the family solicitor are long gone. Even the AA and Tesco offer conveyancing services nowadays.

Most large chains of estate agents also offer an in-house conveyancing service. The good thing about this arrangement is that it tends to be geared to speeding up the transaction, for example by standardising enquiries where possible. Staff at corporate estate agents are normally under strict instructions to heartily recommend their own conveyancers, but if you catch them in an 'honest moment' they may not always be quite so enamoured. What is sometimes

A typical 'legal quarter' in town, the traditional location for solicitors' chambers

gained from streamlining the system may be lost as a result of silly errors by inexperienced staff – plus the price may not actually be as competitive as you might imagine.

Estate agents and mortgage brokers do, however, tend to have a pretty good idea of which solicitors have a reputation for creating problems, and which are efficient and conducive to a successful transaction. After all, they deal with them virtually daily and their income depends on property deals successfully reaching completion. But a word of warning. A practice has now developed whereby solicitors and conveyancers pay referral fees for the introduction of business to them. Although they should disclose this to you, it's advisable to check whether a generous referral fee is the real reason for their warm recommendation.

As a rule, it's best to avoid swanky firms of City solicitors in prime locations. A very expensive solicitor isn't necessarily better. Indeed, with a big firm your low-priority job may end up at the bottom of the pile. A smaller practice specialising in conveyancing may produce much better results. Alternatively, a good compromise between estate agency conveyancers and the small traditional country partnership can be the 'express conveyancing' service offered by some larger specialist firms.

There are now dozens of websites offering low-cost, fixed-price online conveyancing, promising a faster and cheaper service than traditional High Street firms. If one has been recommended it could be worth considering, but it's important to ensure that you can phone or email and discuss your case at any time. You don't have to use a local firm, although it can make all the difference later, saving precious time by dropping urgent documents in and popping round personally to sign contracts. A good local firm may also be better able to surmount local difficulties that might arise, and should know about planning restrictions in the area, having dealt with the same local councils on many previous occasions.

Poor communication is a complaint commonly levelled at solicitors. To be fair, this reputation stems partly from the need for client confidentiality, and partly reflects a desire to not be confronted by crowds of angry people stuck in a long chain all baying for blood. It's not just that it's unethical for one solicitor to speak to the client of another solicitor – they are simply not permitted to do so, which can sometimes be immensely frustrating from the client's viewpoint. However, a good estate agent should be able to liaise with all the various parties, to smooth ruffled feathers and find out why things are moving so slowly.

Lenders' panels

Most people require a solicitor to handle their purchase as well as their sale (see Part 3). If you're buying as well as selling and, like most of us, require a mortgage, your lender will also need a solicitor to register their interest in the property (which will be the security for their loan). So it makes sense to appoint a single firm to simultaneously act for you and your lender, otherwise you'd very likely get lumbered with paying the additional cost of the your bank's legal fees (plus it would add more complexity and delay to the whole process). So before instructing a solicitor it's important to check whether they're on the 'panel' for your mortgage lender. At this early stage you may not yet have decided which bank or building society you'll be using, in which case check that the solicitor is able to act for all major High Street lenders.

To avoid a 'conflict of interest' you are not allowed to appoint the same solicitor as the seller. If it turns out that you *do* have the same one, and you don't want to use another firm, you can always switch to another partner in the same organisation.

Getting quotes

Some online conveyancing services offer 'fixed-price' fees. But to be sure you're getting the correct price for the type

of property, it's best to phone for a quote. You will be asked a number of basic questions, typically the address, the agreed price, whether you want them to handle your sale as well as your purchase, and whether they will also be instructed by your mortgage lender to do their legal work. Charges are higher in the rare cases where a property is 'unregistered' or for leasehold properties such as flats and maisonettes. Be sure to check the quote, because an apparently cheap price can mask all manner of hidden extras, such as additional fees to transfer money or discharge a mortgage etc.

It can be a mistake to make your choice on the basis of price alone. A cheap conveyancer can prove expensive in the long run. Some are notorious for not starting work in earnest until as late in the process as possible. They know that if a transaction is going to fall through it's more likely to happen in the early stages, and they won't want to work for nothing. But by dawdling, both your sale and your purchase could be put in jeopardy. If you pick the cheapest, most of the work will probably be done by an unqualified assistant, or very little time will be apportioned to handle your case. This could result in carelessness and missed details causing last-minute panics, and you may have difficulty getting hold of them when you need to make contact.

Quotes for sale of a property are relatively straightforward, with the average cost of conveyancing for sellers coming in below £600. Quotes for a purchase, on the other hand, can obscure a multitude of charges.

Conveyancing quote – purchase	
Property price	£560,000.00
Subject to a mortgage	Yes
Tenure of property	Freehold
Registered	Yes
Fees	
For the purchase of a property	£750.00
VAT	£126.87
Total fees	**£851.87**
Payments made to third parties on your behalf	
Stamp Duty Land Tax	£22,400.00
Land charge fee, HM Land Registry	£420.00
Land Registry search	£8.00
Local Authority search fee (estimate)	£120.00
Drainage search fee (estimate)	£45.00
Environmental search fee	£30.00
Electronic transfer fee	£35.25
Bankruptcy search fee	£4.00
Total payments to third parties	**£23,071.25**
Fees plus payments to third parties	**£23,923.12**

Solicitors' fees are usually related to the price of the property. However, it's a sobering fact that the amount wasted on conveyancing each year, on transactions that don't complete, is estimated at a mind-boggling £98 million. With this in mind, it might be worth arranging a 'no sale no charge' deal. But bear in mind that firms may then need to reduce their risk by delaying searches etc, which could do you no favours in the long run.

Because flats are leasehold, which involves extra work, there will be an additional charge for these. Leases can be especially troublesome. Buyers sometimes pull out because their solicitor has spotted a 'defect in the lease'. Some mistakes may go right back to the original date of faulty drafting, but if they're spotted in time most such issues can be overcome. This may involve paying for an indemnity insurance policy, or arranging for a 'deed of variation' – permission to change a clause in a lease. In the case of flats, this latter solution means having to contact the freeholder, who may want to charge handsomely for the privilege, or if you're really unlucky may turn out to be an obscure organisation in a far-flung corner of the globe. (See Chapter 17.)

Happily, most properties are freehold and the overwhelming majority are registered, and so should not pose too many problems. Occasionally, however, a complex case can arise with issues such as rights of way, access, maintenance liabilities, separate 'non-contiguous' garden plots, and all kinds of odd restrictions with potentially negative effects on value.

Instructing a solicitor

Apart from being clear about exactly what's included in the price and what isn't, you need to be sure that the firm you're dealing with are experts at conveyancing and don't just dabble when crime and negligence claims are quiet. So ask whether they specialise in residential conveyancing, and who exactly will be handling your job. A few diehard traditional firms still insist on writing formal letters, are not contactable by email, and have partners who disappear to enjoy long lunches and rounds of golf on Friday afternoons. Not what you need when there's a last-minute crisis to resolve!

To start the ball rolling you will have to provide proof of identity and address, to comply with money laundering regulations. The usual drill applies, necessitating fishing out your passport and/or driving licence, along with a selection of utility bills and your current mortgage lender's details.

DIY conveyancing

Once upon a time, solicitors were the only people permitted to transfer property, which made it impossible to buy or sell a house without employing a legal professional. However, this is no longer essential. DIY conveyancing is an option for anyone with their wits about them, with an aptitude for the law, and a fair amount of spare time.

In many cases, conveyancing isn't as complex as it's sometimes made out to be. Much of the job involves asking the right people for information and processing standardised forms and enquiries. The amount of

conveyancing work involved in a typical sale is usually considerably less than for a purchase, so if you're not buying a property at the same time, handling the conveyancing on your own sale can make sense. The attraction is that you can save some of the cost of paying legal fees and also speed things up – by moving faster and replying to requests from the other side's solicitor quicker.

However, in reality there are a number of reasons why it normally isn't worth going to the trouble of doing your own conveyancing, not least because the system is stacked against you:

- You may not actually save much money. Mortgage lenders usually allow the buyer's solicitor to cover their legal work, as there's a fair amount of duplication. However, they won't permit a non-qualified person to do it, and will instead appoint their own legal adviser to protect their interests – at your expense. Unless it's a legal fees-free mortgage, you could get stuck with the extra cost of paying for a separate solicitor to act for the lender, thereby reducing the potential savings from DIY conveyancing.

- Since the advent of HIPs, some of the initial legal work is already paid for by the seller, again reducing potential savings.

- By shopping around, you should be able to obtain some pretty competitive quotes for conveyancing work. Remember that by far the biggest legal expense on your purchase will be tax and fees for searches etc, not conveyancing fees.

- Part of the job involves interpreting searches and replies – for which it helps to have experience. DIY conveyancing is not recommended for more complex transactions, such as those where properties are leasehold, or where the title is not registered (see Chapter 22). But the real killer is that, should you inadvertently miss something, you could be stuck with a property that's worth a lot less when you eventually come to sell. If, on the other hand, your solicitor is negligent, at least you should be able to claim compensation for any loss.

- Rather than seeing this as a sign of your commitment, an estate agent could be rather lukewarm about your offer to their client, the seller. Plus it's not impossible that other solicitors in the chain may close ranks against an 'outsider', perhaps by adopting unnecessarily arcane language.

- If you're a buyer and the seller happens to be doing their own conveyancing, it's best not to do so as well. If both parties on the same transaction are inexperienced there's a far greater risk of legal problems arising. As well as missing something, there's the possibility of overreacting to commonplace and acceptable risks.

Having said all that, in some situations it may still be worth giving DIY conveyancing a shot – such as where there's no mortgage or where you are selling without buying. But be sure to take advantage of the other side's solicitor's knowledge and experience, and if you don't understand something, raise it with them. But if you haven't got the spare time, it's probably best to leave it to the professionals.

> DIY conveyancing guides and printable Land Registry forms are available via the website, **www.home-moving.co.uk**. Other forms are available from HM Revenue & Customs, **www.hmrc.gov/so**. Most forms are also available from law stationers.

E-conveyancing

It seems that people have been complaining about the tortoise-like pace of conveyancing since the days when dinosaurs roamed the land. Now, at last, things appear to be evolving (albeit at a tortoise-like pace). With more than 21 million titles the Land Registry is the world's largest property database, and 'e-conveyancing' is currently being developed in a bid to simplify the whole process, using online registration of land with everything done electronically between computers. It is claimed that this will ultimately dispense with the need for lengthy searches. By 2010 the transfer of land ownership, removal of old mortgages from the register, and registration of new mortgages should all be possible over the Internet. This promises to make buying and selling property in England and Wales faster, easier and more secure than it is with today's largely paper-based system.

The benefits of e-conveyancing include:

- Documents safely signed electronically and delivered instantly.
- 'Data checking' permitting greater accuracy in deeds and forms.
- Applications for registration completed instantly.

Now this all sounds fine and dandy. But despite such grandiose claims some folk are a tad cynical. There have been any number of much-trumpeted billion-dollar government IT systems that promised the Earth and delivered very little (other than short-term chaos and rewards for failure, obviously). And given the Government's track record in looking after our private data, some might question the wisdom of making every last detail of our valuable homes available online. Indeed, the Land Registry website has recently taken action to restrict access to certain scanned documents such as mortgage deeds and leases. These are no longer available

to the public electronically, because of concerns about potential misuse. This may have something to do with the fact that in 2007 and 2008 the Land Registry paid out an incredible £12 million in compensation for fraud or forgery claims. At least it's reassuring to know that if you were to become a victim of fraud, there is a comprehensive compensation scheme in place.

One potential drawback with e-conveyancing is that it could make life harder for DIY conveyancers, who would need to attend a registry office or use a nominated terminal. However, the advent of a super-quick and largely paperless system is still a long-term objective – albeit one not expected to materialise for at least a decade or more, the original ambitious plans having been watered down. At least we now have 'e-registration', which is a step in the right direction, allowing for the delivery of electronic charges and discharges – in other words, electronic communication about mortgages between banks and the Land Registry. Another new innovation is 'e-transfers', allowing conveyancers to send in transfers electronically.

Let's hope it all comes off, but don't hold your breath. As already mentioned, the introduction of e-conveyancing is likely to take many years, and it will have to be introduced in phases.

5 | THE SCOTTISH SYSTEM

There's a general belief that the Scottish property system is far superior to the one that applies elsewhere in the UK. It's certainly the case that the process for buying and selling homes north of the border is radically different. Crucially, it provides far greater certainty once buyers' offers have been accepted, and because of the comparative speed of the process, the twin evils of gazumping and gazundering rarely occur. One of the more visible differences is that there are two types of estate agents in Scotland: 'solicitor estate agents' and conventional 'non-solicitor' agents. Whilst the latter operate in pretty much the same way as their counterparts down south, 'solicitor estate agents' as their name suggests perform the dual role of marketing properties and handling the conveyancing. In addition to carrying out their own marketing activities, most are members of *solicitor property centres*. These are 'property shops' where details of all the homes being sold through local solicitors are exhibited. In some areas such as Edinburgh and Aberdeen some 90 per cent of house sales go through solicitor property centres, whereas in other areas such as Glasgow sales are split roughly equally with conventional estate agencies.

Tenure and tenements

Another big difference with Scottish property is that it's freehold. This makes buying flats considerably easier, since there are no worries with complex leases slowing the process to a snail's pace. Instead, buyers enjoy outright ownership of their property. But whether it's a tenement flat or a house, ownership is subject to title conditions, known as 'burdens', which are generally enforceable by neighbours to protect amenity. With flats or tenements, communal areas like the stairs and hallways, as well as the building's foundations, roof, external walls and guttering are owned equitably by all the various co-owners in the block. Professional estate managers (known as 'factors') are often appointed by the co-owners to maintain the common parts and arrange an insurance policy for the block.

Before you buy

In Scotland making an offer on a property is a serious business. Unlike in the rest of Britain, once your offer's been formally accepted both parties are legally committed to the purchase. This means that a lot of the donkeywork involved in making the various checks and enquiries has to be done in advance – rather as you would when buying at auction.

The downside of this system has traditionally been that potential buyers risked incurring abortive fees for surveys, mortgages and legal work should their offer later be rejected. However, it is essential as a prospective purchaser to know how much you can afford before arranging viewings and, if possible obtain an 'agreement in principle' from your mortgage lender. Without this, you could risk finding yourself legally committed to buying a property without being able to come up with the money to proceed – and pulling out of a done-deal doesn't tend to go down well in *Taggart* country.

Noting interest and making an offer

When you spot a property you like, the person you need to contact first is your solicitor. They will then contact the seller's solicitor or estate agent on your behalf to formally 'note interest'. If there is more than one party interested in the property, the selling agent will invite all interested parties to submit written bids by a set closing date. If there is no other party interested then you have a free hand to make a written offer through your solicitor.

Although homes in Scotland are occasionally marketed at fixed prices, normally asking prices are set several thousand pounds less than the seller expects to achieve. This is in stark contrast to England & Wales where asking prices are normally set slightly above the anticipated sale price (except in rare cases where 'offers in excess' of the stated price are invited). So the challenge facing most prospective purchasers is how far to pitch their offer above the asking price. This is more of a problem in a buoyant market when you would expect to have to pay a significantly higher amount. Sometimes guide prices may be set at strategically low bargain basement levels in order to stimulate bidding – a technique used at auction. Fortunately, guidance should be close at hand from solicitors who have the appropriate knowledge to advise what price to offer. And of course there's plenty of free information online showing what other properties in the street have sold for.

Needless to say, making an offer can be considerably more nerve-wracking where there's competition to buy and bids have to be submitted by a set closing date. In such cases you only have one chance to offer and you won't know the quality of the bids that rival buyers make. The best advice is to do your sums carefully in advance and make the best bid you can afford. If you're successful, the amount others bid won't matter, and in any case it's not normally possible to find this out retrospectively.

Once you've decided how much you're willing to stump up to acquire the property, your offer will need to be made formally through your solicitor. Making a written offer can be something of a fishing expedition because in addition to the price you're prepared to pay, your offer will be subject to a number of conditions – such as any additional items included in the price and, crucially, the 'date of entry', which is the date the buyer proposes to pay the money in exchange for the keys and the title to their new home. Offers are also subject to certain reasonable assumptions, such as the seller actually being the true owner with 'good title' to sell, and there being no 'impediments', such as adverse planning or building control issues. Once your offer has been made, the seller usually has a period of 24 hours to get back to you and indicate their verbal acceptance. In most cases offers are also 'subject to survey' and buyers are expected to have the property surveyed and confirm the price within a further 48 hours. If the surveyor 'downvalues' the property or raises concerns about the building's

condition, buyers may seek to reduce the price, or arrange further detailed specialist reports, or they can simply walk away. Once an offer has been accepted, buyers should waste no time in submitting their mortgage application to the lender.

Surveys

As in the rest of Britain, rather than arrange a private survey, many buyers have traditionally just made do with a copy of the lender's mortgage valuation report - a cheaper but riskier option. But in 2008 a major change was introduced, with sellers now legally required to commission a 'Home Report' when putting their property on the market. Home Reports include a professional survey which is made available to all prospective purchasers. So each property now comes with its own survey.

A Home Report contains 3 parts:-
- A survey by a RICS surveyor showing the condition and providing a valuation.
- An energy report and Energy Performance Certificate (EPC), valid for 10 years or until resale of property.
- A property questionnaire completed by the seller, providing general information, such as parking arrangements and provision of cable TV services.

The Home Report differs from HIPS elsewhere in Britain which don't normally include a survey or a valuation. Although good news for buyers, this has obviously added to sellers' costs. However, there are doubts about whether mortgage lenders will accept them (since Home Reports are instructed and paid for by sellers), so in most cases a

separate mortgage valuation inspection will still be required. There are also concerns about their shelf-life and the cost and frequency of updating them.

Conveyancing

Once the purchase price has been agreed, and any necessary surveys carried out, the seller's solicitor should write back to confirm their *qualified acceptance* of the offer. Usually they will delete or amend some of the conditions attached to the offer and insert new ones, such as a requirement for the buyers to pay compensation for any breach of contract (e.g. should the buyer later pull out). At this juncture, the buyer's solicitor is normally allowed a further 7 days to respond and agree the new conditions. If the terms are acceptable to the buyer, and their mortgage funding has been confirmed, the buyer's solicitor will then issue a formal letter concluding the 'bargain'.

This process, from *exchange of offers* through to *qualified acceptance* and the *concluding letter*, is know as 'the Missives'. Together, the Missives form the legal contract, which will be binding on both parties. So the seller will now be legally obliged to sell and the purchaser obliged to buy in accordance with the terms and conditions contained in the Missives. These cannot now be varied, nor can one party withdraw without the agreement of the other, otherwise there is a breach of contract with severe financial consequences to the defaulter. However, should the buyer's solicitor uncover something seriously unsavoury and their enquiries produce adverse entries, buyers may still be permitted to withdraw from the Missives without penalty provided they do so within a short time frame of a few days. Nonetheless, it is the element of certainty that is one of the great strengths of the Scottish system, in dramatic contrast to proceedings south of the border where buyers and sellers remain free to gazump and gazunder to their heart's content or to back out of agreed deals on the slightest whim.

Bolstered by such commitment, the conveyancing process can now proceed at full tilt. The seller's solicitor will examine the title deeds, and obtain various search reports (at the seller's expense). The searches include a 'property enquiry certificate' which shows whether there are any planning proposals or repair notices affecting the property. The solicitors also check that any structural works for extensions etc have been lawfully carried out and any necessary 'building warrants' and completion certificates have been obtained. A search of the government property registers will confirm that the seller is in a position to complete the sale. The buyer's solicitors will also need to send their client a 'title report' confirming ownership of the property and alerting them to any restrictions and title conditions.

Once these enquiries have been carried out, assuming the purchaser's solicitor is happy to proceed, they will then draft a *'disposition'*. This is the document that will ultimately transfer ownership of the property to the buyer. When the details have been hammered out between the solicitors, the seller will need to sign it. The buyer's solicitors will normally also be acting for the mortgage lender, and will prepare the mortgage deed (known as the 'standard security') for signing by the purchaser. At this stage the purchaser will be asked to pay their solicitor the deposit money, along with the legal fees and other costs,

notably Stamp Duty (where applicable) and government 'land registration dues'.

The date of entry

The day before the agreed 'date of entry', the buyer's solicitor will draw down the mortgage funds, check the final search reports, and advise the buyer when and where to pick up the keys. The funds for the full purchase price will be transferred by *solicitor's cheque* delivered to the seller's solicitors (solicitors cheques are guaranteed by the Law Society of Scotland so normally there is no need to send funds by telegraphic transfer). In return, the seller's solicitor will send the signed *disposition* and title deeds to the purchaser's solicitor. On the date of entry, once the buyer has been advised by their solicitor that the sale has 'settled', they are free to collect the keys. Upon moving in, new owners should immediately advise their solicitors of any problems, for example if the heating is not working, otherwise they will lose their right to claim against the seller. This just leaves the buyer's solicitor with the task of registering the title deeds in the Land Register to confirm the new ownership.

PART 2

SELLING

6 | THE SALE PROCESS

The selling game

The stages you go through as a seller will run something like this, although not always in this precise order. If you're buying your next property at the same time, some stages will overlap, as shown in Part 3. All are all discussed in detail in the following chapters.

■ Getting your Home Information Pack (HIP)

One of the first tasks is to arrange your HIP, containing an energy report and key legal documents that will later be used by the purchaser's solicitor.

■ Appointing your conveyancer

It helps to have your legal team ready in good time – in case your property is snapped up by an eager buyer!

In most cases, the major obstacle to a successful move is the problem of first having to dispose of your existing property. Unless you live in rented accommodation or you're a first-time buyer or an investor, before you can get down to any serious house-hunting achieving a successful sale will be key to getting what you want.

Despite reassuring promises of a quick and easy sale from smooth-talking estate agents, selling a property means embarking on a major journey, littered with traps and potential pitfalls. So let's start by checking exactly what the sale process involves.

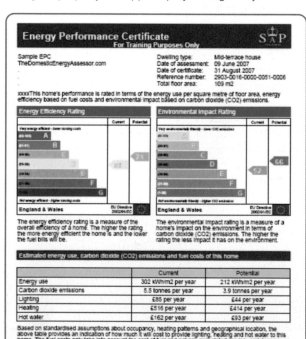

■ Putting it on the market
Having decided on an asking price, select a suitable estate agent and/or sell it privately.

■ Viewings
You or your agent act as tour guides, showing prospective buyers round the house.

■ Negotiating the sale
Sooner or later an offer is made, and it's down to you or your agent to negotiate the best price.

■ Conveyancing
The legal process of transferring ownership can now fully proceed. See below.

■ Valuations and surveys
Most buyers will need a mortgage and most lenders require an inspection for the mortgage valuation. Often the buyer's private survey can be done at the same time.

■ Exchanging contracts
When both sides' solicitors are ready, contracts can be exchanged. Only now is the deal legally binding.

■ Moving and completion
Take the money and move out!

Photo: www.pickfords.co.uk

The legal framework

Once your property is under offer, the main way of measuring progress is by checking how far it has advanced along the legal framework. This consists of a series of key stages where various questions and documents fly (or sometimes crawl reluctantly) back and forth between the solicitors acting for the buyer and seller. This lasts for what seems like an eternity, often becoming bogged down at various points along the way. Trying to understand the reasons for the inevitable gridlock means understanding the legal framework.

The following are the key stages in the route that your solicitor/conveyancer will follow until your sale safely reaches exchange of contracts.

1 Sending out 'vendor questionnaires'
The first sign that things are moving is when you receive two long lists of questions from your solicitor, known as 'vendor questionnaires'. This involves filling in a lot of boxes in preparation for stage 4 below. They will want to know everything from whether you're including light bulbs in the sale to whether you bothered to get planning consent for an extension. Be careful how you complete this, and keep a copy, as disputes can often arise later over the smallest issues, such as whether curtains and carpets were included. If you're not sure of the answer, ask your solicitor.

2 'Office copy entries' ordered (included in the HIP)
Nearly all properties are registered, but this needs to be confirmed by applying to the Land Registry for what are known as 'office copy entries of the title'. These tell you a number of important details about the property, including any mortgages or other loans secured against it. There is also a plan showing the borders of the plot being sold. Anyone who's ever played Monopoly knows the value of the Title Deeds, which traditionally provided proof of ownership of a property. In the past these were usually held by the mortgage lender (the 'mortgagee'), but are now in most cases held on computer at the Land Registry. If the property is unregistered obtaining proof of ownership is more complex. (See Chapter 22.)

3 Preparing the draft contract
This starts life as a fairly standard document setting out all the terms of the sale, such as the agreed price and the amount of the buyer's deposit. However, at this early stage a space is left for the proposed date of completion, which needn't be inserted yet. Most solicitors often draft their own contracts based on a standard template, although anyone can purchase a ready-made contract such as the Law Society's standard contract. This will then be sent to

the buyer's solicitor for them to read through and suggest any changes. It normally bounces back and forth between the solicitors a number of times until both sides are happy with the final draft.

4 'Preliminary enquiries' answered

Your solicitor should by now have received a list of questions known as 'preliminary enquiries' from the buyer's solicitor. These investigate matters such as whether the property is connected to mains services, and whether there have been any disputes. Of course, the only person who can truthfully answer the majority of these questions is you – the owner. So a copy will duly arrive in the post. Some questions may need to be answered jointly with your solicitor. Although replies must be honest, in practice they tend to be a touch evasive, with answers such as 'not to our knowledge' or 'please rely on your own inspection and survey'.

5 Final contract prepared

Once the draft contract has travelled from one side to the other several times and any outstanding issues have been clarified, there will come a time when the final agreed version of the contract can be drawn up. This is known as the 'engrossed' contract. Each side keeps a copy.

6 Contract signed by seller

Before you can exchange contracts, both parties need to sign their copy of the contract. Anyone who jointly owns the house, such as your partner, must also sign.

7 Exchange of contracts

These are magic words, because only after exchange is your sale binding on both parties. If the buyer pulls out after this stage they will lose their full deposit. The amount of money the buyer is required to put down as a deposit will have been agreed earlier. Although contracts generally refer to deposits of ten per cent of the purchase price, in most cases smaller sums are acceptable (typically five per cent). Your side will also want to obtain confirmation from the buyers' solicitor that the necessary funds for the purchase are now all in place (which means the buyers must have received their mortgage offer – unless, of course, they're cash buyers). When all this is done and dusted, you should be able to exchange contracts – and you're home and dry (nearly).

8 Post exchange

There are normally five or so additional tasks for your solicitor to deal with after you've exchanged – see Chapter 12.

Answering questions

Unnecessary delays are sometimes caused by sellers being slow to answer questions and return forms in the early stages. One of the first forms that needs to be filled in, which also happens to be one of the lengthiest, is the 'vendor questionnaire', described above. Additional questions may have been raised to complete the various HIP documents, although providing much of this information is currently optional.

It's not unusual for the same questions to crop up again later in the sale process, with increasing urgency, often designed to elicit more detail. Despite the irritating repetition, in most cases this should be fairly straightforward to deal with.

But what if there's something about the property that you'd really prefer not to broadcast, or certain information that needs to be handled sensitively? Perhaps one reason you decided to sell is because the neighbours from hell have been parking their kebab van on your prize roses and this has led to angry confrontations. Nothing could be more natural than wanting to play down or even bury such unfortunate events. You certainly don't want to present them in a blaze of publicity to potential buyers.

This is where you need to be very careful in the way that purchasers' enquiries are answered. Of course, it's perfectly possible that the new owners of your house will get along famously with the folk next door, perhaps sharing a common interest in the finer points of doner and sheftali kebabs. But it's more likely the history of your dispute will sooner or later come to light, and the first thing they'll do then is go back to their solicitors to check your replies. This is dangerous territory, so answers need to be considered carefully. The black art of spin and lies should be left to those who can afford libel lawyers.

Everybody needs good neighbours – and clearly defined boundaries

True story

A legal case in 2006 involved the sellers of a property who had written to their neighbours to complain about the anti-social behaviour of their teenage son. But when they later came to sell their house they ticked the box on their Home Information Pack to say there had been no disputes.

However, after the purchasers had taken up residence they experienced similar problems with the neighbours and eventually found out about the original dispute. Accordingly they sued the sellers, who had to pay almost £70,000 in compensation to the family who bought their house.

Boundary disputes

Few things seem to inflame neighbourly relations more than an errant garden fence or wall. A disputed inch or two can grow to enormous proportions in the minds of the wronged.

But before formally tackling your neighbours over any contentious issues bear in mind that if you are planning to sell your home in the near future, you will be under obligation to disclose any history of disputes. Complaints that you've made to them in writing, or perhaps via the police or the Council, will obviously be a matter of record. Legally, just because there is no written evidence doesn't automatically absolve sellers from their duty to disclose disputes. But in practice, it could make it considerably more difficult to provide proof in any subsequent claim for damages. So it can pay to tread lightly if such matters arise. Taking an informal approach with neighbours could prove to be a better option.

It may be possible to settle a boundary dispute amicably by having the correct position verified independently. It's a simple matter to obtain a copy of the map of the area from the Land Registry. Then a specialist land surveyor can be employed to produce a digital survey. But even if the report shows that the boundary is in the 'wrong' place this may not help. When a neighbour has left it a long time before making a complaint, and the 'new' boundary has been in position for several years, it may be argued that that's where the boundary now correctly lies.

Taking legal action should always be seen as a last resort, because once you start to involve lawyers then legal fees can swiftly escalate to thousands of pounds. In which case it would probably be cheaper to buy your own meadow.

7 | GETTING READY TO SELL

Before you sell

Before finally taking the plunge and opening up your wallet to estate agents and lawyers, and inviting hordes of complete strangers to tramp through your home, some key questions need to be answered:

■ Is it a buyers' or sellers' market?

In a booming market, properties sell themselves as buyers shove each other aside, competing to buy your highly desirable residence and get a rung up 'the property ladder'. Conversely, in a slow market serious buyers are in short supply, so sellers have to work harder. It's rare for supply and demand to be perfectly balanced – the market normally tends to favour one side or the other. At this stage it's important to get a feel for the way the wind is blowing, as this will determine your negotiating strength as a seller. Clearly the media have a major influence here. Screaming headlines have a tendency to distort or hyperbolise, feeding back into the real world and affecting attitudes and behaviour.

■ Timing

The best months to sell are traditionally from March through to June, or, failing that, during the early autumn. But even in the gloomiest markets there are always some buyers about.

■ Are you tied in?

Before selling, check whether you're likely to suffer a penalty with your existing mortgage if you have to redeem it early. This typically applies to fixed or discounted rates, which commonly run for two-, three- or five-year terms. If it does

Let's be clear exactly why you want to sell. In most cases, the main point of selling is to obtain enough hard cash to facilitate a move to a new home that better suits your lifestyle. You may be trading up to a larger and more expensive residence, or perhaps moving sideways as an independent 'newly single' home owner. You may even be 'empty nesting' and heading off to enjoy retirement in the sun.

Whatever your circumstances, the sale needs to be seen as part of the bigger picture, an essential stepping-stone to achieving your main goal. It's helpful to put things in

perspective as you prepare for the battle ahead. It may become strategically necessary to lose a few minor skirmishes along the way in order to win the prize you seek – the successful completion of your sale and, ultimately, the new lifestyle you want.

turn out that there's a penalty, all may not be lost. Your mortgage may well be 'portable', allowing you to take it with you and secure it on the new house.

■ Selling a flat

Flats are usually a whole lot more complex from a legal perspective because of the lease. As a seller, the sooner you start digging out information the better. Indeed, some of this information will be required at the outset for your Home Information Pack – see below.

If possible try to fish out the service charge accounts over the past few years together with the estimated charge for the current year, and make copies ready for the purchaser's solicitor.

Often the questions asked by solicitors require a response from the freeholder/landlord or their management company. This is a common cause of delay. Each request for information can incur charges for the buyers, so they may be discouraged from submitting some questions early in the process for fear of incurring multiple fees.

Where you're on good terms with your freeholder/landlord (perhaps where you own a share of the freehold of the block) a spot of gentle chasing is often beneficial at this stage.

Arranging your Home Information Pack

As noted earlier, getting your Home Information Pack organised is one the first major decisions sellers need to make. Also known as 'sellers' packs', HIPs are compulsory for all homes being sold in England and Wales. The packs contain the title documents to

HOME INFORMATION PACK

HIPcode

What's in your Home Information Pack?

HIPs must contain the following documents:

- **Energy Performance Certificate** (EPC) – An assessment of how energy efficient your home is.
- **'Terms of sale' statement** showing whether it is freehold or leasehold, and confirming that it's being sold with vacant possession (as opposed to someone remaining in occupation).
- **Home Contents form** showing what fixtures and fittings, carpets, curtains etc are included – but sellers can opt to not disclose information at this stage.
- **Property Information Questionnaire (PIQ)** includes information on flood risks, gas and electrical safety, service charges, structural damage, and parking.
- **Home Use form** with information about the condition of the property and boundaries etc – but sellers can opt to not disclose information at this stage.
- **NHBC warranty** (or equivalent) for new or recently built properties.

The following documents are also compulsory, but can be added to the pack later if there are delays in obtaining them (but you need to provide proof that they've been commissioned):

- **Proof of ownership** – 'Office copy entries' from the Land Registry that provide evidence of 'title' (for registered properties).
- **Local land charge search** – The local authority search covering planning, highways etc.
- **Drainage and water search**
- **A copy of the lease** – for leasehold properties, or equivalent documents for commonhold flats.

Sellers can additionally opt to pay for a mini survey known as a Home Condition Report (HCR), but this is not recommended as buyers generally mistrust them. HCRs are a very basic type of survey, consisting largely of standardised phrases, not tailored to suit individual needs. Crucially, unlike conventional RICS Homebuyers or Building Surveys, HCRs can be carried out by 'home inspectors' who may have relatively little experience and in most cases will not be qualified chartered surveyors.

your property, along with local searches and an Energy Performance Certificate (EPC) that provides buyers with an energy rating for the building.

On average a HIP will set you back between £300 and £400. Marketing your house without one is against the law and leaves you liable to fines (although currently the fine is not massively more than the cost of the HIP). It will also hold up the sale, as buyer's solicitors now expect to be swiftly provided with the pack, including up-to-date local authority searches. Since April 2009 it has been illegal for sellers to market their property without a HIP having been prepared – although there is 28 days' leeway to complete the more complex items, such as searches. A Property Information Questionnaire (PIQ) must be completed as part of the HIP. In reality this can take anything from 9 to 25 days to prepare depending on where in the country your property is located. So HIPs need to be completed (not just ordered) *before* you can begin marketing the property.

Before HIPs appeared on the scene, it was possible to put your property on the market without paying a penny. Those in favour of HIPs claim that adding this up-front cost has helped weed out casual sellers who were just 'testing the water' and unlikely to proceed, thereby wasting everybody's time.

The downside for sellers is the expense of having to pay for a HIP, whether the sale turns out to be successful or not. But it's good news for purchasers, who traditionally had to stump up for the costs of obtaining things like searches and deeds. So if you're buying as well as selling, then effectively you should get some of this outlay back.

HIPs are especially good news for first-time buyers, whose costs have fallen as a result.

The importance of HIPs is that some key legal documents now have to be obtained much earlier, which can obviously help to speed things up. The HIP will remain valid until the property is taken off the market or sold – there is no obligation to refresh or update pack documents. However, there is also no obligation for buyers' solicitors to use the legal information contained in a HIP and some prefer to do their own searches. Also, some mortgage lenders may be reluctant to rely on the local authority search, and will want to submit their own fresh one, especially where documents are more than three months out of date. In case of any errors, HIPs carry £5 million indemnity insurance, plus an additional £250,000 cover for the local authority search component.

There are a number of cases where a HIPs is not required:

- Right-to-buy sales of Council or other social housing
- Where there is no marketing involved, *eg* a sale to a family member or friend
- Seasonal holiday homes
- Properties to be demolished
- Shops with flats included
- Properties without vacant possession – *ie* sold with someone living there
- Portfolios of multiple properties
- Non-residential properties

Energy Performance Certificates (EPCs)

At the heart of every HIP is an Energy Performance Certificate. This gives the building an energy rating similar to those on new fridges, from a super-eco-friendly 'A' down to an embarrassingly chilly 'G'. It also suggests ways to improve the building's energy consumption. Only certificated Domestic Energy Assessors are allowed to prepare Energy Performance Certificates.

Older properties are likely to fare less well in the energy stakes, especially those with solid walls. Having said that, there are plenty of 1960s and 1970s homes with paper-thin wall panels and minimal insulation, making them some of the worst offenders.

But despite government claims that Energy Performance Certificates will save the planet, the reality is that for the vast majority of buyers EPCs are of little interest. There are so many major considerations that you need to make when buying, that for most of us energy efficiency comes a long way down the list. There is no evidence that these have any great influence on people's buying decisions, although they may be a bit more relevant when selecting a newly-built property. However, if your buyer is planning to let the property then the EPC will be welcome, because one is required when flats or houses are rented out.

So if most buyers aren't that bothered, how concerned should sellers be? There is a risk that, finding their home has been damned with a low rating, sellers could be tempted to rush into paying for misguided improvements in a bid to make homes more saleable. For example, double glazing is not a particularly cost-effective improvement. It can take well over 70 years for double glazing to pay for itself on the basis of lower fuel bills, and even modern plastic replacement double glazed units only have a projected lifespan of around 30 years. Energy reports will mark properties down for having single glazing, forgetting that restoring original sash windows not only uses less energy, but can add real value to period properties.

However, there are some improvements that you can carry out to beef up your home's energy rating without breaking the bank. To prepare your property for the visit of the energy assessor, it makes sense to upgrade your loft insulation to a snug 300mm depth. And if your house has cavity walls, having cavity wall insulation injected is another highly effective improvement (but must not be applied to timber-frame houses). Grants may even be available.

Instructing your HIP

There are plenty of people who will be only too keen to make money by arranging your HIP. Your estate agents may kindly offer to arrange the whole thing for you with no up-front fees whatsoever. Delaying payment until completion of the sale (or until withdrawn from the market) can be an attractive proposition for cash-strapped sellers, and arranging HIPs has become a useful part of agents' bait for reeling in new clients. But attractive though this offer may seem, HIPs from agents can work out relatively expensive. Many solicitors are also geared up to arrange HIPs in a similar fashion. However, in both cases it's likely that the instruction will simply be passed to a large corporate HIP provider in return for a commission payment. The time it takes to prepare the HIP will depend not only upon the speed of the local authority search but also on how quickly the Energy Assessor can gain access to the property. Once complete, HIPs are made available online as pdf documents, and can be accessed by prospective buyers (using a code) and printed out.

DIY HIPs

It is possible to put together your own Home Information Pack. The only part of the HIP you can't do yourself is the EPC, and these can be purchased privately. Some of the preliminary legal information about your home can be checked with a little detective work by looking at the documents dating from the time when you bought it. However, before embarking on the DIY route ask your solicitor whether insurance is required to cover you in the event of any errors. The process for compiling your own HIP is explained on our website and title documents can be obtained from **www.landregistry.co.uk**.

> **Further information**
> **www.home-moving.co.uk**
> **www.landregistry.co.uk**
> **www.rightsurvey.co.uk**
> **www.homeinformationpacks.gov.uk**

8 | PUTTING IT ON THE MARKET

Photo: www.JNP.co.uk

At this stage, you naturally want to crack on with your sale and get your property on the market. But before entrusting your main asset to the hands of a local agent, it's worth taking time out to plan your campaign. If all's fair in love, war and property, it helps to have a battle plan.

What's it worth?

To get a realistic idea of how much you can afford to spend on your purchase, there is one fundamental question that needs to be answered – how much is your present home actually worth? If you can nail this down early in the process, it will help you stay on course later when buyers start haggling for price reductions.

This, however, is a subject with potential to seriously ruffle feathers. Valuers know from bitter experience that informing proud home owners that their property is worth less than they'd fondly imagined is tantamount to hurling a personal insult. The same holds true at a national level. Voters will tolerate all manner of dishonesty and ineptitude from politicians, but if house prices start to slide, governments generally do too.

Into this maelstrom of sensitive egos and personal financial wellbeing steps the estate agent, tasked with divining the property's true value. To muddy these waters even further, estate agents have their own agenda – to win business, which is rarely achieved by proffering cautious estimates of value.

There's an old adage that if you ask three different agents you'll get three different opinions of what your house is worth. To be fair, even highly qualified valuation officers assessing properties for tax purposes accept that there is a permissible leeway of up to ten per cent accuracy. But there's no good reason why local estate agents should be too far apart when valuing conventional properties. For example, there is normally no shortage of standard three-bed semis around town to use as comparisons. So unless an agent is incompetent or desperate for business, significant differences of opinion are only likely to occur with odd, one-off properties, such as converted chapels or sprawling period residences.

How to value

When it comes to valuing our own homes, there's a tendency in all of us to view them through rose-tinted

Right: A tricky one to value – unique nautically-themed 1930s concrete bungalow

Officially recorded 'sold' prices can be found online

specs. It's self-evident that our personal good taste in flowery wallpaper and coloured bidets must make our house worth considerably more than that ghastly place down the road that was on the market last year at an outrageous price.

So how do the professionals do it? Residential property is normally valued by making comparisons with recent sales of similar types of houses in the local neighbourhood. Accurate valuation requires an ability to stand well back and take a long, hard, objective look. But as noted earlier, this puts estate agents at an immediate disadvantage, because there's an obvious conflict with the need to win business. Disappointing potential clients with honest, but lower than anticipated valuations is not necessarily the best way to do this.

Agents rarely have formal qualifications in valuation, but those with experience and good local knowledge usually have a pretty shrewd idea as to what price a property will actually sell at – which is why surveyors routinely phone them for comparable evidence and frequently seek their opinion of value.

Comparing one property with another isn't the only trick in town when it comes to valuation. For example, you could instead base the property's value on its investment potential, a method widely employed with commercial and retail property. This involves assessing the amount of rent the property is likely to generate in the space of a year. This rental income is looked at as equivalent to the interest you could earn from a sum of money sitting safely in a building

What adds most value?

A higher value can sometimes be justified because of improvements. But some improvements add more value than others:

■ **High value improvements** – around 100 per cent of the cost recovered
Adding an extra double bedroom
Loft conversion
Adding an extension
Redecorating in neutral tones

■ **Medium value improvements** – around 50 per cent of cost recovered
Refitting the kitchen
Refitting bathrooms
Adding off-street parking

Photo: Capel Kitchens

■ **Low value improvements** – less than 25 per cent of cost recovered
Double glazing
Swimming pool

The precise addition to value will depend on the type of property. Swimming pools will clearly add more to an up-market home than to a small terraced cottage. The amount of value added very much depends on the extent to which an improvement overcomes a major drawback with the property, such as a lack of parking.

Some 'improvements' can actually reduce the value, such as plastic replacement windows fitted to period properties, artificial stone cladding, or polystyrene foam ceiling tiles. Extensions that massively eat up your garden space may also not add much value.

society account. The question is, what capital lump sum (or value of property) would you need in order to generate this annual income? Because of the relatively high risk involved in collecting rent (your tenant could disappear without paying), you would expect to earn a higher interest rate or yield than you'd get from a 'safe' High Street savings account. So if banks are paying five per cent interest, you might expect to earn a rental yield of eight per cent. By working backwards you can calculate a property's approximate 'capital value'. Suppose the annual rent is £10,000, and you need a yield of eight per cent, then the property would be valued at £125,000. Needless to say, calculations aren't always this simple. To judge what sort of return you need to earn it's necessary to weigh up the benefits of any additional future growth in the building's value against drawbacks, such as property being a notoriously 'illiquid' investment – *ie* you can't get your money out in a hurry by suddenly 'liquidating' your house or flat. You also need to take into account the projected returns from alternative investments such as stocks and bonds, the term and quality of the lease and how yields and inflation are expected to perform over the years ahead. Nonetheless, this can still be a useful rule of thumb in helping buy-to-let investors judge whether a property is overvalued.

Detective work

To get an idea of the true value of your house, a good place to start is by checking actual Land Registry sale prices of other properties in your street. This information is widely available online, so you can see the actual selling prices your neighbours accepted for homes – a tempting proposition even if you're not selling!

Another useful guide to the true value of your property is to take the price you paid when you bought it, and then 'index it up' using one of the leading online house-price calculators such as Nationwide or Halifax – see website. Obviously you also need to add something for any improvements you've made to your home. But this doesn't mean just adding the price you paid for your conservatory or loft conversion. As we saw earlier, what you spend on a

home improvement and the amount it adds to the value can be two very different things.

If, when you bought your property, you managed to negotiate a substantial discount to the original asking price, it can be tempting to believe that the property is worth considerably more. But this is not always the case. It sold for the best price the seller could get at the time, and may not have been such an amazing bargain if, for example, the original asking price was set miles too high.

Setting the asking price

Before negotiating your sale it's important to set two figures in your mind – the lowest price you are willing to accept, and the ideal price you would like to achieve.

Pitching your asking price correctly is a key strategic decision. Buyers normally expect to get something knocked off the asking price, so it needs to be set a few percentage points above what you consider the 'true value' to be. This leaves room for buyers to negotiate a lower figure and enjoy basking in the warm money-saving afterglow.

As noted earlier, prices are sometimes set too high where agents are desperate to win business or where sellers have an unrealistically high opinion of value and insist on a stratospheric asking price. Testing the market with a high asking price is sometimes justified on the basis that 'you can always come down later'. The trouble is, such properties can become a drag on the market, even after the price is later reduced. Buyers are wary of 'dinosaurs' that have been around forever, and may attempt to drive a hard bargain. Greed can make you miss a buyer.

There is another approach, widely employed north of the border. When a property is hard to value, agents sometimes set a relatively low 'offers in excess of' guide price designed to stimulate interest. As with an auction, this is designed to generate competition, with rival buyers bidding the price up, sometimes way above the true market value.

Crucially, when setting an asking price you need to take account of stamp duty thresholds. A property priced even £20,000 or £30,000 above a threshold is realistically likely to stick just below the point where stamp duty kicks in. It has to be priced significantly higher for reluctant buyers to make the 'jump' and swallow the big hike in tax.

Getting the best price in a market downturn

It's understandably very hard for home owners to regard falls in prices as anything other than bad news. But if you want to trade up to a more expensive property, it can work in your favour, as the extra money you have to pay gets smaller. For example, if you are selling a £200,000 flat and prices have fallen ten per cent, you will receive £20,000 less. This will be more than offset, however, by the £40,000 you get off the £400,000 house you want to buy. In other words you can take a hit on your sale safe in the knowledge that you will do at least as well when negotiating on your purchase. As they say, you can get away with being greedy on your sale or cheeky on your purchase, but rarely both. The best strategy is to research your local market, and work out how big a hit you are prepared to take on your sale. When the market eventually bounces back, so too will the price of your next home.

However, in a falling market, prices of different properties tend to drop at different rates, as supply and demand varies across the spectrum of property types. Depending on what the planners have permitted in a particular area, there may be a local oversupply. Flats can be especially vulnerable in a market downturn because of the high number of first-time owners who may have had to borrow up to the hilt, with limited income to manage interest rate hikes. This in turn may lead to greater numbers of repossessions and quite dramatic falls in value, depending on local conditions. Small flats have a habit of 'bombing' in a downturn, only to catch up again when prices boom.

In a downturn, buyers can become incredibly sensitive to the slightest problem. Being too close to a road or near a farm, or simply in a postcode where there has been flooding, are suddenly major issues. It's often fringe areas that suffer most. These may be the very same places that are labelled 'up and coming' during boom years. But there are some potential issues that you can do something about. As property-makeover programmes never fail to remind us, you can increase the price that someone is prepared to pay for your house with surprisingly little effort. Some carefully chosen quick-fixes prior to viewings can work wonders. (See chapter 10.)

Deciding what's included

Before putting your property on the market, it's worth considering what 'fixtures and fittings' you are prepared to leave behind. These can later be a useful bargaining chip,

enhancing your negotiating position. So if you're sick of the sight of your carpets and curtains, they may save a buyer a lot of hassle and money, and are worth throwing in. Normally one of the first documents your solicitor sends you as a seller is the 'fixtures, fittings and contents form'. However, at this stage it is not always advisable to mention this in the sales particulars because it's rarely an issue until the time when you come to negotiate the sale. If you do make a big thing about including them, some clever Dick could later demand a discount for not wanting them, on the grounds of 'saving you the trouble of having to remove them'.

This subject becomes more contentious when you realise that no one actually seems to be 100 per cent certain precisely what constitutes a 'fixture' or a 'fitting'. Of course, there are rules of thumb. A fixture is something that's permanently fixed in place, and being attached to the building can't be picked up and walked away with. Fittings, on the other hand, can be easily removed and are normally packed up and taken away. The test is whether removing the thing would damage the property. So things like light pendants and laminate flooring are considered to be fixed, and are left in place, as are TV aerials, fitted hobs and ovens, and anything that is obviously part of the house, such as the doors! But it's the grey areas that can be a fruitful source of argument. Plant pots can be moved, unless of course they're incredibly heavy, and what about shelves and curtain rails?

Appointing an estate agent

The time-honoured way of selling residential property is to put it in the hands of a local estate agent. Although it's true that agents have enjoyed years of easy pickings, their job is rarely as simple as we sometimes like to imagine. Much of the hard graft, such as accompanying endless viewings and patiently holding chains together, gets carried out below the public's radar. Although it's now

The law says...

Under the Consumers, Estate Agents and Redress Act (2007), all estate agents are required to join an approved ombudsman service that can resolve disputes and offer compensation.

The industry is additionally regulated by a hotchpotch of legislation, like the Estate Agents Act and the Property Misdescriptions Act, some dating back 30 years. This makes it an offence to give false or misleading descriptions, but many breaches go unchallenged or cannot be proved.

The law says that:

■ Agents must pass on all offers promptly and in writing to their client – the seller. This includes those made long after a property goes 'under offer'. The only exception is where the seller has told the estate agent not to pass on certain offers – for example, all those below a certain price.

■ Agents are legally obliged not to deliberately mislead or misdescribe something.

■ Property Misdescriptions legislation also requires agents to state in their sales particulars if anyone working there is a 'related person' to the seller. This is to avoid potential conflicts of interest arising. So if you want to buy or sell a property that your estate agent (or one of their associates) happens to own or have an interest in, they must declare their involvement.

Complaining

In the first instance a written complaint should be sent to the firm's head office. If this doesn't resolve the problem, write to local trading standards. Write to NAEA if the firm is a member, or ask the Ombudsman for Estate Agents to review your case. If they support your complaint, they may award compensation. Estate agents 'regulated by RICS' have stricter complaints procedures.

See **www.naea.co.uk**, **www.oea.co.uk** and **www.rics.org**.

easier than ever to sell privately, the vast majority of properties are still bought through estate agents, who are by far the biggest source of property.

Selecting the right agent

You need to be careful about who you instruct. Anyone can set up in business and grandly proclaim themselves as 'estate agents and valuers'. No licence or qualifications are required – which is all the more surprising given that these are the people we entrust with the keys to our homes and details of our personal finances. These are also the people whom we rely upon to vet total strangers before they are shown around our homes. In fact agents are the only part

of the home-buying process that are not regulated. To be fair, there is overwhelming support for a minimum level of competency and compulsory licensing from the industry itself. Many who pride themselves on their professionalism are only too conscious that their reputation is tarnished by a minority of unqualified and unscrupulous agents. It is the Government that has consistently blocked such demands.

Urban folklore in Britain is rife with stories of alleged abuses, such as 'fly boarding' – putting up Sale boards outside properties that aren't for sale – and arranging sexual liaisons in properties to which keys are held. This perception is underpinned by a record number of complaints from unhappy clients – currently more than 8,000 a year received by the Ombudsman for Estate Agents (OEA).

So how do you go about picking a good agent? A good way to start is to look for one who is a member of the National Association of Estate Agents (NAEA). Even better, pick one of the (relatively few) estate agents who are also qualified members of the RICS (Royal Institution of Chartered Surveyors), since they are subject to a strict code of practice. But just because some estate agency firms describe themselves as 'surveyors and valuers' doesn't mean they are qualified RICS members. At best there may be a genuine chartered surveyor somewhere on the payroll at head office, but the people you deal with day-to-day will often have zero qualifications. The NAEA has more than 10,000 members, representing around 60 per cent of the industry. Although it's a voluntary body, members follow a professional code of practice, which if breached can land them with fines, suspension or expulsion. One recent positive move in the right direction is that all estate agents are now required to join an ombudsman service that can resolve disputes and offer compensation.

Ombudsman for Estate Agents A free, fair and independent service for buyers, sellers, tenants and landlords of residential property in the UK

So much for consumer protection. But what you primarily want, of course, is a firm who can sell your house for the best price in the shortest time. Appointing someone with good experience and local knowledge is usually the best way of achieving this, so one of the first questions to ask is how long they have personally been doing the job in this area.

Different firms tend to have their own market niche, specialising in different property types and price ranges – although there are often exceptions where a 'posh' agent may have the occasional starter home on their books, and occasionally a mainstream agent is appointed to sell a minor mansion. But as a rule it's best to stick with agents who sell other properties like yours, be it studio flats, executive homes or country houses. As with different brands of cars, someone looking to buy an economical hatchback won't necessarily consider looking in a Bentley dealer's window. That said, the Internet is starting to make the precise brand of agent a secondary factor when searching.

Many branches of estate agents are not independent, but form part of a larger group. When you look at who owns what, it quickly becomes apparent that it's rather an incestuous world. Many chains are owned by large banks or private equity firms attracted by the potential for sales of lucrative financial services. Any recommendations you receive for associated services such as conveyancing, surveys and especially mortgages and insurance are likely to be primarily geared towards maximising revenue within the group.

The oldest trick

Whatever the market conditions, from time to time all agents become short of clients, and to secure new business they could be tempted to be overoptimistic when valuing your home. Getting the property onto the books is often the primary objective. Getting it sold can be worried about later, even if it means having to slash an overly optimistic asking price down to the value an honest agent would have put on it in the first place. This does you no favours at all, because in the process you might have priced yourself out of the market and missed a perfectly good buyer. At the end of the day, it's important to remember that estate agents are sales people, and as a potential customer you will be squarely lined up in their sights. By putting a value on your home that far exceeds your expectations, the hope is that you will be suitably impressed by their confidence and appoint them over their competitors.

We can all be susceptible to a spot of flattery, and agents make full use of this. Having lavishly complemented your taste, and waxed lyrical about your charming home, you will be left in no doubt that there are dozens of eager buyers queuing up desperate to make offers, and that your property will be snapped up. In a strong market this may indeed happen. But more often, after a number of fruitless viewings the agent provides 'feedback' telling you all the negatives about your property that somehow they hadn't noticed earlier. This is the process of 'managing your expectations downwards'.

Agents sometimes like to suggest that one of the advantages of appointing them is that you'll recoup the cost because they will skilfully 'negotiate' a higher selling price. In reality, securing their commission is usually more important than getting the best price for the client, and when push comes to shove, 'negotiating skills' may actually be employed to persuade you, the seller, to drop the price.

So before making the final decision, test your agent. Ask them how many sales they have made in the last three months, and how many hits they get on their website.

Another deception, occasionally employed by small provincial agents outside London, is to have a second branch apparently based in Mayfair, London WC1. This piece of prime real estate is milked for all its worth as a promotional tool, appearing prominently on their literature, and negotiators will stress their firm's ability to attract cash-rich London business people looking to buy 'out of town'. But in reality this Mayfair 'office' may be nothing more than a shared mailing address.

Marketing tools

Different brands of estate agent will try to convince you that they have a unique ability to conjure up potential buyers. But although some brands are more highly regarded than others, these days most buyers simply contact the agent who happens to be selling the property they've seen on RightMove or some similar website. A lot of buyers also make a point of registering with all the main agents along the High Street. So in effect there's a huge amount of common ground, with most agents employing pretty much the same marketing tools – ads in the local press, mailshots, online listings and For Sale boards. In the battle to gain competitive advantage, some will offer extra features such as online 'virtual tours'.

But if there is one overriding difference to look for it is the quality of their staff. This can vary from branch to branch even in the same firm, so look for experienced, switched-on individuals who demonstrate ability and motivation, rather than dozy, wet-behind-the-ears school-leavers. It's also true to say that some agents have worked hard over many years to build their local reputation and gain credibility, so that when it comes to picking an agent to put their property on the market, sellers will opt for a trusted brand, rather than the cheapest.

The usual marketing tools in the estate agent's armoury are:

Sales particulars

Traditionally agents would write the most appallingly flowery rubbish, blatantly misdescribing gruesome old dives in the most serene language. The Property Misdescriptions Act (1991) largely put an end to this by making false or misleading claims a criminal offence. So agents now ask their client sellers to check their draft details – and validate any spurious claims. In the author's experience it's not unusual for draft details to be riddled with silly errors and spelling mistakes. Terraced houses are described as semis, 1970s houses become 'period properties', even addresses get misquoted. So sellers need to tread carefully: by approving a pile of misleading blurb, a seller could unwittingly become an accessory to a criminal offence – not the best start.

Photos

Most agents manage to come up with pretty impressive photos. Blue skies, roses round the door, even going so far as to 'photoshop out' inconveniently located pylons and chip shops. But this can be a double-edged sword if a brilliant wide-angle photo leads to a first reaction of disappointment when prospective buyers see the property in the flesh.

A blue sky is essential for that 'killer photo'

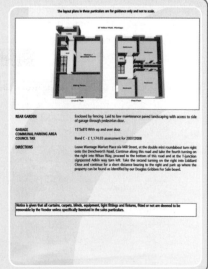

Mailings and phone calls

In days of old, long before email and the Internet, selling a house required a lot of hard graft – and a great deal of licking – which was largely restricted to stamps and envelopes. Jealously guarded lists of applicants would be 'mail-shot' on a weekly basis until they capitulated from beneath a blanket of property particulars. After viewing, prospective buyers would be subjected to a ruthless telesales operation, arms being twisted until they finally submitted and made an offer. Telephone follow-up calls are, of course, still an important part of the sales operation, but emails have largely superseded the mailshot. Yet reports of its demise are premature, since one problem with relying on emails is that they're often deleted or filtered as spam before they're ever read. A well-designed, colourful, glossy sales brochure arriving on your breakfast table can be far more effective at grabbing the attention.

Online advertising

In recent years the Internet has revolutionised residential property sales. The once all-important High Street shop windows are now primarily used to impress new sellers, the British public having well and truly embraced the Internet as the best and fastest way of researching the marketplace when looking for a home. Over 80 per cent of property buyers now start their search online, so if there's one thing the agent needs to get right, it's listing your property on the best 'trade' property portals. There are several well-known sites, including RightMove, PrimeLocation and PropertyFinder. Of these, RightMove is the most dominant, claiming to list the properties offered by more than 90 per cent of all UK estate agents, which in a good year can total almost a million properties at any one time. RightMove is also ranked in the Top 20 most popular websites in the UK. But in response to complaints from agents about the cost of subscribing to such sites, the National Association of Estate

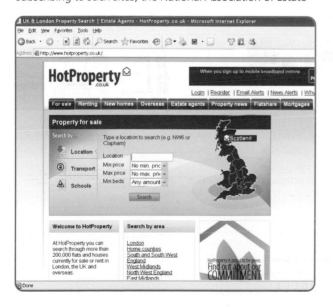

Agents (NAEA) launched a free listings site for its members – PropertyLive.co.uk.

Regardless of the claims made by the various competing sites, one thing's for sure – just about all estate agents now rely on the Internet to attract buyers, largely via a handful of dominant trade portals.

Advertising

Another tradition that retains a useful place in the agent's repertoire is local press advertising. The reason is simple – it works, because the vast majority of buyers come from within a 15-mile radius. However, this can prove a significant expense for agents, especially in a slow market where repeat exposure is required. So be sure to check that there are no hidden extra charges for advertising, and how frequently your property will be featured.

Ads in national papers are formidably expensive and in most cases relatively ineffective for local property. Only when you get into the prime property market does it start to

become viable. Buyers of a high-net-worth with squillions to spend tend to look at a smaller number of properties spread over a wider area (a prospect doubtless made bearable with an executive jet to whisk you between mansions).

Agents' websites

Agents will list properties for sale on their own websites. These will generate a number of enquiries but are insignificant compared to listings on the big trade property portals with their immense 'pulling power'. That said, some large corporate agents' websites might achieve higher search engine rankings than a small local operator.

Home movies

Virtual tours anyone? A video trek through your home can, in theory weed out nosy-parkers and time-wasters who would otherwise be chronically dismayed by your taste in wallpaper. So everyone who then decides to physically

Take a snoop around suspiciously tidy homes with an online 'virtual tour'

come and view your property will already know what to expect, and are therefore more likely to be serious buyers. But there is always the risk that showing too much too soon can actually put people off.

For Sale signs

Sale boards were traditionally regarded as one of the agent's most effective marketing tools. In some areas more than 30 per cent of all enquiries are believed to derive from boards, so without them an agent could lose a lot of business.

To attract viewers, Sale boards are still a useful device, and it is still claimed that properties with signs outside sell quicker than those without. And it's true that boards attract some non-Internet potential buyers. It's surprising how many people notice them, although to some extent their effectiveness depends on the local area.

Agents are extremely keen on them because they are a form of free advertising. Like shop windows, they also help attract fresh sellers. Indeed, one measure of success in a local area is the 'board count', and those with the most boards planted around town will shamelessly boast of percentage market share – an easy statistic to manipulate. The general idea is to leave the boards erected for as long as possible, ideally displaying the word 'SOLD'.

Under existing planning and advertising regulations, agents can place boards on a building or land that is for sale, but signs erected elsewhere require special permission.

Needless to say, some rogue estate agents ignore this and regularly erect signs on the sides of blocks of flats, in communal gardens, in car parks, or public lavatories, inviting the threat of legal action.

Contravention of the regulations is a criminal offence under the Town and Country Planning Act. In addition, the Property Misdescriptions Act 1991 dictates the maximum size for a single board at $0.5m^2$, or a slightly larger $0.6m^2$ where two signs are joined together.

Sole or multiple agency?

Should you appoint just one estate agent? Or is there a better chance of achieving a sale by using two or even three simultaneously? Most sellers appoint a single agent, until things get a bit desperate, at which point a fresh crop of different agents' boards will suddenly sprout from the ground.

These are the options – in all cases the arrangement should be 'no sale no fee', so you normally only pay the agent upon completion of a successful sale:

Sole agency

By far the most popular choice. Here your estate agent is the *only agent* with the right to sell your property. Fees for

What exactly do estate agents do?

- Value the property
- Draft sales particulars with photos
- Advertise online and in the local press
- Mailshot applicants
- Take enquiries and make viewing appointments
- Conduct viewings
- Negotiate a sale price
- Manage the process to completion

sole agency are less than for multiple agency (see below). Importantly this leaves the door open to selling privately, if you wish, for example, to place your own advert in a local newspaper or on a website. You are perfectly free to find a buyer yourself (since you are not an estate agent) with no obligation whatsoever to pay the estate agent's commission.

Apart form the relatively low fees, the attraction of sole agency is that, being the only agent, it should inspire the confidence to spend more time and money promoting your home.

However, sellers have sometimes been badly caught out where they have later switched to a different agent, who then successfully introduced a buyer. If you read the small print, the contract you sign normally ties you in to the first agent for a number of weeks, or even months. During this period they are the *only agent* with the right to sell your property, so it's best to tell them that you only want to sign up for a short period – no more than four to six weeks – which leaves you free to terminate the contract if they fail to perform.

Multiple agency

With multiple agency you're free to appoint any number of agents, each with the right to sell your property on a 'winner-takes-all' basis. From the agent's viewpoint there is a greater chance of wasted effort and expense, which is why the fees quoted will be higher. This again leaves you free to advertise and sell privately alongside the estate agents. But because buyers often register with lots of competing agents, disputes sometimes arise between rival agents as to which one actually introduced the successful buyer. Apart from the expense, the drawback is that a sea of boards outside your house can smack of desperation.

Joint sole agency

This is the caring, sharing approach. Here you appoint two agents who co-operate with one another. Both agents share commission, usually with the lion's share going to the agent that actually introduces the buyer and therefore

can genuinely claim to have sold the property. It is sometimes used as an alternative to multiple agency, perhaps when a property sale is struggling. Commission rates are usually a little higher than for sole agency.

Sole selling rights

This is the one to avoid. It means the estate agent is the *only person* with the right to sell your property. It differs from sole agency in that if the property sells to a buyer you found yourself, you still have to pay the estate agent. So if you wanted to sell to a friend or family member the agent could still claim thousands in fees. Essentially it also stops you from having a go at selling privately.

Fees

Competition between local agents is normally keen. For some agents their primary objective is to get the most 'instructions' and maximise the number of properties placed on the market with them. Some target-driven corporate firms have 'negotiator of the month' incentives to this end. As we have seen, the easiest way to win business is to appeal to sellers' greed by overvaluing.

The other way is to offer lower fees than the competition. So what level of fees should you expect to pay? This can vary anywhere between one and three per cent (plus VAT). Deals below one per cent do exist but are rare. Budget agents charge low commission, but are unlikely to spend much on marketing your home. In common with dearer agents, they still have fixed overheads, such as staff and premises, so the only thing they can cut back on to enable them to charge less is advertising and marketing. To achieve the best price for your home it is necessary to ensure that it is presented to the widest possible audience, so by saving half a per cent on an agent's fee you could lose thousands through poor marketing. This, of course, doesn't mean that a dearer agent will do a better job; they may just spend it all on flash cars. But a good agent should recoup the difference in the fee for you by creating more buyer interest. However, you may still be able to negotiate lower fees, for example if you're willing to show prospective buyers around yourself.

Agency terms

Estate agents normally qualify for commission upon the successful completion of a sale to a buyer they have introduced. However, watch out for contracts that refer to introducing a buyer who is 'ready, willing and able' because it means that if an agent simply finds a buyer who is ready, willing and able to buy, you may be liable to pay the agent's commission if you later decide to pull out for any reason, regardless of the fact that the sale never completed. Estate agents will think nothing of suing you for commission.

As noted earlier, it's important to check the minimum term stipulated in the small print of their contract when instructing sole agents. Many sellers sign up for several months, promising not to instruct an alternative agent within the specified time. But if your sole agent then fails to perform, you are unable to appoint another estate agent to market your property until the agreement expires. Watch out for a clause saying that only by serving a two-week notice *after* the minimum term has expired may an agreement be terminated.

Commission wars

Nasty disputes occasionally break out between rival agents. It's not unknown for one agent to poach a property from another, and both then claim commission for selling it. Disputes occasionally go to court.

This happened in a recent case when London agent Foxtons had arranged for an applicant to look round a £1.15 million property, but no offer was made because the house needed too much work. So no deal was reached. Some months later, the same buyer agreed to buy the property after the seller was contracted to another agency, Hamptons. Foxtons claimed their £20,000 commission fee from the seller on the grounds that they'd 'introduced' the buyer. But the Courts held that an agent has to do more than simply introduce the buyer to the property – they have to introduce them to the *purchase*. So commission

was paid to Hamptons and Foxtons went home empty-handed.

This ruling suggests that commission should only be payable if an agent has already persuaded the buyer to make the purchase. So if they introduce a prospective buyer who then goes away and later makes an offer through another agency, they cannot claim commission fees.

Before you sign an estate agent's contract, always check the small print

Checklist

- What is the minimum term/tie-in period? Four to six weeks should be acceptable.
- How much notice is required to terminate the contract? It should be no more than two weeks.
- Is it sole agency or multiple? Avoid sole selling rights.
- How will the agent go about marketing – which websites and papers will they use?
- Is all advertising included? Check that they don't expect you to pay towards the cost of ads.
- Are sales particulars or a brochure included or is there an extra charge?

Estate agent scams – selling

The following scams are all highly illegal and are today extremely rare – so don't have nightmares:

- **Undervaluing** – The agent deliberately undervalues the property. If the owner accepts the agent's assurances that this is the best price they'll get, the agent quickly buys the property through an associate and then sells it 'back to back' for its true higher value, thereby making a profit. As a seller, the antidote is to instruct several agents to value the property.
- **Price manipulation** – The agent accepts a backhander from an associate to put a particular property to one side while they arrange their mortgage. In the meantime the agent deliberately fails to fully promote the property to the market and fobs off requests for viewings or information from genuine buyers. The seller is eventually told 'there's no interest at this price, so we'll have to reduce it'. In extreme cases prospective buyers may be told that it is already under offer. After a hefty price-cut the friend steps in and buys it cheap, perhaps immediately selling it on 'back to back' at the full value, netting them a juicy profit. This scam has even succeeded on occasion in defrauding major banks

selling repossessed properties. A variation of this theme is for the agent to open any sealed bids and then bin the ones that are better than their briber. The obvious antidote as the seller is to arrange for a colleague to put in an offer and see if the agent passes it on.
- **Flyboarding** – Several well-known London agents were recently fined for a spate of 'flyboarding', where bogus For Sale boards appeared around town in a rash of free publicity. Foxtons had to apologise after an unsolicited board was erected outside the home of 'spin doctor' Alastair Campbell.
- **Board wars** – A Scotland Yard investigation was launched after violent 'board wars' erupted in Central London on a major scale some years ago. As many as 500 rival agents' signs were ripped down each week by organised gangs under cover of darkness in an attempt by one well-known agent to boost their share of the lucrative London market.

9 | SELLING PRIVATELY

It's surprisingly difficult to hold a conversation about property without the words 'estate agent' cropping up within the first few sentences. Love them or loathe them, agents have come to dominate the residential market – indeed, they have become our interface *with* the market. After all, how else would buyers and sellers come together? Actually, when you come to ask that question, there are a number of ways that buyers and sellers can deal directly with one another, the obvious one being by advertising privately. But as in every other walk of life, the Internet has made dealing direct considerably easier. On the other hand we're not simply flogging an old banjo on eBay here, so you have to ask whether it's actually wise to cut out the middleman when selling such a highly valuable and complex asset as a house.

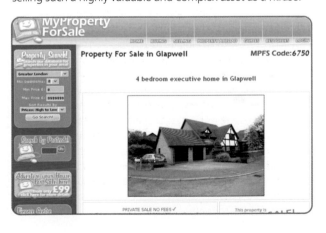

Big business

The UK home sales market is worth around £4 billion. This is the total amount we pay in estate agents' fees in a typical year. When you then factor in additional sales of financial services an average firm's turnover can swell by at least another ten per cent. This means that over the years a lot of agents have made a lot of money, despite, in some cases, offering a less than brilliant service. So the idea of selling privately, and saving several thousand pounds in agent's fees, can be a tempting proposition.

Is the traditional estate agency model flawed?

Currently less than ten per cent of UK residential property sales are conducted without an estate agent. This is despite the fact that the majority of their customers have a negative perception of them. Recent research by ITN discovered that estate agents' customers hold the following views:

- 64 per cent don't trust estate agents; of these, 77 per cent think agents are more interested in profit than in their customers.
- 54 per cent think estate agents have a reputation for being dishonest.
- 43 per cent think estate agents charge too much money for the work they do.

These are pretty damning statistics, which suggest that if there was a really viable alternative, many of us would give it a try.

The role of the middleman

Despite the big potential savings in fees and VAT, managing your own house sale is not for everyone. For busy people, a major attraction of employing an agent is the assumption that everything will be done for you. As we've already seen, that should include drafting accurate property particulars with photos, promoting the house to the market, handling enquiries from buyers, vetting purchasers, accompanying viewings, negotiating a sale and steering it all to a successful completion.

Some agents will do all this brilliantly. But the reality for many sellers is that they still end up devoting a lot of their own time. This starts when you invite three or four local agents to value your home, and then appoint one of them whilst fending off aggrieved calls from the unlucky runners-up. Before your house goes on the market, you will need to check and if necessary amend the draft details. More time is then spent taking calls from the agent to agree times for viewings, and possibly being present for viewings and answering buyers' questions, followed later by long discussions with the agent about viewers' negative 'feedback'. When an offer is forthcoming, more time needs to be devoted to negotiating the agreed sale price via the agent. There then follows a period of weeks or months anxiously chasing the agent and the solicitors trying to ascertain how far the sale has progressed. In total that's a lot of hours of precious time.

A good agent is one who manages the whole process on their clients' behalf, and regularly communicates with them. But in many cases it could be simpler to deal with your buyer direct. Communicating on a one-to-one basis is usually easier than a *ménage à trois*. A triangular relationship means prospective buyers phone the agent who then has to phone you. But because you happen to be out, messages have to be taken, and calls returned, and so on…

The really time-consuming part of the process is conducting viewings, a job in which home owners sometimes end up participating anyway. There's some sense in this, when you consider who's best qualified to talk about your house – an agent who's spent 20 minutes there, or the person who's lived there for years? (However, in some cases, agents are more likely to appreciate which aspects of a property are the *right* ones to talk about!)

Conducting viewings can be very time-consuming

Photo: www.the-wooden-hill-company.co.uk

Another reason that agents have a stranglehold on the market is because it's widely assumed they 'do the paperwork' and look after the legal side of things. But this is a bit of a myth. Agents have no legal qualifications and the reality is that staff are often unqualified and low paid, hence in some cases the quality of service can be poor.

One of the tricks to maximising the profitability of an agency business is to involve sellers as much as possible in their own sale, with the agent dispensing guidance. Profitability depends on paying low basic wages to sales negotiators whose income is largely commission-driven. Minimising time-consuming accompanied viewings is best done by encouraging sellers to participate, or better still by arranging weekly group viewings. The estate agent's role becomes essentially secretarial, booking suitable times for both buyers and sellers.

Some agents claim to 'pro-actively' market your property, and will reel off a host of obscure websites that they will list it with. 'Pro-active' marketing often means ordinary marketing with a bit of added enthusiasm for the first few weeks. The test of a good agent is whether they have the stamina to keep pushing, rather than letting your house slip down their priority list as the weeks go by and new properties come onto their books. The upshot of this is that it's perfectly possible for agency tasks to be undertaken by private home owners – because in many cases you end up doing much of this anyway.

One of the big benefits of selling privately is that you establish a direct relationship with the buyer, even before they visit your property. As a rule, people are less likely to mess you about on a one-to-one basis, whereas they may have fewer scruples about fibbing to an estate agent.

Selling without an agent: preparation

The main attraction of selling privately is obvious: no hefty sale fees (plus VAT). Of course, buyers know this and expect a share of the booty, so the trick is to keep your price down but pitch it so that you still end up making more money than if you'd sold through an agent. But before you can reap the benefits of a DIY sale, the first step is to plan your campaign. You will need to tackle some of the preliminary tasks normally done by the agent. Indeed local agents can be a good source of free guidance.

Your marketing plan

Before you try to sell anything, it's always a good idea to sit down and work out what kind of person it will most likely appeal to, by 'defining your market'. This forms the basis of your marketing plan, and helps you select the right media in which to promote your property. Professional media buyers at advertising agencies do this by comparing magazines, newspapers, TV programmes and websites in terms of 'cost

Ready for inspection

per thousand', calculating what it costs to reach a thousand readers or viewers who match your target audience – *ie* the type of people most likely to be interested in your property. Looked at in this light, posting a video of your house on FaceBook may not be such a brilliant idea after all, when you consider how many people are likely to be surfing it at any one time who just happen to be in the market for a three-bed semi in Clacton (or wherever).

Your marketing plan can also help focus on the best way of describing your property, stressing the features that are most likely to appeal to your target audience. So if you're selling a small flat, aimed at first-time buyers, the features you choose to emphasise are going to be very different from those likely to appeal to buyers of four-bedroom executive homes.

Whatever media you decide to use, it's essential to clearly communicate your message. So here's a handy tip used by professional copywriters. 'AIDA' may sound a bit like a cheapo supermarket, but it's actually the secret behind every successful advertising campaign. If an advert doesn't first attract your *Attention*, it's a total waste of time. But to be of any real use the ad has to swiftly convert your attention to *Interest*. If it's interesting enough, *Desire* will next grip the reader/viewer until they take *Action* to make enquires about buying. Of course, with a Saatchi-sized budget that's easier to achieve than a tiny classified ad. But the principle still applies.

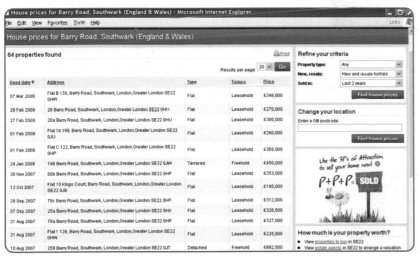

Valuation

Valuing, as we saw in the last chapter, isn't rocket science. There's nothing in the world to stop you from obtaining free opinions of valuation from local agents. This can then be verified by searching online to discover actual sale prices achieved in your street, as well as checking the asking prices of similar nearby properties on the market. Bear in mind that agents commonly talk in terms of an asking price that's pitched to actually achieve a lower sales figure, which is sometimes presented as a range of 'between £X and £Y'. In truth, it's often the lower of these two figures that's the one they consider realistic, whilst simultaneously keeping sellers happy with the prospect of achieving a bigger number.

To cut through the sales waffle, ask them for a realistic opinion of value. If they turn the tables and ask you first what you think, say you don't want to influence their opinion and want an honest valuation.

Writing your own property details

Before embarking on any kind of private sale, you're going to need something that's professional-looking to hand out, post or email to interested buyers. This means writing a page or two of your own property details.

If your house is already on the market with an agent, you could base it on their details (which in turn were probably based on what you told them anyway). The trick is to keep it simple – don't make amazing claims that lead to grave disappointment when the property is viewed. Always stress the best features, such as any views, potential to extend, plot size, improvements etc. Browse a few sets of details on other properties to get the general idea.

When done, finish with a disclaimer at the bottom of the page:

These particulars are believed to be correct and are intended as a general guide only. They don't constitute an offer or any part of a contract. Purchasers are advised to take independent legal advice and rely on their own surveyor and solicitors.

Photography

Central to creating a good impression is the killer photograph. This is something most agents do extremely well. But taking a decent picture of your own house shouldn't prove too difficult. Of course, there are a few tips to bear in mind. A blue sky makes a massive difference to perception; and, obviously, clearing assorted wheelie bins and rusty old bikes out of the picture before snapping can't do any harm. A wide-angle lens can also help. Again, emphasise your property's best features.

Sale boards

Most people move within about 15 miles of their current home, so if you're selling privately it's usually worth erecting your own private sale board. It's surprising how many people notice these, even if you live in a cul-de-sac. Neighbours, postmen and passers-by can all help spread the word. A board is especially worthwhile if there are similar properties for sale nearby. That way you will channel all the viewers that agents have attracted at considerable expense round to your property. No one's going to make an offer to buy a neighbouring house

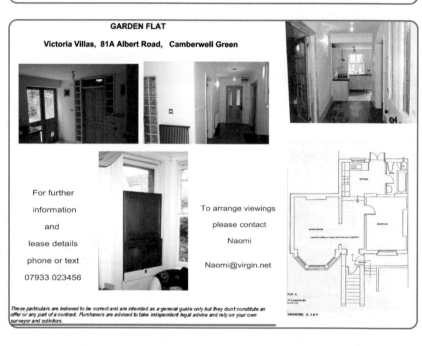

without first checking-out yours. Strictly speaking, because your sale board is part of the marketing process it shouldn't be erected until the HIP has been ordered.

Selling without an agent: the risks

Before rushing out to tell the world about your property, there are two very important issues that you need to consider:

Paying commission

Many sellers choose to have a go at selling privately at the same time as marketing their home through an estate agent. This is perfectly OK. The Office of Fair Trading states that if you find your buyer by selling privately, you do not have to pay the agent commission – as long as you haven't signed a 'sole seller' agreement. As we saw in the last chapter, this is a very different thing from a conventional 'sole agency' agreement.

'Sole seller' contracts are the ones where even if your friend or a family member buys your house, the agent can still claim commission. Fortunately such arrangements are extremely rare, usually only occurring where customers don't realise what they've signed.

Sole agency and multiple agency contracts, on the other hand, are by far the most common forms

of contract, and both leave you free as the owner to sell privately.

However, there's a potential trap here for home owners promoting their properties online on 'private seller' websites, because some of these are actually classed as online estate agents. If you're already contracted on a *sole agency* basis to a High Street firm, then they are the only estate agent you're allowed to use. So there's a potential risk of getting stung for their fees, even if you sell your house privately online. This is not a problem if you have a multiple agency agreement (since any number of competing agents can sell it for you), or if the website you pick isn't classed as an online estate agent (see below).

The key terms in your sole agency contract with the agent are typically described as follows:

You will be liable to pay estate agent's fees if the property is sold to:
   a. *a purchaser introduced by us during the period of sole agency*
   b. *a purchaser introduced by another agent during that period*
   c. *a purchaser with whom we had negotiations about the property during that period.*

Of these, 'c' is the one that is most open to manipulation by the agent. Ideally you should cross out this vague term before signing the contract. Of course, many potential buyers register with agents over the course of a year but often don't get as far as viewing any properties. And on rare occasions, a buyer whom you attract privately – perhaps someone who replied to your private advert – may have previously registered with your estate agent.

To defuse such potentially explosive situations, the first question you have to ask is whether your private buyer is already listed on the agent's books. Even if they are, just being registered isn't enough. To earn their commission the agent normally has to prove that they *introduced* your buyer to the sale (see previous chapter). In such cases the best approach is to ask your buyer to confirm in writing that the agent did not introduce them to the property and that they did not have negotiations with the agent about the property.

Security

For some sellers, security is paramount, and one of the big attractions of using an agent is that they claim to vet interested parties before they set up a viewing. However, most purchasers have no particular recollection of any 'vetting' process being carried out by agents, other than the financial variety aimed at selling you a mortgage.

Just because you live alone or are fearful of strangers visiting the house, it doesn't mean you can't sell without an agent. Managing your own viewings is simply a matter of being businesslike. When making appointments over the phone, note the applicant's name, address and phone number, and then call them back to confirm.

You can effectively interview buyers over the phone before they come for a viewing. Ask them questions about their own situation. Are they in a chain? Are they first-time buyers? Do they have their mortgage arranged yet? It should be possible to weed out time-wasters and raving loonies. Equally important, this allows potential buyers to ask you questions prior to viewing to ensure that the house is suitable, and save them making wasted trips.

Selling privately

There are several methods you can use to sell property privately, and in the process pocket all that lovely commission. A significant number of sales each year come about 'through the grapevine' via friends, work colleagues or family. Indeed, there are a number of very useful marketing tools in the box, some of which are free. But of these, listing your property online is probably now the most essential part of any private sale.

Selling online

The Internet has become firmly established as the optimum way of selling just about everything, from cars to antiques. This is certainly true with residential property. Despite the dominance of the Internet, traditional estate agents' shops are still in fairly abundant supply, having propagated wildly in the boom years. But this old 'shop window' business model is fast becoming redundant, as most prospective buyers are now reeled in from a handful of leading websites. So why not cut out the middleman and simply list your own property online?

The first thing to note is that the websites used by

estate agents are 'trade only'. Unlike eBay or AutoTrader, which happily accept trade and private sellers' listings side by side, the online property world is fragmented. As a private seller you can't phone up or email RightMove or PrimeLocation and simply list your property. This restriction is understandable when you consider that if an estate agent is already paying good money to list your house, they obviously aren't going to be overjoyed at the prospect of direct cut-price competition from their own client.

However, the harsh fact remains that being frozen out from the big trade portals with their immense pulling power means that private sellers are effectively relegated to the relative backwaters of the web. At present this is probably one of the main reasons for selling through an estate agent (whilst also reserving the right to market your house privately). To make up for this, private sellers need to devise a more canny approach to marketing. Selling privately online means that instead of paying a large sum in commission to an agent when your property is sold, in most cases you instead purchase an advertising package.

Picking private seller websites
There's a surprising number of private seller websites available. Links to all the main ones can be found at **www.sellersNET.co.uk**. Prices vary from as a little as £9.99 for a basic listing, but are more typically £100 to £200. But fees can vary wildly, with some charging a fixed half per cent of the asking price.

Of course, a website may look absolutely brilliant, but it's entirely possible that virtually no buyers will ever find it. So to judge whether a particular site is right for you, you need to know what the viewing figures are – how many hits the site routinely attracts. If 95 per cent of the traffic comes from China or the USA, it's obviously pretty meaningless. Consider what kind of coverage the site offers for your area and property type. Put yourself in the shoes of potential buyers. Does it boast the sheer volume of listed properties to give it critical mass when searching by town or broad postcode? If your search only elicits one sad-looking house in a given location, it's a fair bet that potential buyers won't be bookmarking the site for future searches.

Double charging
As we saw earlier, you could potentially be in for a nasty surprise if the website you're using happens to be classed as an online estate agent, as opposed to an online publisher. There's no problem if you have an existing multiple agency contract with a traditional High Street estate agent, or if you're selling privately without simultaneously using an estate agent.

But if you're selling through a local agent on a sole agency basis, you don't want to risk being double-charged thousands of pounds in commission. So it's

Photo: www.noestateagentsplease.co.uk

important to take the precaution of checking that the website you plan to use is actually an *online publisher*. To be on the safe side, even where a website claims not to be an online estate agent, before committing yourself get them to agree in writing to indemnify you against any claims for double commission.

Online listings

Listing your property online is basically a glorified classified advertisement . To list your property for sale you need to give as much information about it as possible and upload plenty of good-quality photographs. Potential buyers browse the website and get in touch with you directly if they're interested. The portal should assist with the design, or at least have a standard template, so your property is displayed professionally.

Some even send a representative round to your house to take photos, prepare particulars and post it on to the Internet. Potential buyers may be able to contact you through a discreet messaging system. By choosing a private 0870 number, enquiries can be directed to your landline, keeping your personal number and email address private.

Friends and family

Meanwhile, back in the terrestrial world, the obvious first step to selling is to make the most of your friends, workmates, neighbours and family. By extending your reach even further to 'friends of friends', it's amazing how many like-minded people can be reached by simply trawling your old address book. Then there's all the contacts in your email address book (both work and personal). Of course, you need to come up with some decent incentive to motivate people, so try emailing everyone with the offer of at least £1,000 commission for introducing the viewer who ultimately buys your house.

Selling at auction

The great thing about selling at auction is that it's quick, as well as relatively easy. Although not strictly a private method of selling, it does place you firmly in the driving seat. But auctions aren't right for all properties. It can be a good way to get rid of somewhere that's quirky, hard to value, or in need of modernising. The

Online estate agent or online publisher?

If a private seller's website is defined as a 'publisher', you should be free to simultaneously market your property through a conventional estate agent, without compromising their 'sole agency' contract. But some websites are not warning their customers of the dangers of double charging. So what exactly is the difference between an online estate agent and an online publisher?

The Office of Fair Trading states:

If an internet property retailer does anything for their clients more than simply carry an advertisement, for example if their website has a message board for sellers to contact buyers, they will be doing estate agency work.

Examples of the types of activities that go beyond merely publishing advertisements and into online estate agency include:

- Sending out property particulars
- Arranging viewings
- Dealing with enquiries from potential buyers and passing on details
- Providing a For Sale board where the board contains the website contact details

Even the mighty Tesco fell foul of this distinction in 2007 when their original DIY listings website, offering a full service including sale boards, was deemed to be an online estate agent, not a publisher.

Checklist: questions to ask before selling privately online

- What are the fees and charges?
- How do they generate traffic to their site?
- Are there links to major property portals?
- What is the site ranking for numbers of hits and visitors?
- How easy is it for buyers to find a large selection of properties in your postcode area?
- Do you get control of your listing so that you can update it and manage it?
- Is it listed until sold?
- Do they provide help with design of particulars?
- How many photos can you upload?
- Do they provide a private enquiry phone number?
- Are email enquiries redirected to you?
- Do they offer a sale board?
- Can you upload a virtual tour video?

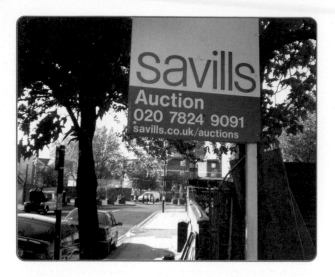

attraction for sellers is that competing buyers may succumb to 'auction fever' and repeatedly bid, pushing up the price.

The procedure for selling is fairly straightforward. The auction house will first value the property, and come up with a non-binding 'guide price'. It will then take photographs and put together details for a catalogue, which will appear about three weeks before the sale, giving prospective buyers time to go on viewings and arrange surveys.

The snag is the cost, which may not actually be much less than with the conventional 'private treaty' method using an estate agent. Auctioneers' commission is usually about 2.5 per cent of the sale price achieved, plus there may be a catalogue entry fee of anything from £300 to £1,000.

You also need to bear in mind that buyers will be looking for some kind of discount or be seeking a bargain, especially in a slow market. And in a market downturn, auctioneers tend to be more selective and won't take properties they consider overpriced.

'Sale By Tender' is an alternative auction-style process where estate agents sometimes invite buyers to submit written competitive bids – see chapter 19.

There are also such things as 'private auctions'. In the exclusive world of the super-rich, these 'by invitation only' events are sometimes held for the purpose of selling unique or highly desirable land and property, with the audience perhaps restricted to family members or neighbours.

Photo: www.SKBauctions.co.uk

Local press advertising

As we have seen, the overwhelming majority of buyers move locally, within half an hour's drive of their present home – which is precisely why most agents advertise in the local papers on a weekly basis. A local press ad can catch casual browsers who may not have been consciously searching for property – or friends on the look-out for someone else.

So why not book your own ad so that potential buyers can get in touch with you directly? Some papers accept free classified ads. But when it comes to parting with hard cash, it's best to avoid paying for a whole series, because even with a discount, this can work out very expensive. Always carefully check the newspaper's circulation figures, and make sure it attracts the right kind of reader. Note that 'readership' figures are not the same as circulation. Newspapers and magazines may assume two or three people read each copy that's actually sold (the dentist's waiting room scenario) and will blatantly quote several times that number as their readership – which all sounds a bit spurious despite being perfectly legit.

A small classified or 'semi-display' ad, perhaps only 4cm x 1 column, is probably the most cost-effective type. You haven't got room to say too much in a small advert. Location and price are the two key factors for most buyers. But you can sometimes create *Attention, Interest and Desire* all in one go by dreaming up a killer headline. Sometimes the less said, the greater the curiosity aroused. But generally you need to 'scream the benefits', stressing positives factors like 'period property', spaciousness, lovely village location, large plot, panoramic views etc. So, for example, if you live in the catchment area of a highly rated school, big it up. The middle classes will move into an unconverted plague pit if they think there are some decent 'A' level grades to be had. Make it sound irresistible: '*Gorgeous Edwardian home with consent to extend to a*

Below: Most buyers live locally, within a 15 mile radius

Photo: wikimedia

marvellous five-bedroom residence in one of the town's prime streets within catchment area of league-table topping St Bartholomew's.'

Finally, complete your sales proposition by adding a 'guide price' and contact details.

Local parish magazines can be incredibly good value and are often worth booking a few months' advertising at a time. Also, keep an eye on other people's 'wanted' ads. If response is slow, keep at it – new buyers come onto the market every day.

National press advertising

Only about one per cent of buyers move more than 100 miles, so the vast majority will be focused on their local areas. Advertising in national papers and glossy magazines is formidably expensive, which is why it's only posh agents that use them for advertising premium properties that are likely to appeal nationally, such as those with paddocks, multi-acre plots, bell-towers or butler's quarters.

Specialist media

LOOT made its name in the 1980s as the 'free ads paper'. Sadly it no longer accepts property ads for free. But there are other 'freesheets' that may be worth considering, though much of this classified ad business has now gravitated to online listings services, such as Gumtree.co.uk. Again, check out the 'wanted' ads.

Publicity

The great thing about publicity is that it's effectively free advertising. But you don't need to employ a PR agency to get results. Local papers are often short of interesting 'human factor' stories, so if your house has a quirky history, or you're moving somewhere unusual, send the journalist a press release with photos of yourself and your property.

Otherwise you can make it a more interesting proposition by offering to leave the Porsche in the garage for the lucky buyer (which may still be cheaper than paying agents' commission).

Approaching developers

Does your property have development potential? Houses with large plots, corner plots, or those suitable for extension or conversion to flats may be hidden goldmines, worth considerably more than the normal market value for that type of house. If you appoint an estate agent the chances are they will have immediately spotted this and promptly tipped off one of their developer chums. Any extra development value will end up being shared between them.

So it can make sense to cut out the beady-eyed middleman and approach developers direct. Even without planning permission some will pay an agreeable price, if the risk is judged acceptable.

But watch out for those who make an offer and then proceed to string out a purchase, before pulling out at the last minute if the planning situation looks shaky.

To really boost your property's value it may be worth first submitting your own planning application. Sites with consent are always worth more than those that are speculative. Even getting planning for an extension can add significant value.

Property search agents

Wealthy buyers sometimes employ 'search agents' to save their time by doing the donkeywork and shortlisting suitable properties to purchase, so it can be worth approaching such agents directly. They will have a list of clients looking for property in the area, and if one likes the look of your home you can arrange a private sale. This costs nothing since the agent is paid by the buyer. People looking in this way tend to be high-net-worth individuals not interested in anything much less than a million.

eBay and YouTube

Though not an obvious marketplace, eBay may possibly be worth a shot in order to reach millions of web surfers. For a fairly small outlay you can post details and pictures of your property in the form of a classified ad. Your listing can include a 'Buy It Now' price together with the option for buyers to 'Make An Offer'. If you instead opt for a conventional eBay auction listing don't forget to include a reserve price in case Mr Smartypants bids £5 and then claims he owns your home.

YouTube isn't usually the first stop for people wanting to buy a house, so it's a bit of a lottery. However, it's free, and your property will be seen by a lot of young and/or trendy web surfers who wouldn't be seen dead on a property portal. Upload a video of your home and prospective buyers can take a two-minute virtual tour, accompanied, if you so wish, by your own taste in haunting music.

House swapping

The general idea of house swapping is to exchange your house with someone else who also wants to move. Sellers register their home and list where they would like to move to and the site searches for potential swaps. In actual practice, it's rare to find someone who just happens to want to swap their property for one just like yours and at the same price, so any resulting sale is likely to involve money changing hands. (See website for links.)

10 | VIEWINGS AND OFFERS

It is sometimes claimed that 'houses sell themselves'. But TV 'Property Doctor' Ann Maurice probably wouldn't agree, having forged a career persuading struggling sellers to zap their homes into shape, and thereby achieve a quicker sale at a better price.

This, of course, is all very well, but in the real world there's a never-ending battle going on with messy kids and pets, so trying to keep your house looking like a pristine show home isn't going to be easy. After all, why should you be forced to feel like stranger in your own home just to tickle the fancy of a few capricious home snoopers? The answer is: because there's some serious money at stake. Selling a house for its top price is hard work, but there's potentially a very big payoff. The best strategy from now on is to stop thinking of it as your home, but instead as a product that has to be sold so that you can move on.

Temporarily changing your lifestyle to sell your house is not unlike appearing in a TV reality show with a big cash prize at the end.

Presenting your property

The killer fact is that messy houses sell for less, or don't sell at all. It's also true that a lot of buyers buy with their emotions, not with their heads. And their emotions can be easily swayed by all kinds of relatively minor things. Get these right, and you can earn yourself a sale.

So before a thundering herd of strangers come trooping through your living room passing judgement on your taste in décor, it's worth taking a little time to smarten things up. The first rule is to keep it simple. There's a lot you can do without spending much money – as little as £500 carefully spent can repay itself tenfold.

A few hours spent de-cluttering is about the easiest and cheapest way to transform your home, making it appear more spacious and therefore more valuable. Be ruthless. Chuck out all those half-dead plants and old magazines you never got round to reading. Clear away bits of old timber and boxes you've kept in case they might come in useful. Donate to Oxfam all those clothes that are two sizes too small and crowding out your wardrobe. Say goodbye to Sammy Snake the draught excluder that everyone trips over. Be minimalist. The fewer items you have cluttering up your house, the bigger and more appealing it will look.

As TV shows frequently remind us, the Number One turn-off for many viewers is doggy smells. So keep it

Left and below: It's worth taking a little time to smarten things up

Photo: www.charlesgrosvenor.co.uk

smelling fragrant. A good blast of fresh air, a spot of hoovering and chucking out old mats and beer-stained carpets can work wonders. This is probably the easiest several thousand pounds that you will ever make. Getting busy with spray and duster can make all the difference.

A well presented house shouts 'Buy Me!'

Cosmetics

It's sometimes said that half of all potential buyers have decided whether or not to buy a property before they reach the front door. Most of the other half probably decide within the first five minutes. So, in order to achieve your home's market

potential pay particular attention to the hall, which is where buyers get their first and last impressions, and to the main reception room or kitchen diner, where most time will be spent when negotiating. If your entrance looks tired and the paint is peeling, give it a fresh lick of paint or varnish. Simple cosmetic improvements are the most worthwhile. A freshly painted front door, front wall or railings can really make a difference. Corroded old letterboxes and door furniture are cheap to replace. Doors that stick or creak make a bad impression and should be adjusted. Decaying timbers to windows and fascias can be overhauled and painted.

First impressions count very much. Sorting out smelly bins, rusty bikes, messy gardens or a broken gate can make a real difference to how a house is perceived and remembered by a prospective buyer. Weedy driveways can

be disguised with neat gravel and a few judiciously placed shrubs in pots can work wonders.

Internally, after tidying up the next best way to make a residence highly desirable is to spend a little time with brush and roller. Now if anyone knows the tricks of presenting property for sale, it has to be the nation's corporate house builders, whose businesses live or die according to how successfully their products appeal to buyers. And newly constructed homes are routinely finished with industrial quantities of magnolia emulsion. By taking a leaf out of Barrett Homes' book, and swapping

Photo: Capital fireplaces

dark colours for neutral tones, formerly cramped rooms can be made to take on surprisingly grand proportions. With the walls nicely spick and span, a fresh bright coat of matt white on the ceiling (preferably applied to a smooth skim plaster finish) will boost the amount of natural light reflected.

Updating

What if your bathroom and kitchen are looking a bit '1970s'? Surely it would be a good idea to refit them? Well, yes…and no. As a general rule, it's only worth spending serious money on stuff that you can take with you. On the other hand, nice new fittings can add some 'wow factor'. The problem is, the cost of such big improvements would need to be added to your asking price. And it's sod's law that your potential buyer's taste in

It's rarely cost-effective to replace old fittings – but it's essential they're sparkling clean (keep loo seats closed for the more discerning visitor!)

styles of kitchen will be totally different from yours. It's not unknown for new owners to rip out perfectly good, freshly fitted kitchen units and chuck them into a skip. Bathrooms are cheaper than kitchens to refit – buying a standard new suite can cost less than £400. But then it's all the associated works such as tiling and flooring that can really bump up the cost. Labour is a major part of the cost, so you can make a useful contribution if you're DIY-confident. On the other hand, if you're not the world's greatest wall tiler, now is not the time to experiment – a rushed job will show.

Big stuff

But where should you draw the line? Carrying out major works just to help sell a property is rarely advisable. Obviously you can add value with loft conversions and extensions, especially in a rising market, but you could end up pushing your asking price over a stamp duty threshold. Better to promote the property's potential for enlargement instead. On the other hand the property's fundamentals must be right – no one is going to be impressed by a CP Hart bathroom suite if the roof's leaking.

Pretty vacant

Occasionally you may find yourself responsible for selling a property that isn't your home. Perhaps it's time to sell off a buy-to-let investment, or you're selling a bungalow on behalf of an aged parent. Being at the 'top of the chain' gives you some negotiating clout, but bear in mind that holding out for a high price isn't always a shrewd move. A property that lies empty for months on end costs money, because of the interest it could otherwise be clocking up in a savings account; plus chilly, bare, empty houses are usually less appealing to purchasers than a warm, nicely decorated home.

If a property is seriously shabby, confronting the situation head-on can be a good alternative. A drawback can be turned into a virtue, by aiming at a slightly different market. Advertising a property as 'with scope for updating – would suit DIY enthusiast' can be a very attractive proposition in a buoyant market.

Home staging

It's been described as the 'hot new trend' in selling property. 'Home staging' is about temporarily furnishing and dressing your property to add a touch of magic and maximise its potential. Because buyers sometimes find it hard to visualise a property's scope, a 'dress to sell' service can really help fire viewers' imaginations and give your home the wow factor, by temporarily stuffing it with posh furniture, rugs and artwork. It is especially useful for empty or sparsely furnished places that would otherwise look sad and lonely. Home staging firms offer a makeover and design service for all rooms, providing everything from bed covers and works of art to rugs and mirrors – which makes for far more impressive photos in the sales particulars. Of course, hiring all these lovely antiques and assorted objets d'art isn't free: it can cost around 1.5 per cent of the sale price, so this may be something you're better off arranging yourself. But the benefits claimed are quicker sales and higher prices achieved (10 to 15 per cent more than comparable properties).

The great outdoors

Somehow, when looking round a property with a neat, well-kempt garden, we subconsciously imagine that it will magically remain in pristine condition. A well-presented garden can help sell a house, but the opposite is also true. So be sure to spruce up the garden before putting the house on the market. In most cases it's simply a case of cutting the grass, doing a spot of weeding and de-cluttering the drive. But you may also need to take any

Photo: Heritagebathrooms.com

DIY house doctoring

In a downturn 'House Doctor' services seem to pop up everywhere. Firms suddenly appear offering 'cosmetic surgery', 'facelifts' and 'detoxes' for your home, promising to transform its market appeal and achieve the best possible price. For such services clients are typically charged around one per cent of the property's value. But this isn't magic. Most is common-sense stuff that you can easily do yourself:

Cleaning and presentation

It's amazing how much stuff you can do without. But you needn't waste money employing a 'personal clutter consultant' who will relish telling you the obvious, ridding you of toys, mementoes and quite possibly your children and pets. When it comes to clearing stuff out, you have to be ruthless. Make sure that surfaces such as windowsills, dressers and tables are clear of unnecessary clutter. Get rid of the half-eaten chocolates on the mantelpiece, wipe away the layers of dust on the telly. Polish the furniture, wash the blinds and blast that weed growing out of the bathroom window. Make sure everywhere is spotless, especially bathrooms and kitchens. Above all, cleaning the windows can make a surprising amount of difference.

Redecorate

Experimental colour schemes that seemed a good idea at the time can be seriously off-putting. So paint over those vivid lime and purple walls. Bright, neutral, clean and uncluttered properties are the most appealing to the broadest range of buyers. But to prevent them looking too bland, buy some cushions and accessories with strong contrasting colours.

Flooring

Old carpets can harbour remarkably dodgy smells, as well as looking terrible. If they're beyond cleaning, replacing them with even budget carpet can give a very positive impression.

A polished wood floor will contrast nicely with white or pale walls, lending the room a spacious 'art gallery' ambience.

Fix things

Do basic repairs. Go through each room and do any outstanding minor jobs to improve the finish at minor expense – *eg* touch-up paintwork, straighten cupboard doors, polish or replace door handles. And get busy with the Polyfilla – cracks can seriously worry buyers, even though they are rarely structurally significant. Also reseal around baths, basins and showers, and remove any mould. Mend dripping taps, replace cracked panes of glass, and stick down peeling wallpaper. Make sure the doorbell works.

Kitchens and bathrooms

If your fitted units are looking tired, it shouldn't cost much to replace the unit doors or just paint them. Either way, this will be much cheaper than buying a totally new kitchen. If the units are in fairly good condition but look dated, just replace the doorknobs or handles. Fitting new taps can make a big difference. Another economical trick is to fit good quality worktops onto existing units. A tired bathroom can be transformed by lots of white fluffy towels and posh body pampering products. Where necessary, showers can be descaled and tiles regrouted for next to nothing.

Lighting

Buyers respond to light, so capitalise on natural light sources and supplement them with lamps, candles and reflective surfaces. It needn't cost a lot to change old light shades and swap old dusty and dated lamp fittings for cool modern ones.

Furniture

Experts reckon symmetry is all-important, so pull the bed out from the corner and procure some matching bedside tables. Temporarily replacing old MFI furniture with a select few antique items can transform a room's appeal.

Layout

Is the 'flow' of your home right? Are rooms in their optimum places? If not, could any of the reception rooms be knocked through and opened up together? Alternatively you could simply change the way some rooms are used.

Fragrant aromas

Smell is important. Get rid of killer pet smells and old laundry. Odour of dog or cat is one of the all-time top turn-offs, so be sure to banish dogs along with smokers and potties before viewings. The smell of drying washing isn't the most inviting of aromas either, so bundle away the drying sheets and open the windows to get some air into the room in good time. Avoid strong food odours – don't cook curry or kippers, and avoid frying onions or garlic before a viewing, as the smell will linger.

Flowers, herbs and a bowl of fruit will brighten up a room and create an appealing background ambience. Use scents that say 'home' – freshly baked bread or biscuits, vanilla, cinnamon, coffee and, of course, the best scent of all – clean fresh air. Open the doors and windows to ventilate and freshen up rooms and air the house before viewings.

Sounds

To help mask exterior noise that you can't control, light background 'mood music' can be very effective indoors, and water features or subtle wind chimes can be soothing in outdoor spaces.

Lifestyle

People like to 'buy into' success, so 'lifestyle visuals' – such as a cool flat-screen TV or a hot new laptop – can make all the difference in the form of subliminal signalling. Best of all you take these things with you when you leave!

Keep wheelie bins tidy – and ideally out of sight

heaps of junk to the tip, fix sticking gates and remove old estate agents' boards in case they give the impression the property's a bit of a dinosaur. Some people love walls bedecked with climbing shrubs; others hate them, so the best advice is probably to keep them neatly trimmed.

A sumptuous oasis can be hewn from the most squalid and depressing patch of land, and can add significant value for those buyers to whom the garden is the key selling point. Architects increasingly aim to design kitchen/diner extensions that bring the garden into the house, opening the whole thing up. This can be magic in the summer, even for small low-maintenance gardens. But spending time and money making a large garden highly ornamental can backfire. Most people who need a large garden have young children and want green, open spaces for them to play in. If you are trying to appeal to the family market, it may be worth trying to create compartmentalised spaces with football areas discreetly hedged or located out of sight.

Top selling tips
If your house isn't shifting, try following these tips:

- Drop the price. It's important to pitch this just right, because going too low on price can make the property look blighted so that it fails to attract interest.
- Check your presentation, especially the 'kerb appeal' to the front.
- Invite a crassly tactless friend round, tell them your property's on the market and ask their honest opinion.
- If the months go by and your house is sticking, estate agents need to 'do a Madonna' and reinvent the presentation so that it doesn't become stale. For example, a house may have a great view that was underplayed in the initial marketing. By taking some fresh photos that aspect of the house can be emphasised as part of a package to re-market the property at a revised price.

House names
Change your house name is a fairly straightforward process that involves notifying the local council. Houses with the words 'old' or 'cottage' in their name have sure-fire appeal when it comes to attracting viewers. Of course, you can't just label a bog standard ex-Council semi 'The Old Farm Barn'. It helps if there's a grain of truth in the name. For many smaller homes, not necessarily just period properties, 'cottage' may sound appropriate, perhaps paired with the name of a popular shrub or cute creature, such as holly, ivy, robin or skylark. Names like 'Sea View' or 'Park View' may be a bit uninspiring, but they at least draw attention to a positive feature. In a similar vein, a house in Oxford that is truthfully named 'Martins The Newsagent View' may not invite so many viewings. As a rule it's best to avoid dark humour, like 'Haunted House', 'Crack House' or 'The Old Whorehouse'.

Conducting viewings

Your mission, should you choose to accept it, is to invite complete strangers into your home in the hope of enticing them to take up residence and begin a new life there. As we have seen, despite paying an estate agent to sell their property many sellers don't feel comfortable with their house keys being made available to strangers, potentially compromising security. But whether you're selling privately or through an agent, from now on you may need to devote a fair amount of your valuable time to playing tour guide.

By sorting things out in advance you will remove the excuses that buyers can use to justify putting in lower offers. The house has to shout that it's worth the money. So be sure that viewers don't have to clamber over old bikes and bin bags blocking the hall. From a security viewpoint it's obviously sensible not to leave cash and valuables on display. Clear the decks and tuck your precious family photos and knick-knacks neatly away in a drawer. To create a welcoming atmosphere, nothing beats a roaring log fire.

There is, of course, another quite different possible scenario. Just when you'd got your house all beautifully spick and span, a massive anti-climax could be in store. What if the phone doesn't ring and there are no viewings? It's a bit like getting all dressed up and no one turning up to the party. Even in a quiet market, it's the agent's primary task to generate interest, so if it's all quiet on the western front it's very likely that they're not doing their job properly. This means checking the property isn't priced too ambitiously, that the particulars make it sound attractive, and that it's being promoted in all the right places. If you're not around personally, check with your agents that potential buyers aren't just being shown around by their 'Saturday boy'. You may want to consider switching agents or beefing up you DIY sale efforts. Sooner or later the levy will break, and the guests will arrive.

There is an art to showing viewers around. Most of us gabble too much, even going so far as apologising for anything that falls short of perfection. The first task is to smooth your guests' path by warmly inviting them in and then showing them round in a relaxed manner. You need to allow people the freedom to look around. They may already be interested in buying your house, so don't keep gassing the whole time – be a listener as well. If possible make them aware that other potential buyers are interested. Probably the best approach is to enter each room first, inviting the viewers to follow you. Point out any nice views, perhaps opening cupboards (unless you're anticipating an avalanche of towels, hoovers, bras and knickers). Don't apologise for you home's appearance to viewers. Modesty isn't going to get you anywhere. Remember that people buy into other people's lifestyles, so answering the door wearing a decrepit old shell suit with dribble stains down the front could be enough to scare off some buyers.

Be relaxed and sociable. Make small talk – 'Have you come far?' – but don't let the conversation drift away from the main subject for too long. Resist the temptation to proudly boast about all your guarantees for damp and dry rot treatments, as this can induce negative thoughts. Avoid switching off lights as you leave each room. But it is a good idea to switch off blaring TVs and radios that divert attention.

If they ask how long your house has been on the market, and the truthful answer is 'A bloody long time,' try instead saying 'Actually, houses in this road/village are never on the market long.' If they press the point, you might want to explain any reason for a slow sale, such as 'It was under offer so we did the decent thing and took it off the market, but were let down when the buyer who couldn't get a mortgage.'

Some folk may like you so much that they never know when to leave. A prolonged viewing can be brought to a close by saying 'We're expecting someone else shortly. Could you let us know by Tuesday, as there's a lady coming back for a second viewing next week.'

You don't need to go so far as baking bread to create the delightful aroma and the right ambience, but the waft of freshly brewed coffee during a viewing isn't a bad idea. Also make sure the house is light and airy, with curtains drawn well back in daylight hours. Leave doors open to allow light into halls and landings.

If viewings have to take place on a dark evening, be sure to make the home cosy and warm, with some soft lighting and ideally with a fire blazing merrily in the grate. Some subtle ambient background music can be soothing, with the exact choice tailored to suit your market. It all helps buyers visualise their new lifestyle and encourages them to buy.

A viewing is also a good chance for you to interview *them*. Ask how far they've got with their own sale, or are they ' just looking'? Inevitably there will be some time-wasters who didn't get weeded out in advance on the phone, but in group viewings they can play a useful role bumping up the numbers. Even so, when, after a lengthy viewing, a couple announce that they won't be making an offer because of something blindingly obvious (such as 'It's too far from Maidenhead' when the property's located in Birmingham) you begin to wonder.

Buying signals

Showroom salesmen are trained to recognise 'buying signals'. Whether it's the subtle act of touching a fridge that a potential customer has subconsciously decided to buy, or asking questions about delivery dates, buyers' body language may unwittingly reveal their true intentions. But playing psychologist with house hunters is a tougher call. For one thing, during the crucial weeks or months following the decision to agree the purchase, the buyers initial euphoria is likely to slowly disperse, like an outgoing tide exposing the jagged rocks of house-purchase reality.

All the same, it makes conducting viewings a tad more interesting if you're able to read the signals. For example, sensitive viewers may only say nice things so as not to upset your feelings, but secretly detest the place. Team viewing partners such as husbands and wives will want to chat amongst themselves to compare observations, and need space in which to do so. Sometimes those who appear totally disinterested, barely uttering a murmur, actually turn out to be serious buyers. Conversely the loud, cheery, backslappers may just be having a laugh. The best policy is to treat every viewer as a potentially serious buyer, even viewers who make obviously critical comments about your pride and joy. Rather than just being rude, it's possible they could be gearing up for negotiation, employing a technique to lessen your expectations and get a lower price.

As a seller you need to know how 'proceedable' potential buyers are. In order of preference, you want the following:

- A cash buyer who doesn't have a property to sell
- An investor or first-time buyer with a provisional mortgage offer
- A buyer who has already exchanged on the sale of their present property

Photo: wikimedia

- A buyer whose house is under offer
- A buyer who has yet to sell their present property

But things are not always what they seem. People sometimes tell the most astounding porkies in order to elbow ahead and secure a deal. The claim 'We're cash buyers' sometimes turns out to be totally untrue. So it's best to ask for written proof of their position before accepting an offer from self-proclaimed cash buyers.

Who are you dealing with?

As endless groups of people trudge around your home, it can be interesting to play 'spot the decision-maker'. It's sometimes said that men have a tendency to dominate financial decisions, and women lifestyle decisions. But given that house purchase normally combines a large quantity of both, it probably depends more on the personality of the individuals. In a complex, high-risk purchase decision such as this, buyers – especially first-time-buyers – tend to place a lot of importance on the views of others, especially family and friends. So if a trusted work colleague announces 'I'd never want to live in a timber-frame house,' their opinion can carry a lot of weight (whether it's technically valid or not). Even children can influence parents not to consider a certain property because 'The garden's too small for football' or 'I don't want to go to a new school away from my friends.' The opinions of experts and media pundits can also exert considerable influence.

Sometimes the person who's negotiating eye-to-eye with you to buy the property isn't actually the one who's going to live there. Perhaps they're a search agent acting for their client behind the scenes, or perhaps they're buying a flat for a student son or daughter; in which case, even if they love the place, if on a second viewing the client or student in question doesn't like the look of it, then the deal may never happen.

Opening negotiations

As we saw in Chapter 3, there are two essential figures you need in your head before starting to negotiate. The first is the best price you realistically think you could achieve for the property. The other is your bottom line figure that's the minimum acceptable. You also need to keep in mind the state of the market – in a buoyant market you're obviously more likely to be successful holding out for a higher sum.

When it comes to negotiating, up to a point you can 'make your own weather' by being discreet about what you disclose to whom – a bit like playing poker. Of course, the estate agent is on 'your side' – you are their client after all. But even if they're on your best buddies list it can be a mistake to reveal your hand too early. For example, suppose you confide in them that you've just had your offer accepted on a brilliant property and you can't wait to move in. Knowing how keen you are to move, the agent could be tempted to mention this to the buyer, who then feels encouraged to submit a lower offer.

Similarly, never tell the estate agent your rock bottom price that you will accept, because their main concern is to get your property out of the way in order to earn commission. If they were tempted to tell prospective buyers how low you can go, it could seriously weaken your bargaining position.

If, directly upon arrival at your house, a viewer promptly enquires 'Will you take an offer?' try kicking the subject into touch by replying 'By all means please take a look around and we'll have a chat about it,' before changing the subject with 'What sort of properties have you seen so far?' Of course, you may not need to bargain at all. Some folk hate the very idea of haggling, and if your asking price is too high it will put them off.

Don't be the first to raise the sordid subject of money. The best approach is to be super-nice so that with any luck viewers won't want to offend you by offering too low a price (well, it's worth a try!).

Sometimes you have to play a long game. Depending on the market, it may be worth accepting a lower offer so that you can then focus on your purchase. Alternatively, it may suit you better to hold out for a higher price. In the meantime, be prepared for every other estate agent in a 30-mile radius to bombard you with outrageous mailshots claiming they have dozens of cash buyers waiting for your house. This can be interpreted to mean that they're desperate to win a 'negotiator of the month' bonus prize holiday.

If your home is clean and tidy and priced realistically, you will get your buyer sooner or later. Reject bargain-hunters, and just keep on showing viewers around until it's sold.

The effect of the market

Your negotiating strategy must take account of the strength or weakness of your position as dictated by the state of the

housing market. If prices are stagnating or falling in a slow market, buyers have the upper hand. As a seller it's natural to be reluctant to sell 'too cheap', but in a tough market you may have to be flexible. Instead of nursing your losses, focus on recouping them when you buy your next property at a bargain price. Swings and roundabouts.

Conversely, in a booming market it's not unknown for prices to increase at the astonishing rate of around two per cent *a month* (as occurred in 1988, 2002 and 2007). In a rapidly rising market sellers and agents alike will try to second-guess future increases by setting optimistic asking prices. In a boom year, it's not unusual for several competing offers to be received on the same property, some of them above the asking price.

Hard bargaining

At some point a serious offer will materialise, usually via your estate agent. When this happens, no matter what the figure is, the best strategy is to look shocked. As with Moroccan souk traders, the first offer is normally not

Photo: JNP.co.uk

True story

Some years ago Connells estate agents in Basingstoke sent out sales letters claiming they had several people specifically interested in buying property in a particular street. Unfortunately for the estate agents, a Trading Standards officer lived in one of the properties and received a sales letter. When challenged, the agents were unable to provide evidence to support their claim. Indeed, the letters had been sent despite a previous warning from the Office of Fair Trading to the same branch in 1995 against sending such letters making misleading claims.

accepted outright. If you do immediately jump at it, the buyer will think he could have got it for less, and may eventually pull out. On the other hand, don't say something like 'No way mate – how dare you insult my intelligence with such a pathetically low offer.' It's important to always leave the door open for a subsequent higher offer. As a rule, the harder a buyer has to work to get a deal, the more satisfied they will be with it. One useful first response is to say that you weren't expecting to have to haggle, which is why the asking price was originally set at a very reasonable price. Or explain that because you are keen to move swiftly, you set a competitive price despite being told you could get more.

Before responding to an offer, ask if they have already sold their property and have their mortgage arranged. How soon could they complete? Bargaining involves a lot of speculation and guesswork, so the more facts you have the better. There's an art to 'controlled inaction' when bargaining – sometimes deliberate delay can be a useful weapon.

One benefit of selling without an agent is that buyers sometimes feel more relaxed because they may think you're an amateur, which can actually strengthen your position.

Even if you were intending to leave things like curtains and carpets all along, they can still be thrown in as bargaining chips. You could counter a revised offer by announcing that you couldn't possibly include the carpets and curtains at that price (and then negotiate separately for these).

This is where some agents or sellers find their integrity can become a tad flexible. Upon receiving their first offer they may be tempted to say 'We've already had an offer for this amount.' But if the buyer checks this fact and it turns out not to be true, it could well backfire. Or the buyer may then increase their offer to an acceptable level but turn the tables by suddenly reducing it at the last minute.

It doesn't do any harm to keep reminding prospective purchasers of the incredible bargain they're getting compared to other properties elsewhere – they must already think this, otherwise they wouldn't be spending time trying to buy your property. If your price is pitched just above a stamp duty threshold you will most likely have always anticipated having to come down to that level, but you can still stress the favour you're doing them by saving them lots of tax.

When the deal has at last been agreed, make it clear that this is the final contractual figure and that no further discussions will be entered into. This is to try and guard against manipulative buyers who later try to 'gazunder' by pulling a further price reduction just before exchange.

Accepting an offer

You could be lucky and receive an offer directly your property goes on the market. But if you do receive a very swift offer in the first few days, it may not be wise to accept it too eagerly, because after a few weeks you will start to think 'If it sold so quickly, we must have priced it too low.' Alternatively, you may find yourself playing host to endless viewings for groups of strangers invading your space for months on end before receiving an offer.

If you accept an offer from someone who hasn't yet sold their property, there's a good chance the process will drag on for ages while they struggle to sell, until quite possibly they'll let you down some six months later. This is a risk you can't afford to take. Of course, there's nothing to stop you accepting the offer subject to imposing a time limit, perhaps saying 'We'll give you 4 weeks to sell before putting it back on the market.' Or you could provisionally agree to a deal, saying something like 'I really hope you'll be able to buy it, but until you've sold your property we'll have to keep it on the market. But you're at the top of our list and we promise not to sell to anyone else without contacting you first – that's fair, isn't it?'

If you can't find a property to buy

With your home already under offer, what can you do if you then can't find a place to buy, or your purchase falls through? First, don't panic. Second, don't rush out and in

be difficult, you could always make your acceptance subject to being able to find a suitable property. It might be wise to level with your purchasers and suggest they do not proceed with their mortgage valuation or conveyancing, to minimise their abortive costs if things don't eventually proceed.

Alternatively, if as a seller in a rising market you later feel it necessary to 'renegotiate' the agreed sale price with your buyer it can cause real trouble. There may be plenty of other eager buyers out there ready to bite your hand off, and legally there's nothing to stop you doing this, but 'gazumping' is unethical and being greedy can backfire, should the new buyer later pull out – a bird in the hand is sometimes worth two in the bush.

If you can't find a property to buy within the agreed timescale these are usually the three best options:

■ Move into rented accommodation temporarily

It shouldn't be too hard to find a suitable property to rent for 6 or 12 months at a reasonable rent. It doesn't have to be the last word in luxury, just somewhere warm, dry and conveniently located. The obvious downside is the hassle of having to move twice, and possible issues with storing furniture etc. But the cost should be recouped later by being in such a strong position to buy.

■ Persuade your buyers to hang on

Everyone understands the traumas of moving, so your buyers may well be prepared to delay their move to fit in with you. The question is, will *their* buyers further down the chain be as understanding? If they really want your house, perhaps they will be prepared to move into rented in the meantime, maybe with a small inducement in the form of a slightly reduced sale price.

■ Withdraw

You may have to tell your buyers that you are no longer able to sell to them. Until exchange of contracts there is nothing to stop either side pulling out.

desperation buy any old property on the rebound – moving to the wrong house could mean having to move again a year or so later.

In a buoyant market buying is far harder than selling, so if you don't find a suitable property to buy within a few weeks of accepting an offer on the place you're selling you will be at a disadvantage, as prices continue to rise after you have accepted a fixed sale price.

In such a situation it's usually best to play straight with people. If you think finding a place to move to is going to

11 | INTO THE VOID

Managing the waiting game

Great news – your property is now officially 'Under Offer'. The first visible sign of success is when the words 'FOR SALE' on the estate agent's board magically morph into 'SOLD' – followed in tiny letters by the all-important phrase 'subject to contract'. Celebrations at this stage would be a tad premature, because of course nothing is actually binding until exchange of contracts. Right now, it's rather like peering across a vast canyon, knowing that you could be in for a bumpy ride before making it safely across to the other side.

In the meantime, you will have to endure the longest 'cooling-off period' known to man, during which buyers and sellers alike are highly sensitive to other influences. A good estate agent will know the importance of correctly managing the waiting game during the tense days that lie ahead.

Progress

Now your conveyancer can really swing into action. You're off to a flying start, with your HIP already containing some of the preliminary legal searches and enquiries. As we saw earlier, progress will be measured against the legal framework. So let's remind ourselves what your conveyancer will be doing:

- Obtaining the title deeds for the property being sold, to prove ownership
- Ordering 'office copy entries' (or a copy bundle of the deeds for unregistered properties)
- Preparing the draft contract, and sending it to the buyer's solicitor
- Sending evidence of title to the buyer's solicitor
- Answering 'preliminary enquiries'
- Preparing the final 'engrossed' contract
- Arranging for the seller to sign the contract
- Exchanging contracts

Whilst the draft travels interminably backwards and forwards, and various searches are pursued, there will be some other matters to keep you busy closer to home.

Surveys and valuations

The mortgage valuation and survey is a key stage that can be a tiny bit nerve-wracking. Some sellers liken the surveyor's visit to a trip to the dentist. On the plus side, at least it's not you who's paying for it.

The mortgage valuation

At some point in the next two or three weeks you're likely to get a phone call from your estate agent, or directly from a firm of surveyors. Most buyers will need a mortgage, so their lender will probably require an inspection to be booked for the mortgage valuation. This is basically to confirm to the

To pre-empt such risks, it's worth digging out some supporting comparables in advance for the surveyor. Note that asking prices aren't much use – to be relevant, prices need to be either 'under offer' or 'sold', ideally within the last six months. A lot can be discovered online, or by phoning round local estate agents. Better still, get your agent to do the work and come up with some evidence to justify it – after all, they were the people who originally valued it and decided what your home was worth. It's also advisable to take the trouble to present the house reasonably well. Piles of old laundry, filthy bathrooms, criminally dangerous electrics and clusters of dog poo in the garden (or living room) aren't going to help instil an overall impression of quality. But in many cases agents singularly fail to advise their sellers on the importance of taking such precautions.

lender that the property is worth the money being paid, and that it provides suitable security for their loan. In some cases however, a physical inspection of the property may not be required as lenders sometimes rely instead on simple 'drive by' or 'desktop' valuations. At least one in every five buyers will also instruct a private Homebuyer or Building Survey (see below) which in most cases will be carried out at the same time as the mortgage valuation.

Most sellers leave this stage up to their estate agent to handle, but it's comparatively rare for agents to do more than simply dish out the keys (some even struggle with that). But this is a critical part of the sale that needs to be managed. The main worry is that should the surveyor decide to 'downvalue' your property, then the buyer may accordingly decide they want to renegotiate the price. A lower valuation can also mess up the buyer's mortgage offer, which will have been calculated on the basis of the agreed sale price.

Avoiding downvaluation

Surveyors value houses by assessing evidence of recent sales of similar properties in the same postcode area. In most cases this shouldn't be too hard to find, but where properties are unusual, or the sale price is on the high side, a lack of good comparable evidence can lead to the surveyor cautiously valuing the property lower than the agreed price.

The survey

Armed with ladders, damp meter and an industrial-sized tape measure, the surveyor duly turns up on your doorstep. Whereas a typical mortgage valuation inspection will take about 25 minutes, a Homebuyer survey should take between one and two hours, and a Building Survey probably half a day. Some surveyors start in the loft, others start outside. Either way, it's worth trying to be helpful and answering questions about any recent improvements you've made, the dates of extensions, and any guarantees for work you've had done. Some surveyors may be immune to charm, but a cup of tea can go a long way.

When the job's done ask them what they think. Are there any significant defects? Just about all houses can be criticised in one way or another on a technical level, but often such defects are 'normal' for the age and type of property. Even a certain amount of damp, and a few old wood beetle boreholes, are very common in period buildings, and needn't be a deal breaker. An experienced surveyor should know when not to overreact.

In most properties, surveys will flag up routine matters such as electrics and heating systems that need some updating. In older house they may even recommend a drains test, or timber and damp treatment. This is not particularly unusual. Surveys also often point out the presence of asbestos-based materials, which are extremely common – for example in the form of asbestos cement soffits to eaves and corrugated sheeting to garage roofs – and aren't as scary as they sound.

What can go wrong?

Even the hardiest souls can find themselves reduced to gibbering wrecks over the long weeks leading up to exchange of contracts. Most people will be trying to manage a purchase at the same time as their sale, so there's the potential for double trouble. One thing to consider is that there's less chance of buyers pulling stunts if you've built a good personal relationship with them directly, rather than communicating blindly via the agent.

Never think that no news is good news – poor communication is a deal-breaker. If trouble does strike, remember that it's extremely rare in any transaction for everything to run perfectly smoothly at this stage. Apart from the property being valued below the agreed sale price, or potentially expensive defects being spotted by the surveyor, there are a number of classic problems that can blow up. But for each problem, there is a possible solution.

There are many reasons why buyers may decide to pull out of an agreed sale. If such a calamity happens to you, all you can do as a jilted seller is try to put the inevitable anger and frustration to one side and focus instead on getting to the bottom of the problem in order to address the real issue.

A break in the chain

Of all the things that can go wrong, a break in the chain is probably the worst, since it's the one you have least control over. You're dependent on each transaction in the whole chain going smoothly, so the longer the chain, the greater the chances of trouble. The weakest link is usually the bottom of the chain, where a first-time buyer may need a very large loan, perhaps combined with a relatively low income and minimal savings for the deposit and fees. It's by no means unknown for over-optimistic assumptions about mortgage finance, or a relatively minor downvaluation, to wreck carefully constructed calculations.

When a chain is threatening to collapse, estate agents will be only too aware that their commission is likely to swiftly follow it down the plughole. Some are better than others at 'sales progressing', and if things do go wrong you're going to need their help to pinpoint where the problem lies.

Any of the following problems can strike at any point in your chain:

Gazundering

'Gazumping' is a well known problem for buyers in rising markets, where they find themselves pushed aside at the last minute in favour of a higher bid from a rival buyer. 'Gazundering' is the greedy ugly cousin of gazumping, and can be a problem for sellers in a weak market. When buyers are thin on he ground, gazundering (aka 'bid and chip') occurs when your house is already under offer. Having agreed the sale price long ago, your buyer suddenly threatens to pull out unless you come up with a hefty price reduction. Unscrupulous buyers sometimes pull such a stunt at the last minute, just prior to exchange of contracts. This, of course, is pure blackmail. Underhand and unethical it may be, but it is not illegal. It is a perfect example of the absurdity of a home-buying system that allows either party to pull out at any time, for any reason, all the way up to exchange.

If there's any justification for such action it might be found in a steeply falling market where the sale has dragged on for months and property values have plummeted since the price was agreed. But when a sale price is negotiated, any likely increase or decrease in the market over the next couple of months should already be factored in.

The solution to gazundering isn't to go round and knock seven bells out of your buyer for being such a devious git (although it might make you feel better). Instead, the first thing to do is to call their bluff. Buyers will have clocked up a lot more costs than sellers by this stage, which they'd have to write off should the deal fall through.

One possible solution is for both sides to inoculate themselves in advance against such shenanigans by signing a 'lock-out agreement' at the time the offer is accepted. This is the same antidote as is used to preventing gazumping, where buyers and sellers agree to be faithful to each other for a certain period of time, the only get-out being if the buyer discovers some major structural or legal defect. Your solicitor should be able to draw up a suitable contract and agree a non-refundable deposit of, say, one per cent of the sale price each from you and your buyer. However, it has to be said that the success of lock-out agreements relies very much on the goodwill of both parties, and they are not the cure-all panacea they are sometimes made out to be. (See chapter 22.)

Some agents have introduced measures to pre-empt gazundering by stipulating a strict timeframe that buyers must abide by. But in a slow market where numbers of buyers are extremely thin on the ground there is little competition to buy, and such deterrents may have limited effectiveness.

Physical defects

Where potentially expensive defects have been spotted, specialist reports are sometimes required to get an idea of the cost of repairs. Surveyors also occasionally request a second opinion as a precautionary measure to cover their backs. A structural engineer's report may be required as a condition of the mortgage valuation if

apparent structural defects have been noted. But in many cases the engineer will give the property a clean bill of health, so this needn't be anything like as serious as it sounds, and the report may even come in useful one day when you come to sell. On older properties, the requirement for timber and damp reports is fairly common, as well as precautionary checks on the electrics or drains.

However, things that should have been evident at the time when the price was negotiated shouldn't be a reason for renegotiation now – for example an obviously dated heating system or decrepit windows.

Where a property has a history of subsidence or underpinning it may raise alarm bells with insurers, in which case the usual solution is for the new owners to simply take over and continue the existing building insurance policy. (See Chapter 22.)

The buyers see a better property

No house is perfect. As a purchaser, you always end up having to compromise on something. But if your buyer suddenly pulls out halfway through the sale process because they've just seen 'the house they've always wanted', there's not much you can do other than point out to them the risks they're taking. By withdrawing now they will stand to lose money, having clocked up abortive charges for such things as valuations, surveys and legal fees. By going back to Square One they will be messing their own buyer about and could well risk losing their sale. Plus they may be assuming their mortgage can stretch a lot higher, which could prove unrealistic. In addition falling in

love at first sight with the other house may well mean they have yet to perceive some of its negative qualities. Again, a lock-out contract can help prevent such flights of fancy and disloyalty.

Insufficient funds to exchange

Ideally, the amount of deposit should be known reasonably early in the process, but in actual practice, where there's a long chain, this sum may not be revealed until very close to exchange. Last-minute panics are not unknown – for example, where a buyer's solicitors request permission at the eleventh hour to pay a much reduced deposit.

Traditionally, sellers' solicitors would not exchange contracts until they knew that the buyers' solicitors were in receipt of funds for the deposit. But today this isn't always the case. Imagine a typical chain of linked transactions, in which all parties have agreed to exchange simultaneously. On the day of exchange, the deposit paid by the person at the bottom (often a first-time buyer) will need to be passed up the chain, from one solicitor to another, so it may be that your own buyer is reliant on deposit money filtering up from the depths of the chain below.

As we saw earlier, the amount of deposit is normally less than the official ten per cent stated in the contract. Although smaller sums of, say, five per cent are usually acceptable so as not to stall the exchange of contracts, in a market downturn, a larger deposit will provide valuable reassurance between exchange and competion.

Problems agreeing a completion date

Sometimes a mutually acceptable completion date cannot be agreed. This may simply be down to bloody mindedness and a reluctance to compromise. Suppose you've already accommodated your buyer's every whim on top of accepting a substantially reduced sale price, why should it be you who's inconvenienced? Why should it be you who has to move the family into a caravan for a week just to make life easy for those awkward sods? Whose side ultimately ends up compromising is likely to depend on the strength of the market, which will dictate whether the negotiating power rests with buyers or sellers.

Completion often takes place a couple of weeks after exchange, but it can be any time you agree. Perhaps a longer period of a month or more might suit everyone better, although the requirements of the chain as a whole will have some bearing here. To keep your sale on track, you could consider moving into rented 'holiday' accommodation, or even arranging a bridging loan. It may mean moving home twice, but that's still cheaper than paying aborted fees and starting all over again. One compromise is to agree a contribution towards your costs if it makes the whole chain work and everyone else also benefits.

To prevent such problems arising in the first place it helps if you can agree your completion date reasonably early on. But in reality, even where you and your buyers are able to mutually agree this date, it's still not advisable to immediately book your removals, or arrange a week's annual leave. Such agreed dates aren't actually binding until exchange of contracts and have a nasty habit of coming horribly unstuck. The longer the chain, the more likely it is that unforeseen delays will arise somewhere along the line. All it takes is a delay with a mortgage offer for one person in the chain to screw the dates up for everyone else. Then tempers get frayed because plans for removals and time off work are totally scuppered. So by all means work towards your proposed completion date, and notify your solicitor and estate agents accordingly; but don't be too rigid – it pays to remain flexible until you've exchanged.

Strictly speaking, completion doesn't have to wait until after exchange – the two can be carried out simultaneously, something property dealers and developers sometimes do to save time. Unfortunately this isn't quite as simple as it sounds, and is only a realistic option where there's no chain, so that it's just between you and your buyer. But even then there's a potential problem, which once again is all down to the fact that the completion date isn't legally binding or certain until exchange, which means that there's no obligation on either party. So there's nothing to stop the other side from suddenly changing their mind at the last minute and announcing that they want to put the completion date back another week. Which would be a bit of nightmare, because in the meantime you've booked the removal firm for that day, and you'll incur cancellation fees. Worse, there's the small matter of the mortgage funds that had to be ordered a week in advance – so now hundreds of thousands of pounds of mortgage money swirling about in cyber space will have to be returned, incurring multiple banking fees.

Disputes about what's included

One of the first tasks when selling is to complete a detailed list of what's included and what isn't. Despite this, many a sale has hit the rocks months later over the most trivial issues – arguments over the ownership of toilet roll holders, shelves or light fittings. It may sound laughably petty, but fixtures and fittings can sometimes be the straw that breaks the camel's back – ultimately becoming 'a matter of principle'. In other words, the process of selling a house can get you so stressed out that you're prepared to lose the sale just to teach them a (no doubt well deserved) lesson.

If this happens, take a deep breath. No matter how annoying the other side are, don't let them ruin your plans. Keep your eyes on the big picture and be prepared to lose a few quid on minor bits and pieces. Don't be bloody-minded just to prove a matter of principle. If they really want your greenhouse complete with prize-winning marrows, let them have it. You could buy 100 of them for what it would cost to let the deal fall through.

FIXTURES FITTINGS AND CONTENTS

Address of the property

1. Place a tick in one of these three columns against every item.

2. The second column ("excluded from the sale") is for items on the list which you are proposing to take with you when you move. If you are prepared to sell any of these to the buyer, please write the price you wish to be paid beside the name of the item and the buyer can then decide whether or not to accept you to sell.

	INCLUDED in the sale	EXCLUDED from the sale	NONE at the property
TV Aerial/Satellite Dish			
Radio Aerial			
Immersion Heater			
Hot Water Cylinder Jacket			
Roof Insulation			
Wall Heaters			
Night Storage Heater			
Gas / Electric Fires with any Surround			
Light Fittings:			
Ceiling Lights	☐	☐	☐
Wall Lights	☐	☐	☐
Lamp Shades	☐	☐	☐
If these are to be removed, it is assumed that they will be replaced by ceiling rose and socket, flex bulb holder and bulb			
Switches			
Dimmer switches			
Electric Points			
Fluorescent Lighting			
Outside Lights			

This form comprises 6 pages. Please complete all sections on all pages

A typical contents form for sellers to complete – all 6 pages!

Downvaluation

If the surveyor doing the mortgage valuation decides to value your property at a lower figure than the agreed sale price, it may prompt a re-think on the part of your buyer. In a rising market this doesn't always worry buyers unduly because they know that the value of the property will grow in the months ahead. But in a less buoyant market buyers may demand blood if the house is officially judged to be worth less than they've agreed to pay. Hence the importance of managing the valuation and survey process.

As we saw earlier, if your house does get unreasonably downvalued it should be possible to challenge the valuation retrospectively. Note that surveyors typically work within an acceptable margin of error, and do not normally downvalue within five per cent of the purchase price. It may be worth having your agent phone the surveyor to discuss the comparable evidence they used to reach their opinion of value. Valuers should operate within a radius of 25 miles of the property to ensure that they have good knowledge of the local market. In cases where the buyer's mortgage depended on the property 'valuing up' the buyer may be willing to take a gamble and pay for a different valuer to be instructed in the hope that they come up with a more optimistic valuation (probably via a new mortgage lender).

Mortgage problems

The most common problem that buyers face is arranging mortgages. Problems can be divided into those relating to the property – surveying and legal issues – and those concerning the applicants' financial status.

As the seller, there's not a great deal you can directly do about your buyer's income or credit problems, but you may be able to suggest solutions. Difficulties range from their employer being slow to return income references through to questions about how to count earnings from bonuses, overtime and commission. Credit scoring can be affected by innocent errors such as where someone's name and address is absent from the electoral register, perhaps because they're renting somewhere temporarily. Genuine mistakes sometimes occur, such as where a former flatmate has run up debts affecting other occupants' credit references. But such concerns can often be resolved. Past debt problems with a CCJ (County Court Judgment) can sometimes be cleared by applying to a credit reference agency to have it removed.

A good mortgage broker can sometimes save the day, by reapplying to a different lender with more relaxed criteria. Buyer's income and credit scores should have been checked at the preliminary stages, so as not to waste everyone's time, so it can particularly annoying if this turns out to be the problem.

Another risk with mortgages is where lenders decide to play fast and loose with their mortgage deals. This happened in 2008 as lenders suddenly decided en masse to withdraw higher loan-to-value mortgages and to drastically ration buy-to-let funding. In a matter of months maximum loan-to-value ratios collapsed from 125 per cent to around 90 per cent whilst interest rates rocketed. This caused problems particularly at the vulnerable lower end of the market, and many chains spectacularly collapsed. This was also the year when for many people the word 'banker' became a term of abuse.

Legal problems

Apart from mortgage difficulties, there is rumoured to be one other major cause of sales collapsing: slow solicitors. Of course, it's unfair to blame our learned friends for every problem that can vaguely be labelled 'legal', but for many sellers the conveyancing process still isn't as transparent as it could be.

This might be because in a typical transaction, it's buyers who are directly affected by legal problems more than sellers. But of course, their legal problems can very quickly become the seller's problems, as they threaten to mess up a sale or, indeed, sink the entire chain.

To avoid duplication, we look at all the common causes of delay due to legal issues – and show what you can do about them – in Part 3 (see Chapter 22).

Just the bare facts – a typical mortgage valuation report won't tell you a lot

Renegotiating the price

It may be possible to salvage a lost sale by renegotiating the agreed price, but this is never going to be easy. Pride and anger may justifiably make you want to stand your ground, even at the expense of your sale collapsing.

The only justification for revising an already done deal may be where new evidence has come to light since the offer was agreed. This will typically relate to defects spotted by the surveyor, which may include issues with the location that the buyers weren't aware of, such as an epidemic of drive-by shootings or floodwater submerging the street. More likely, their solicitors may have discovered that local authority consents weren't obtained for an old extension or structural alteration, or that proposals to widen the road into an eight-lane motorway some 20 years ago are still current. Either way, it's always best to start by getting the facts straight by having a chat with the solicitor or surveyor. Worries about defects can usually be nailed by obtaining quotes and translating them into a sum of money.

Once all the facts are at your fingertips, some last minute fancy footwork on your part might just save the day. But there's an art to negotiating. It helps to be polite and to calmly justify your position. For example, if an estimate for essential drainage works has come in at £2,000 you might suggest going 50/50 with the buyers. Always leave the door open so that it's easy for the other side to call you back and co-operate without losing face.

12 EXCHANGE AND COMPLETION

Photo: www.pickfords.co.uk

When your solicitor finally invites you to sign the contract, it's a sure sign that you've almost reached safe ground. But there's still the potential for thrills and excitement, because until you have safely exchanged, either side can pull out on the flimsiest pretext or the merest whim, shooting down your plans and dreams in the process. Nevertheless, assuming no one decides to pull a last-minute stunt, and that everyone involved has done their job properly, your sale should just about be in the bag.

Planning your move

The process of physically moving needs to be planned several weeks in advance. As we see in Chapter 23, there are a number of options to consider. You could employ a removals firm to do everything, by opting for a full packing service. Or you might prefer to do your own packing and just pay for 'removals only'. Alternatively, if you don't mind a spot of hard work you could save a few quid by hiring a van and, with the assistance of a small gang of highly motivated acolytes, do the whole lot yourself. Whichever option you pick, unless you've agreed a space of four or

Photo: www.pickfords.co.uk

Photo: www.pickfords.co.uk

more weeks between exchange and completion you'll need to set the wheels in motion now.

This normally means inviting three removal firms round to provide written quotes. Bear in mind also that it's incredibly easy to underestimate how long it's going to take to get all your stuff packed and ready. It's not a bad idea to allow yourself double the amount of time that you first guessed this would take. At the risk of tempting providence, some of the packing of non-essential items can be started before exchange. (See Chapter 23.)

Exchange of contracts

Once all the conveyancers in the chain are finally satisfied with the nitty-gritty detail in the contracts, and the various searches and enquiries are finished, the deal can at last be done.

Exchange of contracts, as the name suggests, usually involves each side swapping a signed copy of the same document. Once you have signed your copy, and the buyers theirs, exchange should take place. In reality, exchange will take place verbally when one solicitor phones the other, leaving the physical exchange of documents until shortly afterwards. After this all-important phone call, your solicitor should contact you directly to confirm the good news that exchange has taken place. This is one of those rare occasions when otherwise sober individuals are overcome with the passionate desire to embrace their legal adviser and smother them in hugs and kisses. The sense of relief is overwhelming.

But even at this stage it's not unknown for inexplicable delays to strike. One solicitor may try phoning the other, only to discover that they've skived off to play golf or are enjoying an extended Friday afternoon luncheon. Such 'country practices' are largely a thing of the past, but delays at this stage for whatever reason can send your blood pressure rocketing.

Now that you've exchanged it's highly unlikely that problems will arise within the space of the next week or two, although it's just possible that one of the parties could go bankrupt, the buyers could get divorced or a promised loan from a friend or family might fail to materialise. But, hey, your buyer could also be abducted by aliens or struck by a meteorite. So let's just celebrate having got this far.

What's in a contract?

What the contract basically says is that (a) the seller agrees to hand over the house and (b) the buyer agrees to hand over the money to pay for it. A typical contract will include the following clauses, although these are sometimes changed or additional ones inserted:

- The buyer's and seller's names and addresses.
- A description of what is being sold (a plan is only needed in rare cases where properties are unregistered).
- The agreed price.
- The amount of the deposit (often five per cent of the purchase price).
- The agreed date of completion.
- The capacity in which the seller is selling (referred to as 'full guarantee' where they own the freehold or leasehold; in rare cases where the seller is a lender who has repossessed the property or an executor or trustee selling after the death of the owner, it is known as 'limited guarantee').
- The agreed price of any extras that are being purchased separately (sometimes used as a dodge to reduce the price below stamp duty threshold).
- Covenants – any restrictions on the deeds or 'office copy entries'.
- Whether the property is freehold or leasehold.
- The rate of interest chargeable for any delay in completing.
- Title – confirming how the seller will prove ownership, normally by reference to 'office copy entries'.
- Risk – what happens if the house is destroyed or seriously damaged between the date of exchange and completion, *eg* the buyer can withdraw and ask for their deposit back.

Preparing for completion

Now, at last, you can look forward to moving house with confidence. Typically completion will take place a couple of weeks after exchange, but the actual agreed timescales will be stated in the contract. In the meantime the seller's solicitor still has some key tasks still to perform:

■ Sends evidence of title to buyer's solicitor

A copy of the deeds must be sent to the buyer's solicitor, or a summary of their contents known as an 'abstract of title'.

■ Arranges for seller to sign the final conveyance document

After checking that the transfer document or 'conveyance' is correct, the seller will need to sign it.

■ Receives balance of purchase price and hand over the title documents

The balance of the purchase money (typically the remaining 95 per cent, depending on the size of deposit you paid) must be received by your solicitor before completion. Upon completion, the title documents will be passed to the buyer's solicitor.

■ Pays off seller's old mortgage

Before the property can be handed over to the buyers, the old mortgage secured against it must be paid off. The existing mortgage lender will therefore be contacted as soon as possible to request confirmation of the amount outstanding and any redemption fees and penalties. The seller's solicitor will then deduct this sum from the sale money to pay off the old mortgage so it is 'discharged in full'.

Of course, it's not just the solicitors who need to keep on top of things during this final lap. There are a lot of practical matters that sellers need to deal with.

Removals

Immediately after exchange, you'll need to contact your chosen removal company to confirm your moving-out day (which normally corresponds to the day of completion). Time is short, so don't delay in case they're heavily booked.

Utilities

Be sure to notify your existing suppliers – for gas, electricity, water and drainage, and telephone and Internet services – well in advance. Tell them the date of completion and provide the new owners' details, but explain that the service is not to be discontinued. Remember to read the meters before you leave, so that you can inform the utility firms shortly after moving.

Post

For the first six months it's well worth taking advantage of the Royal Mail's forwarding service, which is good value for money and should prevent any 'rogue' mail from getting into the wrong hands.

Photo: www.pickfords.co.uk

Checklist of things to do before completion

- Confirm the completion date/moving day with your Removal firm
- Return any outstanding documents to your solicitor, signed by you if required
- Have the following meters read:
  Electricity
  Gas
  Water
- Notify the relevant councils of your move and ask for any Council Tax adjustment
- Notify water and sewerage company
- Arrange for post to be redirected
- Notify BT or other phone provider and ask for bill up to date of departure
- Arrange telephone and broadband connection to your new home
- Notify relevant parties of your change of address, including:
  Tax Office
  Department of Work & Pensions
  Child Benefit Agency/HM Revenue & Customs
  Banks and building societies
  TV and/or video hire companies
  Organisations to which you subscribe
  Publications to which you subscribe
- Cancel newsagent deliveries
- Cancel milk
- Cancel Direct Debit for old mortgage
- Put in place new Direct Debit for new mortgage
- Cancel insurance on old home
- Check that insurance has been arranged on new home (from exchange)
- Notify contents insurers of change of address

Neighbours

Some you may be sad to say goodbye to, others perhaps less so.

Council Tax

After exchange, write to your local council and ask for a refund of the Council Tax you have paid, or for confirmation of how much is owed. With your new home, note that you only become responsible for Council Tax when you begin to move your belongings into the property – which in some cases may not be for a while after completion.

Completion day

Come the big day, you still can't afford to take your eye off the ball. Although in 99 per cent of cases everything should go through without difficulty, problems do occasionally arise. The cause of last-minute problems is more likely to rest in the buyer's court than the seller's, which is why this subject is covered in greater depth in Chapter 23.

The area with the greatest potential for hitches is the transfer of mortgage funds, which is usually done by telegraphic transfer (TTF). If someone in the chain doesn't receive the money for the sale of their house, it will prevent them from completing, which in turn can delay completion throughout the whole chain until the next day. This of course is a potential nightmare, because removal firms are all booked and ready. Solicitors cannot force buyers to complete and physically hand over their money on the actual day of completion, even though buyers are legally obliged under the terms of the contract to do so. But if they delay completion, purchasers can be held legally liable for interest and expenses incurred by sellers.

Keys

Normally, sellers leave a set of keys with their estate agent or solicitor, with instructions to release them as soon as full

payment of the completion monies has been received. This is also a useful solution if the house is to be left empty for a while after you've moved out. However, buyers sometimes prefer to arrange with sellers for a direct handover of the keys. Either way, until your solicitors have received the completion money it's essential that the keys are not handed over. No matter how nice the buyers are, you can't risk letting them move in because they could still fail to complete. So keep in touch with your solicitor on the day until they confirm that that the funds have cleared. Delays in the release of the keys are more likely the further up the chain you are. Each seller in the chain has to be sure that funds have been paid before releasing the keys, and with a long chain it can sometimes be quite late in the day before the final keys can be released.

Timing

Fortunately, most completions go without a hitch, so you should find yourself waving goodbye to the old place by lunchtime or soon after. You should normally aim to be packed up and ready to leave by about 2:00pm. Buyers arriving too early can be extremely irritating as you try to remember a thousand things to ensure a successful move. Of course, there's nothing to stop you agreeing a different time between yourselves, but sellers are not allowed to remain in occupation after the completion date.

Be sure to take all the agreed contents and fittings with you. If, however, the task of moving all your old stuff turns out to be more demanding than anticipated (which it always does) then the buyers may be champing at the bit, while you're still hard at it. If you're really struggling to move everything out in time, one compromise may be to store some stuff in a garage or shed until the next day, with the new owners' consent.

After completion, your solicitor will need to pay off your existing mortgage. Your estate agents' fees are normally paid through your solicitor, but they will probably not make payment without first notifying you of the amount and giving you an opportunity to check the bill.

True story

Avoiding identity theft

Every year credit reference agency Experian receive over 4,000 calls from victims of identity fraud. Moving house potentially poses a big security risk. Just one document with key information can be enough to get an ID fraudster started, as Katie Baxter discovered when she moved:

'I'd forgotten to tell a company that I'd moved, so they sent some information to my old house, which the people living there at the time got hold of. With that address and my name, they managed to spend £8,000 on clothes and furniture.' This was all bought in Katie's name, leaving her responsible for the tab. Katie continues: 'I am so surprised at how easy it was for them to set up these accounts in my name. What shocked me the most was that they set up a different date of birth. Debt collectors' letters followed, and catalogues I'd never heard of arrived in my name.'

The fraudsters skipped the country, but the theft of her identity left a grim legacy for the victim. She continued to be turned down as a bad credit risk when attempting to buy things on credit for a long time afterwards.

So the best advice is to arrange for Royal Mail to forward your post to your new address; be sure to write in good time to all your banks, insurers and financial services providers; and lastly, take your address off the publicly accessible electoral roll (there's a box you can tick).
Source: BBC TV 'Identity theft: outnumbered'

PART 3

BUYING

13 | THE PURCHASE PROCESS

Buying should be much more enjoyable than selling, because you can focus squarely on getting that fabulous new home that you really want. Cash buyers, first-time buyers and investors are best placed to buy since they don't have to worry about selling first. The same is true if you're currently renting. But for most of us, quite a bit of time will have already been spent getting this far, with our existing house under offer. Either way, the main task now is to track down the best possible new home within your budget. Then, to ensure success, the purchase process must be carefully managed, so nothing can rain on your parade.

The buying game

The stages you go through as a buyer will run something like this, although not always in this precise order. If you're simultaneously selling your old property some stages will overlap, as shown in Part 2. All of these stages are discussed in detail in the following chapters.

■ Deciding what can you afford

Before you start hunting for your dream home, it's important to work out how much you can afford to borrow. This will depend on your income and the amount that you're realistically able to to pay each month in mortgage intereset, as well as what sort of savings you have to cover the various fees, the deposit and the moving costs. If you have a property to sell, get it under offer first and take a crash course in mortgages (see Chapter 14). Getting a 'mortgage agreement in principle' from a lender at this stage will save time later.

■ Deciding where you want to live

What's an acceptable travelling time to work and school? What's the proximity to motorways and public transport? Town or village? An established area or one that's 'up and coming'? Located on a main road or in a sleepy backwater? How does an area score regarding crime and safety?

■ Deciding what sort of property you want

What do you really need from your new home – how many bedrooms, potential to extend, what size garden etc. Do you want a house, a bungalow or a flat? A classic Georgian townhouse, a Victorian terrace or a 1930s semi? Or perhaps a house on a new development?

■ Appointing your conveyancer

In most cases the same firm will also be handling your sale (see Chapter 4).

■ Viewing

You like the look of a property on paper, but agents' descriptions may not tell the full story! One viewing is never enough, but it will help you decide if you could live there. Does it tick the right boxes? Consider how it compares with other properties, what condition it's in and whether it's in a nice area. Is it worth the money?

■ **Making an offer**
Negotiate the best price and get your offer accepted.

■ **Finalising your mortgage**
Submit your application. The lender makes credit and income checks, and instructs a mortgage valuation before issuing your mortgage offer.

■ **Conveyancing**
The legal process of transferring ownership can now fully proceed. See below.

■ **Getting a survey**
A lot of serious defects aren't at all obvious. Unless a qualified surveyor inspects your new home, you may find there are some nasty repair bills in store for you.

■ **Exchanging contracts**
When both sides' solicitors are ready, contracts can be exchanged. Only now is the deal legally binding.

■ **Moving and completion**
Pay the money and move in.

The legal framework

Once you've found the right property and your offer has been accepted, the legal side of things can really start moving. The key legal steps up to exchange of contracts are set out below. Often two or more of these tasks will be going on at the same time. From now on, progress is measured by how far things have advanced along this legal framework.

1 Draft contract checked and returned
The draft contract sets out all the terms of the sale, although the date of completion isn't normally inserted at this stage. This is the first version of what will eventually become the final contract, confirming the change of ownership of the property. It is prepared by the seller's

Photo: JNP.co.uk

solicitor based on a standard form modified to suit the seller and the property being purchased. It is then sent to your solicitor, who checks it and amends any clauses that are detrimental to your interests, raising any questions with the seller's solicitor before returning it. The main thing they look for is any alterations to the standard text. Although written in a standard format, these can sometimes go through many changes and alterations, before both sides are happy to agree to all the terms and conditions. Then the final versions can be signed and contracts can be exchanged. There are two main parts to a draft contract:

Particulars of sale
Usually printed on the first page of the contract, this states the names of the two parties and provides a brief description of the property and the agreed purchase price etc.

Conditions of sale
Here you will find the details of the proposed transaction. This usually comprises standard conditions of sale (typically the Law Society Conditions) plus any extra conditions added by the seller's solicitors (for example where they specifically require the buyer to insure the house from exchange).
To confirm current ownership of the property, a copy of the title documents (normally the 'office copy entries') usually accompanies the draft contract along with an attached fixtures and fittings form.

2 'Preliminary enquiries' sent to vendor's solicitor
One of the first jobs is for your solicitor to send out a long list of questions about the property to the other side's solicitor. These preliminary enquiries (or 'pre-contract enquiries') are on a standard form, usually with a few extra queries added at the bottom of the list. They ask things like whether the property is connected to mains gas, water, electricity and drainage, whether there have been any disputes with neighbours, and what alterations have been made to the house. Further questions are raised about any known rights of way, who owns the boundaries, and whether any extensions have been built. If you're buying a flat, information about the lease will also be requested.
A separate fixtures and fittings form asks sellers to state exactly what they're including in the sale – *ie* whether carpets, curtains and lights etc are to be left at the property.
In some cases the seller's solicitor will start the ball rolling and volunteer this preliminary information, but if the sellers are not terribly organised these questions may ricochet to and fro between the parties for a number of weeks until satisfactory answers are forthcoming. Of course, it doesn't help that the replies to individual questions are typically vague and unhelpful, such as 'I don't know', 'Not to my knowledge' and 'No, but please rely on your own searches'. But if a vendor deliberately lies – for example by denying

any history of boundary disputes with neighbours – and, as the new owner, you suffer a loss as a result, they could be sued for damages (see Chapter 7).

3 Local authority search

The Local Authority search is one of the most important components of the purchase process. This is because down at City Hall there is a veritable treasure trove of important data waiting to be explored. Here you will find records of planning consents, infringements of building regulations, and warning notices issued for 'dangerous structures' at the property you're buying. They also keep records of compulsory purchase notices – where buildings are zoned for compulsory acquisition so that they can be demolished to make way for a major project, such as a new bypass. Clearly, this is crucial stuff that could drastically affect the value of your property.

So a number of searching questions are sent to the Council, and several different departments are required to provide answers. These enquiries will also ascertain whether the property is Listed or located in a Conservation Area, whether the road is publicly maintained (otherwise the adjoining home owners may be liable for the cost of maintaining it), and if there are any plans to build a motorway in the vicinity. Any council grants secured on the property should be flagged up, along with any planning restrictions on extending the house.

The good news is that local authority searches are included in the HIP that the seller will by now have ordered and paid for. In case of errors, the accuracy of HIPs is backed with indemnity insurance. However, some solicitors and mortgage lenders may not want to rely on this, if the search is out of date, or where some information is missing, in which case a fresh search may be required (at the buyer's expense). Local searches are discussed in more detail in Chapter 20.

Traditionally, an additional set of questions would also need to be sent to the water authority to find out who's responsible for the drainage system. But this may not be necessary as the relevant information should be available

Searchers' delight. Town halls are a treasure trove of information

Photo: wikimedia

in the HIP. However, sometimes other specialist searches are needed, depending on the property's location. If you're planning to move to an area where mining was a traditional industry, a mining search will be needed. Or if your new home faces a common or village green, there's a risk that you might be expected to pay towards its upkeep, so a 'common search' will be required to sniff out any such liabilities (though as a bonus it may be discovered that you enjoy the ancient right to graze your sheep free of charge!).

4 Checking title with the Land Registry

At the same time as your solicitor is mulling over the draft contract, perhaps the most important check of all must be carried out – that the person from whom you've agreed to buy the house isn't an identity fraudster but is actually the true owner with the legal right to sell the property. This is normally done by checking the Land Registry 'office copy entries'. However, in those rare cases where properties are unregistered, your solicitor will need to sift through a bundle of old title deeds known as an 'Epitome of Title' (see 'Unregistered properties' in Chapter 20). While they're at it, they will also confirm whether there are any public rights of way across the garden, and conversely whether you benefit from rights of access over anyone else's property. They will further check any recorded legal restrictions on the use of the property. Any intriguing issues that come to light will then be raised with the seller's solicitor.

5 Checking your mortgage offer

Unless you happen to be that rare species, a cash buyer, you will not be able to exchange contracts until the formal mortgage offer has been received from your lender. This isn't just the agreement in principle you got from your lender ages ago. It's a formal written offer confirming that they will come up with the funds secured on the house you're buying. But first, the mortgage valuation must have been completed and (hopefully) will have confirmed the agreed sale price. It also depends on the lender satisfactorily processing your income references and credit ratings. When everything's tickety-boo, your solicitor will send you the mortgage deed to sign.

You will also need to confirm that you have sufficient money set aside to pay the balance of the purchase price not covered by your new mortgage. Cash buyers will need to provide proof of the existence of funds, such as a bank statement or an impressively bulging suitcase.

Sometimes the bank's mortgage valuation report will flag up issues about potential legal concerns that have been spotted on site. This normally relates to matters like shared access, apparent rights of way over gardens, nearby electrical sub-stations, and tunnel passageways through terraces ('flying freeholds'). They may also point out any extensions or structural alterations that needed planning or Building Regs consent. Such issues will need to be further investigated by your conveyancer. In rare cases lenders may

keep a retention to encourage buyers to repair major defects (see Chapter 21).

Your solicitor will normally receive a copy of the valuation report direct from the mortgage lender, so they can raise questions about anything suspicious noted in the report. But occasionally banks forget to send them one, so it's not a bad idea to pop a copy of yours through just in case.

6 Arranging for the buyer to sign the contract

Once your solicitor is happy with all the terms of the contract, you will be invited to sign it, together with your partner or other joint purchasers. This normally involves a visit to their offices. But before signing it's worth taking a few moments to browse through the contract papers and title documents. As far as possible (without being fluent in legal-speak) make sure that you are happy before you sign and commit to contract.

7 Exchanging contracts

The magic words 'exchange of contracts' mean that the sale is now binding on both parties. It's not entirely unknown for buyers to pull out after this stage, but you would lose your full deposit and possibly be sued by the seller. Before exchange can take place, sufficient deposit money will normally need to be transferred safely into your solicitor's bank account.

Once contracts have been exchanged, your solicitor's work doesn't stop. There are several key legal tasks that need to be carried out prior to completion, for which see Chapter 23.

Timing your purchase

Somewhere in the small print of mortgage adverts it normally states something like 'House prices can fall as well as rise'. Rather disappointingly, it doesn't tell you when this is going to happen. Even the experts consistently fail to accurately predict the timing of market downturns. One thing that everyone is agreed on is that markets are cyclical. As a very rough rule there has been a slump in house prices every 7 to 12 years, and this, of course, is the best time to buy. The problem is, when prices are rapidly rising it may seem as if they will continue moving upwards forever. The fear amongst buyers is that by holding back from the 'property ladder' in the boom times, prices will continue to rocket, making it even harder to save for a deposit in future.

One reason why second-guessing the housing market is such a tough call is that world events, such as inflation, wars, disasters and oil prices, affect mortgage interest rates in the UK, which in turn have a major influence on the affordability of housing.

But it's important to have some idea of the state of the market, before you start in order to gauge the strength of your negotiating position as a buyer or seller.

Buying during a boom

There's a lot of luck involved in buying property. No one wants to be in the position where they have to witness their main asset plunging in value over several years, having 'bought at the peak of the market'. Where prices fall to the extent where the mortgage is bigger than the (now shrunken) value of a house, it means you are in *negative equity*. Plenty of home owners found themselves in this position during the early 1990s slump, and for most it simply wasn't an issue. Problems are only likely to arise should you be forced to sell – for example where you have to move for a new job. If you did sell it for less money than the mortgage secured on it, you would still owe the bank the balance, which could be a seriously hefty sum. The best advice is to just get on with your life, and sooner or later prices will pick up, often quite dramatically.

Buying during a slump

Amidst all the doom and gloom that the media delight in churning out during a slump, it can be hard to know when exactly to take the plunge and start buying. It may be tempting to hang on until prices fall even further, but remember that they won't drop forever. Eventually, as wages and rents increase over time, property becomes more affordable. Bargain hunters buy cheap, and as demand increases prices rise, fuelling media tales of easy money, and then everyone else in the country follows suit and plunges in, pushing prices higher still. Low interest rates, easy finance and full employment are other ingredients that pave the way for recovery.

What if you haven't yet sold?

Suppose you were just idly mulling over the notion of moving house when, quite unexpectedly, you come across your dream home with a For Sale board outside. It's the house you've always wanted, but you haven't even put yours on the market. By the time you've waited for an offer on your place ten other buyers could have snapped it up. So what should you do?

If you seriously decide to buy before selling, the only way your offer will be taken seriously is if you effectively become a 'cash buyer' for example by taking out a bridging loan. (See Chapter 1.) Otherwise, even if your offer is accepted, there's a fairly high chance you'll get pushed sharply aside directly a 'proceedable' rival buyer pops up. And losing a property that you've got your heart set on will obviously cause immense anguish. In this state of mind, given a straight choice between securing the house you really want and 'giving your right arm', it's not inconceivable that the much-loved limb would be the loser.

As a rule, the further the purchase process has proceeded, the more painful it becomes to lose a property. Even after just a week you probably already had all the decoration and furnishing planned to perfection in your head. By the second week you'd mentally built the extension, brought up the family and joined the local parish council. Then suddenly there's a competing bid from someone else who barges in with wads of cash, and promptly proceeds to exchange contracts.

The hardest thing to realise when disaster strikes is that houses are like rather bargains on eBay – if you miss one, sooner or later another, possibly even a better one, will come along.

Relocating for your employer

The greater the distance that you're planning to move, the more hassle there tends to be. This is largely because the home-finding process will involve lots of long, tedious journeys, possibly over many months. Picking the right property is far more difficult if you don't know the local area. But if you're relocating as a career move instigated by your employer, it may well be that all the expenses and fees are fully paid, with most of the hard work managed for you by a relocation company. So in fact this is probably the best way to move house.

The psychology of buying

Advertisers are well aware that, as buyers, we go through a number of distinct stages when making a purchase decision. Indeed, marketing people are trained to spot these stages, so they can successfully target us at the right time with their sales message.

The following steps apply to some relatively simple purchases, such as buying a car, but are probably more evident in more complex decisions like buying a house, where the process continues for several months.

Stage 1 Problem recognition

This is where you – or your partner – recognise a need. In the same way that feeling hungry will prompt a quest for food, so the decision to get married may trigger the need

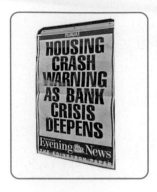

for larger accommodation than a studio flat 'bachelor pad'. Or perhaps the news that a baby is on the way could prompt the need for a third bedroom. Once the problem has been recognised, the main alternatives are broadly considered – in this case renting or buying a suitable flat or a house, or building an extension. Other alternatives, such as living with Mum and Dad, renting a houseboat or buying a caravan may be swiftly rejected, or utilised temporarily as a short-term means to an end.

Stage 2 Information search

Next comes a long period of information gathering – reading magazines and books, taking advice from friends and parents, even some preliminary property searching online. Formerly dull subjects like mortgages and house prices suddenly become formidably interesting, and you start to bore your friends with endless property chat. You become more sensitive and receptive to information.

Of course, this initially fairly relaxed phase may fizzle out as you postpone making a decision. But more often it evolves into actively searching for information. As it becomes more urgent, you notice For Sale boards, check out estate agents, and even arrange to look over a few properties.

Marketing people know that at this stage you're likely to be relatively open to persuasive messages – and equally likely to be influenced by negative messages, such as friends' bad experiences with a particular bank or firm of estate agents.

The main sources of information are:

- Personal sources – work colleagues, family and friends
- Personal experience – previous experiences, trial use of the product (*eg* perhaps you've been renting the property before considering buying it)
- Public sources – media, consumer associations
- Businesses – advertising, publicity and sales people

Of these, personal sources and independent media can be especially important in shaping opinion of what's 'social acceptability'. So if your trusted friend announces 'Only sad morons with hygiene issues live in studio flats,' it could make you even more determined to move.

Estate agents know that bad media publicity has the potential to undermine the carefully honed positive image projected in their promotions. Buying a property is a complex, high-risk decision, so we attach considerable importance to personal testimonials and opinions as opposed to 'managed' commercial messages. Meeting a

disgruntled former customer of an estate agent or mortgage lender can influence your decisions. The role of trusted opinion leaders or local media as influencers can be crucial.

The psychology of buying cars tells us that some brands are 'aspirational' (Bentley, Jaguar, Mercedes etc). 'Aspirational lifestyle groups' are those to which consumers would like to belong, and can be an important influence on buyers. But the lifestyle we aspire to is likely to also depend on what stage of life we've reached – youthful city traders may be seduced by the cool urban chic of a docklands warehouse conversion, whereas older age groups may prefer the lifestyle choice of a splendid Georgian townhouse, a smart new executive home or a classic country cottage with roses round the door.

Stage 3 Evaluation of alternatives
There comes a time when you've received a lot of information and you want to start resolving the problem. Some kind of order needs to be imposed on the chaos of images, data and messages. This means narrowing down your options, perhaps by limiting your choice of neighbourhoods, and making decisions on what's realistically affordable. In other words you begin to get focused on what's really important, such as the numbers of bedrooms, nearness to shops etc.

At this stage you are very receptive to informed opinion. If an estate agent is perceived as genuine, their comments can influence you: 'Of course, ten years ago that was a very popular area, but now the houses are all rented out to benefit claimants – I wouldn't want to bring my children up there'; or 'I think you're very wise considering three-bedroom semis in Southcourt.' Of course, this won't have much affect if you believe that the agent's main goal is to persuade you to buy a tired property that they haven't been able to shift.

Stage 4 Overload
Enough already! Not altogether surprisingly, it's first-time buyers who are more likely to suffer information overload and confusion. At this stage you are reaching crisis point and just want to make a decision, because by doing so, you will feel less confused, more satisfied, more certain and will stop actively seeking information. The problem is, the desire to 'cut and run' often leads to the wrong

decision being made. Indeed, unscrupulous marketeers have been known to deliberately engineer systematic overload of vulnerable consumers for this very purpose. High-pressure timeshare sales techniques were once infamous for this. Energy suppliers have been accused of deliberate 'obfuscation' as have some financial services providers with their unenviable record of miss-selling endowments, pensions and mortgages.

Stage 5 The purchase decision
Ultimately, all the alternative offerings will be ranked in order of preference and a decision made. But it's still possible for purchasers to change their minds, as the decision remains subject to modifying factors, especially the attitudes of friends, family and professional advisers. Buyers are also highly sensitive to potential risks. What if there are hidden faults in the property or there are neighbours from hell living next door? What if mortgage rates rise? Are we doing the right thing?

However, as consumers, we tend to develop our own ways of dealing with risk over time. For example we may only consider buying new homes with an NHBC warranty, or avoid properties that are likely to need expensive renovation work. Buying designer goods, such as branded kitchen appliances, may help provide reassurance about product quality.

This is the critical 'point of sale' phase where marketeers know that, with careful management, they can influence the purchase decision.

Stage 6 Post purchase
The problem with property is that having made the decision to buy, there is then an interminable 'cooling-off period', where buyers and sellers are subject to all kinds of influences that can muddy the water and cause you to pull out. Which is why the word 'SOLD' in estate agent language actually means 'under offer subject to contract and survey and a million other possibly negative influences'.

It's well known that some buyers suffer from 'post-purchase blues'. It's claimed that the biggest readers of car ads are those who've just bought a car. It seems we go on looking for justification that we made the right decision, which is why agents need to continually reassure buyers by bolstering them with positive messages all the way up to exchange.

14 | FINANCING YOUR PURCHASE

There wouldn't be much of a property market without easy access to mortgage funding. This became horribly apparent in 2008 in the aftermath of the credit crunch when, in a state of near panic, banks began to hastily withdraw mortgages, crashing the market into reverse gear. Fortunately mortgage funding is now once again widely available, albeit on slightly less attractive terms than has been the case for some years. So before you start viewing property and mentally moving in to that fabulous mansion, the first question has to be –

How much can I afford to borrow?

You are about to make what is probably the biggest financial commitment of your life. But unless you're massively cash-rich, getting your hands on a prime piece of real estate is likely to involve borrowing large amounts of spondulicks. The average mortgage size in Britain is around £150,000, but to figure out how big a mortgage you can have, the first step is to look at your income and draw up a monthly budget. This will show what sort of payments you can realistically afford to make.

Budgeting

As a general rule, your monthly mortgage payments should be no more than about one-third of your income after tax. If you're comfortably paying rent at the moment, or your existing mortgage isn't too taxing, you could take this as a base figure and add a bit. If the figures look depressingly tight, you might be able to meet your mortgage payments by other means, such as taking in a lodger, or buying with relatives or friends – see next chapter.

But your income isn't the only factor. It helps greatly if there's something in the piggybank. A certain amount of capital, in the form of cash savings, shares or equity from the sale of your existing home, will be required.

Even if your bank is willing to lend as much as 90 per cent of the purchase price, you'll still need to come up with the other 10 per cent. Although this represents a sizeable chunk of money, it should be manageable for anyone who's built up some equity in their present home. But as well as the deposit, as a buyer you have to budget for a number of extra costs, notably stamp duty tax, legal fees and survey and mortgage fees.

Estimated cost of buying a £200,000 property

Stamp duty (at 1% of the *full purchase price*)	£2,000.00
Solicitor's fees	£400.00
Telegraphic transfer fee	£30.00
Local authority search	£200.00
Drainage search fee	£60.00
Environmental search fee	£50.00
Land Registry searches	£10.00
Bankruptcy search (per applicant)	£5.00
Land Registry fee (to register you as the new owner)	£200.00
Lender's mortgage valuation fee	£200.00
Homebuyer survey	£350.00
Buildings insurance	£175.00
Removals	£550.00
TOTAL	4,230.00

All figures are approximate.

NB Most lenders charge arrangement fees and some mortgages may attract additional fees – see below. Some mortgage brokers also charge a fee.

If you are selling as well as buying, you will need to additionally allow for estate agents' fees and a HIP – see Part 2. The average cost of fees for someone moving house is around £10,000. (*Source: BBC Panorama.*)

Stamp duty

Buying a house means you will need a sizeable pot of spare cash to pay the Government. One of the most hated taxes, and one of the hardest to avoid, stamp duty is a tax on moving home paid by purchasers. Rates change from time to time but stamp duty currently catches many struggling first-time buyers, thereby making housing less affordable.

At the time of writing, 'stamp duty land tax' – to give it its full name – must be paid by buyers on all transactions above £175,000. If the property's value is less than this, you will be in the lucky minority which doesn't have to pay anything to the Chancellor. For homes priced between £175,001 and £250,000 you pay one per cent of the property's value. Between £250,001 and £500,000 you pay three per cent, and above £500,001 it's four per cent of the value of the property – see website for updates.

Where the price of the property you're buying happens to be just above a 'stamp duty threshold', one well-known tax dodge was to lower the agreed purchase price below the threshold and then reimburse the seller by paying an inflated price for fixtures and fittings separately. But the taxman is wise to this, and it can be hard to justify paying £10,000 for a second-hand sofa.

The only mildly good news is if you are buying a property in an area designated by the Government as 'disadvantaged', stamp duty may not apply. See website for areas that qualify.

Calculating your borrowing power

The size of mortgage you can borrow depends largely on your income. But there are different types of income, so how exactly do lenders calculate the amount they are prepared to lend?

Income multiples

Traditionally, the amount you could borrow was calculated

Photo: MortimersAylesbury.co.uk

by multiplying your gross annual income by three. If you were buying with your partner banks would allow 2.5 times your joint income. But as interest rates fell in the 1990s this seemed unduly cautious and now 4 times sole salary or 3 to 3.5 times joint income is widely available. So if you're earning £30,000 a year and your partner brings home £15,000, you may be able to jointly borrow a grand total of £157,500. But since, in some parts of the country, this won't buy you much more than the proverbial broom-cupboard, lenders have devised more flexible 'affordability' methods of calculating how much applicants can borrow.

'Affordability' is a more sophisticated but less transparent process that takes account of the applicant's overall financial circumstances. It is meant to take into account the possibility of unfortunate events occurring – such as injury, illness or losing your job. What if one of you had to stop working, perhaps because of an unplanned pregnancy? Suppose interest rates take a hike – as they did in the early 1990s, peaking at 15 per cent. These are all issues the 'affordability' test will weigh up, balanced by possible future good news, such as whether your salary is likely to rise significantly. The risk of bad things happening can, of course, be 'hedged' by taking out insurance for illness or redundancy, and jumps in interest rates countered by arranging a fixed rate mortgage (see below).

Does commission count?

No matter what price range you're looking in, it always seems that the property you *really* want is just beyond your financial reach. The temptation is to stretch a few thousand more. But making the sums add up isn't always easy. The way lenders assess extra income – things like commission, bonuses, overtime payments and company cars – can make all the difference. Basically this will depend on how your employer describes it. If they class it as 'guaranteed' then the bank should treat it as basic salary. More often it will not be guaranteed, in which case mortgage lenders will normally be prepared to include only half the value in their calculations. So if your non-guaranteed commission comes to £10,000 a year, the lender may be willing to add £5,000 to your basic salary before multiplying it up. Best run this past your employer first.

Self-employed

You may have noticed TV ads bragging about how they can lend money even in the toughest cases. Poor credit history? Arrears? Escaped terror suspect? Self-employed? No problem. When it comes to arranging a loan, being self-employed can make you feel like a second-class citizen. Independently earning an honest living seems to get lumped together with assorted high-risk categories and all manner of social ills.

Whereas the average employee simply has to utter the magic words 'PAYE' and provide three months' wage slips or a P60 and everyone's happy, for the self-employed there can be a mountain to climb to produce suitable 'proof of income'.

That said, mainstream lenders should be perfectly happy if you can confirm your income by providing two or three years' worth of accounts. The problem is that your accounts will be drafted to (quite legitimately) minimise your tax liabilities and may not do full justice when it comes to presenting your income for mortgage purposes. This can also be an issue if your business hasn't been running for that long. If proving your income is difficult, perhaps because some of it is paid in cash, a good broker may be able to advise on suitable self-certification products, although the choice of lenders will be limited, ultimately costing you more through higher mortgage rates.

Self-certification and 'non-status'

Many self-employed people find that 'non-status' mortgages offer a good solution. These enable you to 'self-certify' your income by signing a document stating how much you earn. A broker will know which lenders are worth approaching. Most judge cases in terms of overall 'affordability' rather than strict income multiples.

Some lenders have been criticised for 'turning a blind eye' where applicants may have been tempted to grossly exaggerate their income. Obviously a bigger mortgage can lead to problems meeting monthly payments, ultimately ending in repossession. But as a safety net, 'self-cert' mortgages usually require a sizeable deposit, perhaps 25 per cent or more of the purchase price, and rates are often higher than the lender's Standard Variable Rate, because of the increased risk. If the loan is limited to 75 per cent of the value of the property, for a £250,000 home you would need to come up with £62,500 cash. The usual range of mortgages – fixed, capped, discounted etc – are available with self-certification.

Loan-to value (LTV)

Even if you're a big earner, there are limits on what you're allowed to borrow. The size of the mortgage loan compared to the value of the property is fundamental to the maths of mortgages. This 'loan-to-value' ratio, or LTV, will crucially dictate how much the bank will lend. As everyone knows, the days of 125 per cent LTV mortgages are now history (Northern Rock weren't the only lender to offer loans totalling considerably more than the value of the house being purchased). At the time of writing, most lenders have reduced the maximum they are prepared to lend to only 85 per cent of the property's value. Because lower loans mean lower risk for lenders you need to borrow less than 75 per cent LTV to qualify for the cheapest deals. So it's now more important than ever to have at least a sizeable deposit as well as a spotless credit history, because high LTV mortgages will cost you more.

Credit and references

Before the bank hands over hundreds of thousands of their lovely pounds, they'll obviously want to be sure that their money's in safe hands. So how exactly do they go about investigating this?

Would you lend money to...you?

Most of us would think twice about lending money even to our dearest friends if we knew they had a history of absconding without payment. The same holds true for banks – with the notable exception of the US sub-prime lending fiasco, which proved the obvious point that if you lend money to 'un-creditworthy' folk you may as well wave goodbye to your cash. There are three main ways lenders check your creditworthiness:

■ Employer's reference

The traditional way of weeding out applicants with a dodgy fiscal disposition is to take up a reference from their employer. But this apparently straightforward process can sometimes hold up house sales, so to prevent any delays it's best to check that your employer has responded swiftly once they've received the request. A common problem is when employers don't bother to complete the lender's official form, and instead write a letter, which the lender will not accept.

■ Credit scoring

In the same way that car insurers know from previous claims which drivers are statistically more likely to have crashes (young males), banks have a pretty shrewd idea about which mortgage applicants are more likely to default on a loan. For example, research shows that there's a greater chance that first-time buyers will get into trouble, perhaps because their jobs are less secure. It's also true that self-employed applicants are statistically twice as likely to default on their mortgages as those employed in steady jobs. Joint applications from married couples with dual incomes are also viewed more favourably than from singletons.

Every mortgage lender has their own particular credit scoring system. Points are deducted for various risks and if, when your total credit score is finally totted up, it falls below a certain figure, your application will be declined. Typically, you will lose points if:

- You're self-employed
- You've moved home recently or frequently
- You're not on the electoral register
- This is your first mortgage or loan
- You recently started a new job or have changed jobs frequently

Such point scoring systems are obviously a bit rough and ready, and are not always terribly fair. For example, it's not impossible for a millionaire to be refused a mortgage because the computer software automatically marks down their application for other reasons. A whole multitude of factors can affect your overall credit score. For example, failure to register onto the electoral roll when you change address will work against you. Or if you split up with a former partner with whom you shared a bank account

your own score could continue to be affected by their irresponsible financial behaviour.

Most of us aren't even aware of things that could be damaging our rating. (See below.)

■ Credit references

Today, a major part of the lender's assessment of your suitability is carried out online via a credit reference agency. This search will immediately throw up any history of bankruptcy, or CCJs (County Court Judgments – see below), and show whether you have ever fallen behind with payments on any previous loans.

But as newspaper headlines remind us from time to time, the problem is that personal credit records are not always accurate, unjustly condemning innocent individuals to 'debtor status' in the eyes of financial organisations. You can check your credit file by contacting any one of the three credit reference agencies in the UK – Experian, Equifax or Callcredit. See website for links.

County Court Judgments – CCJs

You've seen the adverts proclaiming 'CCJs – no problem'. Actually, the harsh truth is that when you're trying to borrow big money, CCJs often are a problem.

If you have a CCJ for debt registered against you, it's unlikely that mainstream mortgage lenders will want to do business. Instead, specialist lenders who deal with 'credit impaired cases' may be able to swing things, albeit at a higher interest rate and with lots of juicy arrangement fees.

But it's not just ASBO-toting bad lads who get lumbered with CCJs. Right now there are thousands of people walking around completely unaware that their credit rating is besmirched, thanks to the ease with which CCJs for debt can be obtained.

To ascertain if any CCJ has been issued against you, a copy of your credit record can be downloaded online from either Experian or Equifax.

The good news is that CCJs only stay on your record for six years. Where the sum involved was less than about £3,000 and has now been repaid in full (*ie* the debt is 'satisfied') lenders may not be too worried even within a shorter period of time.

However, applications are likely to be declined where you have more than one CCJ, or for larger amounts, or where this wasn't disclosed on the application form.

A good broker may be able to get a CCJ removed, allowing you to get a better mortgage deal with a mainstream lender. Some firms offer 'credit repair', where they aim to remove CCJs or get the money owed reduced. But their fees can be substantial, and success may depend on them being able to spot any procedural irregularities that can be challenged.

Brokers

Mortgages should be straightforward. Essentially you're borrowing money to buy a house and in return paying interest on the loan. But after making a few enquiries, you soon realise that things are not quite as simple as they seem. The problem with mortgages is the sheer variety of types, and the complexity of trying to compare like with like. Even price-comparison websites can struggle to give an accurate picture. There are over 100 different organisations providing mortgages in the UK – not just banks and building societies but also some of the big insurance companies. Most of these offer a range of frequently changing products. Despite drastically slimming down after the credit crunch, there are still several thousand mortgage deals to choose from.

With so many complex deals on the market, and a whole

raft of hidden charges and traps, most experts recommend using a mortgage broker to steer a course through the financial quagmire. A good broker can save a lot of hassle by warning you in advance of any credit-scoring issues, and should identify the best deal and know which lenders to apply to. The snag is, there are plenty of 'jack the lad' brokers who are more interested in maximising their commission than matching you up with the best possible mortgage deal, so it's important to pick a professional mortgage adviser who can access the whole market to find the best deal for you.

Selecting the right mortgage broker

Suddenly every second person you meet seems to be a mortgage expert. Even solicitors sometimes boast a financial services division. But in the financial ocean, there are plenty of sharks circling, having scented blood from many miles away. So where do you look for impartial advice?

Estate agents realised long ago that there's serious money to be made flogging financial services. Which may explain the warm smile greeting you as you amble into your local branch. In-house mortgage advisers employed by estate agents are sometimes linked to a major bank (which may even own the chain of estate agents). So in some cases your choice will be restricted to a small panel of lenders, and it's unlikely you'll get the best deal. You are not obliged to take out a mortgage from an estate agent, although some dodgy firms may try to persuade you otherwise.

What about banks and building societies, surely these are the obvious place to start looking for a mortgage? Unfortunately, this isn't necessarily so, since they only sell their own products. In the same way that a Renault showroom wouldn't offer a test drive in a Mini, your choice of product from a specific High Street lender will be limited by what they have available. Even if they offer

By law, you must be given a Key Facts Illustration (KFI) when arranging a mortgage

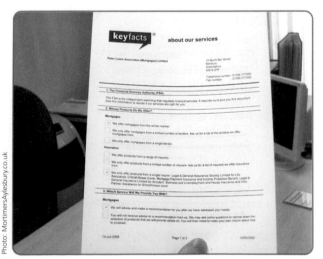

Photo: MortimersAylesbury.co.uk

Getting the best mortgage deal could mean savings of thousands of pounds over the life of a mortgage, so ask a few searching questions before appointing a broker:

■ How long have you been working as a financial adviser and what are your qualifications?
■ How many mortgage lenders do you have access to? (needs to be at least 50)
■ How many different mortgage lenders did you place mortgages with last year? (ideally ten or more)
■ How many mortgages (as opposed to pensions and ISAs etc) did you arrange last year?

mortgages from a panel of providers, the choice is likely to be very limited. Given the amount of money you're spending it's essential to shop around for the best deal. You want an unbiased view of the mortgage market, so the thing to look for is an *independent* mortgage broker.

You want a broker whose expertise is specifically in mortgages, and who knows all the best deals at any given time in an ever-changing market. You want someone who is able to sift through thousands of competing mortgages. So an Independent Financial Adviser (IFA) who covers 1,001 other financial products may not be best placed to advise.

Some supposedly 'independent' brokers actually place most business with a top-five list of big banks who pay them the highest fees (known as 'procuration fees'). But although many mortgage brokers are 'appointed representatives' of one household name insurance firm, so their range of insurance products will be limited, their choice of mortgages may still be reasonably broad and independent.

At the end of the day, it's normally best to go with an independent 'whole-of-market' broker. Although there may still be the occasional deal that some mortgage lenders keep in reserve, the overwhelming majority of mortgages should be accessible via this route. But to be certain you're not missing anything, check the FSA comparison website at fsa.gov.uk/tables.

Lenders normally pay commission of several hundred pounds to brokers for arranging a

Independent Mortgage Solutions

mortgage. The advantage is that you as the customer pay nothing up front, which can really help when budgets are tight. Some, on the other hand, charge you an arrangement fee. Others refund all commissions and instead charge you an hourly fee for their advice. But a reputable broker should be willing to recommend the right mortgage for you, even if it pays him a little less commission.

Quality of service

Believe it or not, some banks can be slow and incompetent. Avoiding such lenders is important not just to keep your stress levels down, but because in a buoyant property market speed may be of the essence. Because you can't exchange contracts until you've got your mortgage offer, there's a risk that someone else with a smarter, faster bank could pip you to the post. Every day spent waiting is an extra day when something can go wrong with your purchase. A switched-on lender should be able to process your application within about two weeks.

Some lenders are also rather accident-prone when it comes to after-sales service, forgetting to collect payments so that you're hit with a enormous bill months later, or even charging the wrong amount (inevitably in their favour). A good broker should know which lenders to avoid.

Mortgages

The time to start arranging your mortgage is before you start looking for a property. If you wait until you've found somewhere, then suddenly you'll be under pressure, which isn't the best position to be in when making a major financial decision. So having already decided what you can afford, and smoothed the way for credit and income references, the next step is to take a long hard look at the products on offer.

Photo: wikimedia

Choosing the right type of mortgage

Politicians are always telling us we need more choice. As we saw earlier, when it comes to mortgages they won't be disappointed. Despite the market downturn, there are a large number of competing loans and these need to be carefully assessed. It's a jungle out there.

There are several key factors to consider when picking the right mortgage – the interest rate you pay, the number of years the mortgage will run, and how you plan to pay it off. But mortgage products are rarely what they seem. Each comes loaded with sweeteners and in many cases nasty penalties to catch out the unwary. Below we explore each factor in turn.

Interest rate options

The amount you pay in interest is largely influenced by the Bank of England's decision each month whether to cut, raise or hold UK interest rates. Lower rates are often used to try to boost spending in a recession, and higher rates to rein in consumer spending and inflationary price rises in a boom. The decision is more difficult when both factors are present – when prices are rising, but the economy's simultaneously stalling, as happened in the 1970s when economic stagnation combined with inflation to produce the bastard offspring dubbed 'stagflation'. More recently the credit crunch raised the price at which banks lend money to each other on international markets, causing mortgage rates to rise. Predicting future rates is a tough call, since unexpected events a million miles away can affect sentiment – a run on the yen, a Beijing stock market shock, a tsunami, bird flu or terror attacks.

In 1992 interest rates rocketed as high as 15 per cent, but have since plumbed the depths at 3 per cent or less. On a £150,000 mortgage that's the difference between paying £1,875 a month and £375 (interest only) – which could seriously affect your amount of spare beer money. So unless you possess a reliable crystal ball, it might be worth opting for the security of a fixed mortgage rate.

■ Variable rates

Each lender will have a standard variable rate (SVR) mortgage – which is typically about 1.5 or 2 per cent above the Bank of England rate – from which all their other deals are calculated. A discounted mortgage might, for example, be 1 per cent lower than the lender's SVR for a couple of years. Sometimes lenders use other names for their key variable rate, such as 'base mortgage rate' (BMR).

A variable rate lets you ride the market waves, cashing in on rate cuts but also having to endure any increases. But this is the bog-standard mortgage and, being relatively uncompetitive, is normally best avoided. It is often better to opt for a special fixed or discounted deal. When these come to an end, they automatically reverts to the dearer SVR, bumping up your monthly mortgage payments until you get round to arranging a fresh deal.

■ Fixed rates

A fixed rate mortgage does exactly what it says on the tin. Locking your rate at an agreed level means your payments are firmly fixed, guaranteed to stay the same regardless of global stock market crashes, rocketing base rates or hell freezing over. With predictable mortgage payments, budgeting is obviously a lot easier and there are no nasty shocks. The downside of being protected from rate increases is, of course, the possibility of missing out on any potential rate cuts.

Fixed rates tend to run for two, three or five years, although longer-term deals can be found. The cheapest rates tend to be for two-year fixed rates, because there's less risk for the lender than for the equivalent five-year deal. During this period you have to stick with the agreed deal or pay a penalty, which isn't an unreasonable stipulation. So if there's a chance that you might need to move in the short term, think twice before fixing. The other thing to avoid is any overhanging 'tie-in' period that continues after the end of the fix (see 'Penalties and hidden fees').

An interesting variation on this theme is 'stepped fixed rates', which are fixed for an initial period but then rise over time at set intervals, so you know exactly what your repayments will be.

■ Discount rates

Usually some of the cheapest deals are available as discounted rates, pegged a per cent or so below the lender's SVR. Discounted rate deals are usually offered over a period of two or three years, and are cheaper for a shorter term. But discount rates move up and down in relation to the standard variable rate, like a basket under a hot air balloon. So you could be in for a bumpy ride (albeit at a discount).

■ Capped rates

Capped mortgages were invented to overcome all the bad habits of discounted and variable rates. They can still go up, but only by a limited amount, before hitting a maximum ceiling or 'cap'. This means you know the worst scenario in advance. Here you get the best of both worlds, reaping the benefit if rates fall while the cap protects you from the worst effects of a rise. Capped rate deals are usually available over three, five or ten years. The drawback is that interest rates tend to be higher than for fixed rate deals and not so many lenders offer them, so there's less choice. And because even the experts find it impossible to predict long-term interest rates, it makes sense not to tie yourself into one deal for more than about five years at a time.

■ Tracker mortgages

Tracker mortgages follow movements in the Bank of England base rate at a set margin, say 1 per cent above it. Trackers offer a significantly better deal than the lender's standard variable rate, and most don't carry penalties should you want to switch to another deal. They are therefore attractive if you want the flexibility to change your mortgage quickly. Unlike discounted rates, which are linked to the lender's SVR, your lender can't suddenly decide to boost their profits by widening the margin. The drawback is that trackers are variable and follow the upswings and downturns of Bank of England base rates, with no certainty. And many have 'collars' that set a floor to how low they will go regardless of how far the base rate drops. Some 'discounted base rate trackers' offer large initial discounts for the first 6 or 12 months, which allows the lender to publicise the deal with headlines quoting a mouth-wateringly low introductory rate.

■ Offset mortgages/current account mortgages (CAMs)

If your mortgage is with same bank as your savings or current account, with an 'offset mortgage' the two can work together to reduce your payments. Although your savings are kept in a separate account, they're offset against the total mortgage debt. So suppose your mortgage is £100,000 but you've got savings of £4,000 and another £1,000 sitting in your current account, they'll only charge you interest on £95,000. This can be worth considering because banks normally pay a miniscule interest on current accounts and not a great deal more on savings accounts. So in effect they're paying you a far higher rate equivalent to what they charge at their mortgage rate, plus you won't get taxed on interest earned. You can still spend your cash in the normal way. There is even a 'friends and family' version where you can persuade others to open accounts at the same bank, and their savings help reduce your mortgage interest payments (see next chapter).

A current account mortgage is similar to an offset, except that you keep all your money (ie your current account, savings and even personal loans and credit cards) lumped together in one account. Which means that when you get a bank statement you may appear to be alarmingly overdrawn to the tune of hundreds of thousands of pounds – roughly the amount of your mortgage! The attraction, however, is that the small change sitting idly in your current account is now gainfully employed eating away at your debt. So when you get paid each month, until you spend your money it will beaver away helping reduce your mortgage. But like offset mortgages, the downside is that interest rates are often at the lender's SVR and are less competitive than for fixed or discounted deals. Consequently you need to have several thousand pounds in savings to make it worth opting for one of these.

■ Portability and flexibility

Most of the above types of mortgage should also be available as 'portable' loans, allowing you to move home and take your mortgage with you to secure on the new house. This saves having to pay a redemption penalty if you're tied in for a number of years.

Some mortgages allow you to overpay when you feel flush with spare cash but then miss a payment or two when times are hard. By overpaying for a while you should be able to build up a reserve, that makes it possible to underpay when the need arises. Some flexible mortgages allow you to take a 'payment holiday', although this inevitably means your mortgage will take longer to pay off.

If you main goal is to pay off your mortgage as quickly as possible, and save shed-loads of money in the long term, many standard variable mortgages allow you to pay up to ten per cent extra per year. A flexible mortgage is good for the self-employed or where your income fluctuates.

The mortgage term

Strange word, 'mortgage'. Scholars may recognise its French origin, which literally translates as 'death pledge' – in other words a 'pay till you drop' life sentence, or the proverbial millstone round your neck.

Traditionally mortgages were taken out for 25 years and you stuck with the same lender through thick and thin. To be sure of repaying it by the end, you would normally pay a bit extra each month to slowly eat away at the mountain of debt (see 'Payback time' below). Today, however, we are all encouraged to be 'rate tarts' – in other words it can pay to shop around, switching lenders every few years to get the best deal. Otherwise your existing lender will reward your loyalty by lumbering you with an expensive standard variable rate loan.

It's still common for home buyers to take out a mortgage for a period of 25 years, although it's a bit academic now that everyone switches lenders every two or three years to get a better deal.

For first-time buyers, the trend is towards longer terms of 30 years or more, because spreading it further into the future can make monthly repayments a bit lower. The downside of a longer term, of course, is that the total cost over all those years will be much higher. In reality, over the last 50 years house price inflation has dramatically boosted the value of our homes in relation to the mortgages secured on them. So what is now a sizeable loan could be peanuts in quarter of a century's time. On the other hand, as prices rise there's a 'feel-good factor' that makes it very tempting to keep increasing the size of the mortgage,

Hey big lenders
The largest UK mortgage lenders include:

- Barclays-Woolwich
- HSBC/First Direct
- Lloyds (including HBOS and C&G)
- Nationwide
- Royal Bank of Scotland-NatWest
- Santander Group (Abbey/Alliance & Leicester/B&B)

Mortgage lenders are regulated by the Financial Services Authority (FSA) and are legally required to present customers with a 'key facts' document containing simple, user-friendly information about their mortgage offer. This should set out the total cost of the loan, including any up-front fees, not just the headline interest rate. New customers have to sign a written confirmation that they have been given the key facts document before the mortgage can proceed.

taking money out to pay for extensions, cars or holidays, so it doesn't actually shrink much over time. Which means there's still the small matter to consider of how to pay it all off before you get too 'old and boring'.

Payback time – paying it all off

Right now, worrying about how you are ultimately going to pay back your mortgage at some point in the distant future probably isn't Priority Number One. The immediate objective has to be completing the purchase of your new home, preferably with a few quid left over each month to afford some kind of social life.

Mortgage payments will be your biggest expense every month over many years, so adding to the burden by paying extra money into some kind of savings plan isn't a tremendously attractive proposition. But before handing over large sacks of their lovely cash, your lender will quite reasonably want to know how you propose to pay it all back. These are the main options:

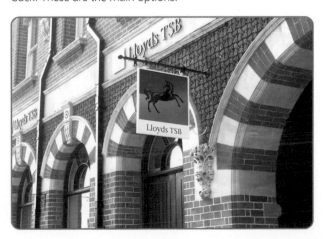

■ Interest only

The cheapest possible option is to pay just the interest on the mortgage and nothing else. Around one in three mortgages taken out are on an interest-only basis. The snag, of course, is that this way you're never going to pay off that enormous mortgage debt – which may be fine if you plan to die young, or anticipate receiving a generous inheritance, or have some other priceless assets that can be liquidated in due course. But for the rest of us the music needs to be faced sooner rather than later.

Your house will probably be your main asset in older age. So you don't want the double whammy of a minuscule pension coupled with an everlasting mortgage mountain forcing you to slave away stacking shelves at the local DIY store until you drop dead. One option is to arrange an interest-only mortgage for the first few years, then when your salary has increased start paying into a savings plan, or switch to a repayment loan, as long as you're prepared for a jump in monthly payments. For a typical £150,000 repayment mortgage over a 25-year term at an interest rate of six per cent, the monthly interest you pay would be £750 a month. But by switching to a repayment mortgage this would typically leap by nearly 30 per cent to about £965.

■ Repayment

The traditional way of guaranteeing that the capital you borrow will be fully paid off by the end of the mortgage term is with a repayment mortgage – still the most popular type. But they may not always be the best option. In the above example with a £150,000 mortgage, on top of your monthly interest-only payment you'd be forking out over £200 extra towards repaying the capital you borrowed. Your monthly repayments therefore comprise mainly interest with a smaller extra amount paying back the capital.

However all these small payments will add up over time, and each year will gradually decrease the amount of capital owed. This means the interest the bank can charge on this smaller outstanding loan is also less, and there will be a reduced amount to pay each month. But rather than lower your monthly repayments, each year the bank will instead increase the proportion of capital repaid, accelerating clearing the debt over time. Clever stuff.

The snag with this is that in the early years of a repayment mortgage your payments mainly comprise interest, so if you keep changing lenders and starting anew every few years the sum won't decrease much at all.

■ Investment

Instead of directly paying off a bit of the mortgage each month, you could instead put a similar sum aside into an investment fund. It is then professionally invested for the long-term in assets such as shares, commercial property or Government bonds. The important thing with all investments is to pick the right asset management or life assurance company with good investment performance, something your broker should be able to advise on.

■ Endowments

'Endowment' is not a word you hear too often these days. In 1986 endowments accounted for 80 per cent of all mortgages, but now they represent less than 10 per cent. This is partly because there are no great tax advantages compared to ISAs and pension mortgages. But crucially, their reputation was fatally tarnished when many were miss-sold in the 1980s and 1990s. Many customers were given the impression by commission-hungry salesmen that by the end of their mortgage term they would be guaranteed to have paid off the mortgage. Some 'with profits' policies even promised money to spare by the end of the term, a veritable overflowing pot of gold. Instead, the bitter reality for many home owners was a shortfall, thanks to generous commissions and fees siphoned off by greedy fund managers despite their investments underperforming. Because the risks had often not been fully spelled out at the time of sale, many customers successfully claimed compensation.

The way any such investment is supposed to work is that you should be given a range of projected end-values at the outset, with varying assumptions about the likely annual growth, which of course depends on market performance.

The idea behind 'with profits' endowments is that your investment is subject to 'smoothing'. Here the fund manager prudently holds back some of the profits when the stock market is booming to compensate for lower returns when the market is flat or falling. If the policy performs better than anticipated, you should get a tax-free surplus sum in addition to paying off your mortgage.

Though there is no guarantee that enough cash will be generated by the end of the term to pay off the mortgage, at least there's the mildly comforting consolation that if you die before the policy matures the life assurance element will pay off the mortgage early.

■ Pension mortgages

Most of us already put something aside every month towards a pension. Pensions are very tax-efficient, since unlike normal savings accounts you don't get stung for income tax on the money you pay in, or on the interest you earn. This means higher-rate taxpayers save the most tax. So it makes sense to use this as a way to save towards paying off your mortgage.

Of course, you can't just take a large chunk of your pension to repay your mortgage and leave yourself with nothing to live on when you retire. But by paying extra money into your personal pension fund each month, when you retire up to 25 per cent of the total pension money you've saved can be used to pay off the mortgage. For a few additional quid in premiums a life assurance scheme will cover you so that if you drop dead in the meantime the mortgage gets paid off.

Pension mortgages are usually arranged by self-employed people, because if you're a member of a company pension scheme you can't have a pension mortgage. But again, they are stock market linked and depend on the skills of a fund manager (who's first loyalty will be to his own wallet). Nonetheless, your savings should still grow quicker even than a tax-efficient ISA.

■ ISA mortgages

As everyone knows, you can invest a few thousand pounds each year in an ISA and you don't get taxed on the interest earned. This isn't quite as good a deal as with pensions, where you also don't pay any income tax on your salary when it's invested, but unlike pensions you can get at your money early (if you wish). And on the plus side, you can have more hands-on control, influencing where your money is invested, with less commission going into the pockets of some anonymous fund manager-gambler. You can build up a personal portfolio of ISA investments yourself or invest a monthly sum into an ISA mortgage offered by your lender, or do it through a pooled investment such as a unit trust.

A mix of cash ISAs and stocks & shares ISAs will help balance the risk.

Unlike endowments, the money invested increases quicker over time as no tax is siphoned off by the Government. Also, investment charges are lower, with a typical initial charge of around 5 per cent of the amount invested, and an annual management charge of around 1.5 per cent.

It's also easy to switch investments if your fund is under-performing, plus you can stop and restart payments. But stocks & shares ISAs are of course vulnerable to stock market fluctuations and cash ISAs are affected by changes in interest rates over time.

Comparing mortgages

Having selected the type of mortgage that would be right for your particular circumstances, the next step is to come up with a shortlist of banks and building societies that can offer a suitable product.

But when it comes to mortgages, comparing like with like is not always easy. Even price comparison websites can struggle to do the broker's job and churn out best-buy mortgages, because of the sheer complexity of rates and hidden charges. How on earth do you compare a mortgage offering free fees and cash back with another offering a two per cent discount for the first year, but subject to redemption penalties? Even mortgage brokers need special programmes to break it all down into digestible components.

Of course, the thing about 'free' incentives is that they often aren't. You normally end up paying in some other way, such as a higher interest rate or stricter penalties. A very competitive headline mortgage rate will usually be counterbalanced by some hidden charges cunningly packaged into the deal.

Incentives and sweeteners

Mortgage advertisements frequently proclaim a host of freebies in a bid to win your business. Some incentives are well worth taking advantage of, but there may be drawbacks, so let's see what these goodies are actually worth.

■ Discounts

Opting for a deal with a deeply discounted interest rate for a limited initial period can be very useful when you've got 101 other expenses to budget for. Savings here can help fund furnishing your new home. But watch out for the nasty surprise of 'payment shock' a year or two down the line when the mortgage reverts to the full rate and your monthly payment may nearly double.

■ Flexible payments

Some standard mortgages now take account of modern work trends such as contract-working, self-employment and part-time employment. So your mortgage may allow you the flexibility to make larger monthly payments when business is good, and to take a 'payment holiday' or reduce payments when money is tight.

■ Cashback

Wouldn't it be nice if your lender gave you a large dollop of cash with your new mortgage? Mortgages that offer the incentive of 'cashback' may be very useful when it comes to paying for furnishing the new home, but they tend to be more expensive in the long run, charging higher interest rates. Such deals are not widely available, and only apply for applicants requiring loans that are low in relation to the purchase price (a low LTV). Unless the interest rate on offer is especially keen, negotiating an overdraft or zero per cent credit card deal may be a better option. The bulging brown envelope is also a favourite incentive with developers of new properties, but can lead to mortgage valuation problems. (See Chapter 16.)

Free insurance

Your lender and solicitor will insist that your new home is covered by buildings insurance from the day of exchange of contracts (even though you won't move in until completion day). It normally pays to shop around to get the best deal. But some lenders will pay the first year's cover in advance, which is well worth having as long as the mortgage itself is competitive. But lenders do this because they know we all get a bit lazy once insurance is set up and don't bother switching. So remember to shop around when it comes up for renewal so that you don't get tied in to uncompetitive cover.

Free fees

A widely advertised headline incentive, fees-free deals can save you quite a bit – except they aren't normally free should your purchase fall through and if the mortgage doesn't proceed. This is evident where for example you have to pay an initial 'arrangement fee' which is refunded upon completion of the mortgage. To compare one mortgage deal with another you'll need to list all the fees the lender charges (or refunds), as these can easily add up to several thousand pounds, making a headline interest rate not as sharp as it seems. Fees-free deals commonly apply to:

Free valuations

Lenders normally appoint a surveyor to carry out a mortgage valuation to confirm that the property is actually worth what's being paid. Lenders typically charge anything from £200 to £800 for this (depending on the purchase price) and may even send you a copy of the report. Although a mortgage valuation is not a survey, and getting it free can be a useful saving, the content may mean very little where lenders are instructing 'drive-by' valuations or using a computer model to 'guesstimate' values.

Refunded application fees

When it comes to thinking up new names and bizarre reasons for fees, no one can beat bankers for creativity – arrangement fees, application fees, reservation fees, higher lending fees and completion fees to name but a few. Some lenders now charge several thousand pounds to subsidise a low headline-grabbing interest rate. To judge how competitive such deals really are, divide the upfront fee by the total number of months that the mortgage deal lasts. For example, a two-year mortgage deal with a £1,500 'arrangement fee' would be equivalent to paying an extra £62.50 per month in interest over 24 months (plus a bit

more for the interest you'd earn on your money by not having to pay it all up front) – which is the same as paying an extra half per cent on a typical £150,000 mortgage.

Free legal fees

Solicitor's fees are often the next biggest expense after forking out for a deposit. The catch here is that 'free' legal fees may only refer to the legal work that covers the lender's interests, or just the basic conveyancing costs for you and them. It also won't exempt you from the whole array of legal 'disbursements' and fees for searches and stamp duty tax. And it may limit your choice of solicitor.

Adding costs to the loan

Even if you're not offered any freebies, your lender may let you add some charges costs to the loan, which can be extremely useful when money's tight as it reduces your upfront costs. But it's not so generous when you calculate how much interest you end up paying over 25 years.

That just about exhausts the range of sweeteners and goodies that you're likely to be offered. But there is another side to this coin which makes sobering reading. To see if there are any nasty penalties or hidden fees lurking in the small print you'll probably need to take a much closer look.

Penalties and hidden fees

Mortgage lenders' marketing departments are becoming ever smarter at devising insidious ways to camouflage fees and charges. Even the most reputable brands in banking are not averse to burying all kinds of nasties in the small print. A well-known TV ad shows a seductive headline deal used as bait to reel in an unsuspecting customer who, having signed on the dotted line, is then subjected to outrageous fees and hidden penalties. The financial services industry is no stranger to accusations of miss-selling, where customers are tricked into buying dubious financial 'products' without being told the full story.

Regrettably today, shopping around for a mortgage is as much about spotting the 'sting in the tail' as it is about

Photo: wikimedia

securing a good mortgage rate. Again, this is where a decent broker can help spot dirty tricks. Below are some well-known nasties to steer clear of:

■ MIGs and HLCs

'Mortgage Indemnity Guarantees' (MIGs) are a one-off insurance premium charged by some lenders where the mortgage is high in relation to the value of the property. 'Higher Lending Charges' (HLCs) are similar to MIGs. Calculated as a percentage of your mortgage, they could add several thousand pounds to the cost of the loan.

Although not so common as they once were, lenders normally find some way of charging you more for higher percentage loans over about 75 per cent LTV, even if it's just by imposing a higher interest rate.

Many home owners were sold MIGs in the late1980s, just before the market took a severe and prolonged downturn, causing some to default on their mortgages – just the kind of situation such policies were designed for. So when repossessed properties were sold for less money than the mortgages secured against them, many owners assumed they were covered. In fact, such policies only protect the *lender* against the risk of losing money. Having paid out to the lender, the insurance companies who provide such guarantees then doggedly pursued the luckless evicted former home owner for the balance.

Although some lenders will add the cost of arranging such policies to the loan, MIGs are best avoided. The best solution is to somehow come up with a bigger deposit, reducing your loan-to-value ratio and thereby sidestepping such penalties. Alternatively look for a more competitive mortgage deal.

■ Early redemption 'tie-in' penalties

Say you agree to take out a two- or three-year mortgage, perhaps at a low fixed rate; it's normally made very clear that you'd have to pay a stiff penalty should you redeem it during this period, for example if you move house and  pay it off. Fair enough. But what has caused grievances in the past are where such 'tie-ins' or 'lock-ins' overhang the initial reduced rate period, perhaps continuing for a couple more years. Here extended penalties tie you in beyond the agreed two- or three-year term at an uncompetitively high rate, usually the lender's SVR. Any earlier savings you made would later be more than recouped by the lender.

But should you instead decide to repay (redeem) part or all of the mortgage before the extended term you'd then get badly stung with a redemption penalty, typically three or six months' interest.

Moral: look beyond the headline rate. And if you're planning to move again in the near future, don't get a mortgage that ties you in.

■ Redemption charges

Being wise to the danger of early repayment penalties, you may decide to wait until the end of the agreed term before paying off the old mortgage and switching lenders. But guess what? A fee of several hundred pounds appears in the small print of your solicitor's final account – it seems your friendly mortgage lender has been busy upping their 'redemption charges' by several hundred per cent since you took out the mortgage, supposedly to cover administration costs. Alliance & Leicester and some other well-known lenders were recently criticised for imposing hefty redemption penalties to customers innocently paying off their mortgages.

■ Annual interest calculation

One sneaky trick employed by some lenders is to calculate the interest they charge you on an annual basis. This will cost significantly more than if it was charged daily.

It works like this. When you make a mortgage payment, that sum of money should immediately reduce the amount of your mortgage debt, which in turn should straight away cut the amount of interest you're charged. But with some lenders, your monthly payments don't reduce your mortgage until 1 January next year, so you're paying interest on a larger sum than you actually owe. This adds up to a sizeable amount over a number of years.

■ Compulsory insurance

Those nice, big-hearted folk at the bank are at it again. 'We'll arrange your buildings and contents insurance when you take out a mortgage with us.' That's very kind, except for one small thing: the cost of the policy is far more expensive than if you arranged it yourself. Some lenders force customers to buy their buildings and contents insurance. This may be the catch with an otherwise cheap deal, so you could be better off opting for a dearer mortgage and shopping around for insurance quotes online.

Some lenders adopt a sneakier approach. When applying for the mortgage online, the website reminds you that building insurance is compulsory. But this is deliberately presented in an ambiguous way that looks like you have to tick the box to proceed. Knowing you'll be stressed out by this stage, and afraid that one false click of the mouse will wipe out all the data you've just spent 45 minutes inputting, they take advantage. Alternatively some lenders charge a fee, say £100, if you don't take out their insurance, which may actually be a better option in the long run.

■ Payment Protection Insurance

PPI is just the latest miss-selling scandal. As the name suggests, these policies are sold to prudent folk who want to cover their monthly mortgage payments in the event of redundancy or injury. Customers pay an incredible £5.5 billion in premiums each year for policies that have so many exclusions when it comes to paying out that in many cases they're not worth the paper they're written on. Avoid.

Doing your mortgage application

Once you've picked the best mortgage deal, all that remains is to fill in the lender's form. Getting your mortgage approved can take a couple of weeks if it's a reasonably straightforward case. It helps if some of the donkey work has already been done by your having previously obtained an 'agreement in principle' – a certificate, valid for up to six months, which confirms how much you will be loaned, subject to valuation and credit checks.

DON'T MISS THIS MONTH'S SPECIAL OFFERS

PLEASE TAKE ONE

Applying online

Ever-growing numbers of people are now applying online. This is fine if you're confident about exactly which deal you want and don't need further guidance. You fill in an application form online and submit it to the lender. But as seasoned form-fillers will know, websites vary greatly. Most of us have experienced the frustration of slogging away for half an hour inputting personal data and then clicking the final 'continue' button only to be informed that 'There has been an error, please try later', and all your data is lost in cyberspace. Sometimes it's easier to be guided through the process by an independent broker who's 'on your side'.

Completing the mortgage application form

Most lenders' application forms run into several pages and typically require the following information:

■ **Name, address and date of birth of each applicant**
If you've lived at your present address for less than three years, you'll also need to give your previous address. A contact number must be provided for the lender's surveyor to call to arrange access to do the mortgage valuation (normally via the estate agent).

■ **Address of the property you plan to buy, the agreed price and how much you want to borrow**

■ **Your solicitor's details**

■ **The amount of your deposit**
To avoid money laundering, lenders may ask where the funds came from (such as from your savings, or as a present from a relative).

■ **The employment details of each applicant**
Job titles, employers' names and addresses, salaries, length of time in employment.

■ **Salary details**
Annual salary, commission, bonuses, company cars etc.

■ **Bank account details for each applicant** including how long you've banked there

■ **Whether you've ever been declared bankrupt** or currently have any CCJs

■ **Any other loans for each applicant** – such as outstanding credit card debts, or personal loans.

Providing proof

In these days of identity fraud, proving who you are may not be as simple as it seems, but hopefully it shouldn't become a Kafkaesque nightmare. A visit to the local branch of your chosen mortgage lender should hopefully be all that's required, or you may even be able to apply by post (recorded delivery). If there's a broker involved, they should be able to organise this. In order to prove who you are and what you earn, a number of key documents will need to be supplied, such as:

■ Passport or UK driving licence
■ Utility bills to verify your address
■ Wage slips for three or six months
■ P60 PAYE statement (summary of the year's salary provided by your employer)
■ Bank statements

UK IDENTITY CARD
NAME
TONY CHARLES BLIAR
DATE OF BIRTH
05-06-1953
NATIONALITY
BRITISH
ID NUMBER
5318008
ISSUED BY WWW.SILLY-GOVERNMENT.CO.UK

Tips to make sure it doesn't all go wrong

Rule Number One is that you can't rely very much on the Government. If it turns out that you're not able to pay your mortgage there may not be too much help at hand.

If you lose your job and are claiming Income Support, or Jobseeker's Allowance, there's a lengthy waiting period of 13 weeks before help with mortgage interest payments is available. The Government will then pay your mortgage interest, but only up to the first £175,000 of your mortgage. Even then, the available support is capped and means-tested, so in order to qualify, you can't have much in the way of savings. Unemployed people will lose this help after two years (if claiming Jobseeker's allowance), and it also doesn't apply to people over 60 who get pension credit. Instead, the Government encourages home owners to cough up for Payment Protection Insurance (PPI), to cover mortgage payments for up to a year – which, as noted above, has been the subject of a major miss-selling scandal.

There is, however, some common sense advice that's worth repeating:

- Don't overstretch yourself by taking a bigger mortgage than you can comfortably afford each month.
- Set up a direct debit to pay your mortgage a couple of days after your salary is credited each month.
- Stick to a budget, so that you watch the pennies.
- Pick a fixed-rate deal for the first few years so that your monthly payments don't increase.
- Take out insurance to cover your mortgage payments.
- Keep a few months' savings in reserve for emergencies.

If you find yourself struggling with repayments, tell your lender. They should be able to work out a package with you to help get you through a difficult patch, and avoid repossession. For example, switching to an interest only deal can significantly reduce payments.

There is, however, a possible glimmer of light for families who find that they can no longer afford their mortgage repayments. Limited funds are available so that local councils may be able to bail them out, in one of three ways:

- A 'social landlord' such as a housing association could buy the home, pay off the loan, and rent the house back to the family.
- It could buy a share in the home, letting the owner pay off part of their mortgage.
- It could simply lend the home owner the money.

See 'HomeBuy' section in the next chapter.

The government have recently announced a 'mortgage holiday' scheme in a bid to cut repossessions. If you lose your job or suffer a serious loss of income (e.g. no bonus or overtime) you may be able to defer your mortgage interest payments for up to two years. If you then subsequently fail to repay your missed mortgage payments, the government claims it will step in and pay the mortgage lender on your behalf. This deal applies to households with mortgages of up to £400,000 where you have less than £16,000 in savings. See website for updates.

What happens next?

Once your application has been accepted, and your income and credit references all stack up, the property you're buying will be valued by a mortgage surveyor appointed by the bank. Within a week or two the lender should write to you and your solicitor with the all-important mortgage offer, confirming the availability of funds for your purchase. The offer will have a number of standard conditions attached – check that you're happy with these, as they are often badly worded – and you are legally bound to comply with them. Then once you and the solicitors are ready, you should be able to exchange contracts.

15 | FIRST-TIME BUYERS

most lenders wouldn't let you borrow half this amount, the figures simply didn't add up. But every cloud has a silver lining. Post-credit crunch, as incomes rise over time, and with house prices at more realistic levels, affordability has significantly improved.

Beaconsfield Road, AYLESBURY

Call 01296 398555 for further details

A very well presented two bedroom terraced home conveniently situated within walking distance of the town centre and railway station.

Entrance hall • 16ft Lounge • Modern fitted kitchen/dining room • Two good sized bedrooms • Refitted bathroom • Gas central heating • Double glazed windows • Enclosed rear garden • Allocated parking • Convenient cul-de-sac location

Getting a foot on the property ladder has become considerably more challenging in recent years. As property prices rocketed in the boom years, affordability became a serious issue. Only as long as banks were prepared to lend 100 per cent (or higher) mortgages at generous income multiples could the maths still be made to work. The rest, as they say, is history. The 2008 credit crunch and resulting mortgage famine hit first-time buyers hardest as deals were hastily withdrawn. And when the lower end of the market stalls, it's contagious. Chains collapse, and the whole market slows.

The changing market

One reason why prices of flats and starter homes reached such astronomical heights was the competing demand from 'buy-to-let' investors looking to acquire smaller properties. But as banks also reduced available funds to investors, they risked kicking away the remaining prop supporting the lower end of the market. The resulting drop in demand has resulted in large price falls in areas suffering an oversupply of new flats.

At the peak of the market, to afford an average property in some areas first-time buyers would have needed to borrow as much as ten times their average salary. Given that

Affordability

Research shows that the average first-time buyer has an income of around £35,000 and is 29 years old. Most borrow just over three times their salary. But if you're a university graduate or a young professional with a decent job, but you don't earn very much, lenders may take your future earnings potential into account, and allow you to borrow more.

To see what sort of property you can afford to buy, the following steps can be a useful guide:

■ Calculate how much you can borrow, using an online calculator, which also shows what your monthly repayments will be. See website for links.

- Add any savings to the amount you can borrow.
- Deduct this total from the purchase price of the property you want, and the purchase fees, and what's left is the shortfall. The next step is to plug this gap.

Budgeting

Since the demise of 100 per cent (or larger) mortgages, buyers need to come up with a decent-sized deposit. There are several ways you can do this. First, by persuading someone else to write you a big cheque – the 'beg, borrow or steal' option is explored below. Second, sell off some assets. If our lives depended on it, most of us could raise a few thousand auctioning off lots of unused stuff, or trading down to a greener and cheaper mode of transport. Third, earn a bit more – perhaps by nagging the boss for a pay rise, or maybe by working in a bar for a couple of evenings a week.

But perhaps the best way of saving for a deposit is to spend a bit less of the money you've got. This means making sacrifices by cutting down on non-essential expenditure. Although the words 'budgeting' or 'economising' have all the appeal of a dose of 1950s austerity, there are some easy cutbacks you can make that should be fairly painless. Giving up smoking, cutting down on takeaways and visiting the pub a little less often may even have the added bonus of seeing you drop a jeans' size or two. Greater savings can be made by cutting out designer labels, or squeezing more miles out of the old banger (the newer the car the more money thrown away on depreciation). Above all, getting a financial grip and religiously paying off credit cards each month will avoid being clobbered with expensive interest penalties.

Tell your friends you're saving for a house, and they may even buy the drinks. Keeping a record of where all the money goes each month is a great way to spot where all your hard-earned cash is being wasted.

Renting a room

A lot of first-time buyers manage to afford a larger mortgage by making their new property earn a sizeable chunk of income. For anyone used to sharing rented houses or flats, the idea of taking in a lodger should hold no great horrors. The attraction of two- or three-bedroom properties is that renting out the spare room can help pay the mortgage. This can make all the difference until you're in a position to comfortably cover the monthly mortgage payments yourself, perhaps after a year or two of pay rises. The obvious downside is some loss of privacy, and clearly you'll need to vet lodgers very carefully.

One major attraction of taking in a lodger is that the income is tax-free. Under the 'rent a room' scheme you're quite legitimately allowed to earn rental income of £4,250 (2008/9 figures) without paying a penny in tax. The only snag is that lenders rarely take this into account when calculating income multiples, but it's worth mentioning.

Your tenant should pay any resulting increase in Council Tax, which is calculated on the assumption that two adults share a property. So if you're a one-man-band, by taking in a lodger you could lose your present 25 per cent discount. But if there are two of you already, adding a third person shouldn't increase the bill.

Lodgers have no legal security of tenure, so giving notice should be straightforward. You don't need any legal tenancy agreement, but to avoid future disagreements always write down the following key points at the outset, and agree them with your lodger:

- How much rent is due and when it's to be paid
- When the rent can be increased
- Any inclusive services that are provided (cleaning etc)
- How much notice you need to give to terminate the tenancy
- How the bills are to be shared

Before taking in a lodger, you need to upgrade your home insurance (for both contents and building), and if you live in a flat you must notify the freeholder. It's also worth checking when you take out a mortgage that the lender is OK about you taking in lodgers, and that they won't try to use it as an excuse to charge you more for a dearer buy-to-let mortgage.

When in comes to paying the mortgage, every little helps, so there may be other potential sources of income that you can unlock in your property. For example, in town centres, or near stations and airports, consider letting out your garage or driveway for parking. Owners of properties in the vicinity of world-class sports centres such as The Oval or Wimbledon can earn generous sums letting their homes at peak seasons. Or perhaps the film crew from *Midsomer Murders* might take a shine to the 'gritty reality' of your des res.

Buying with a small deposit

Saving for a deposit makes perfect sense in a falling or static market. But if prices are rising, by waiting a year or more there's a risk that you'll be priced out of the market. So if you don't want to wait too long, there are some possible short cuts, such as buying with friends, that could help make the maths work in your favour (see below).

One problem with only having a small deposit is that you won't get the best mortgage rate, as lenders will regard you as higher risk. Banks usually find a way to penalise anyone borrowing a very high per cent loan, usually by charging higher interest rates. Where lenders impose 'higher lending fees', these can add a few thousand pounds to the cost of arranging the loan.

In order to afford the home you really want it can be tempting to use all means possible to make the sums add up. But taking a large cash advance on credit cards has to be about the worst possible way of borrowing money and should be avoided, along with unsecured loans at sky-high rates from loan-sharks. It is sometimes claimed that any moneylender who advertises on daytime TV should be treated warily.

Pooling your resources

The most cost-effective way of buying is to do it jointly with others. Buying with your partner, or with friends or relatives, immediately gives you access to two lots of savings and therefore a bigger deposit. With two people, your monthly repayments are cut in half. Although most lenders allow up to four names on a mortgage, the loan itself may only be based on two or three salaries, in which case you won't be able to borrow much extra even if you move in with a busload of all your mates.

Entering into the biggest financial commitment of your life with a total stranger probably isn't the ideal arrangement. But you obviously need to use your own judgement and there are websites such as **Cobuywithme.com** that can help bring like-minded people together. Obviously, it's important to be extra careful when picking your future co-owners, rather than jumping to a decision after a few beers down the pub. Even if you're deeply smitten with each other, experience suggests that the best policy is usually to plan for the worst, just in case. In any event it's sensible to instruct your solicitor to draw up a contract that clearly states who is contributing what to the deposit and the monthly mortgage payments, clarifying each party's share in the

Watch out!
Couples who buy a property together can sometimes be a little misty eyed, knowing their relationship will endure forever. But insisting on a clear contract that records each others' contribution needn't sink a loving relationship.

In one recent case, because the mortgage had been taken out solely in the boyfriend's name, when the couple broke up his girlfriend had no claim to the property, even though she had been paying her share of the mortgage to him in cash every month.

property. It will also specify what happens if one wants to quit, perhaps giving the others first option to buy them out. This way, if you do end up hating the sight of each other at least this will be one major thing you won't have to argue about. Legally there are two main ways of buying with others:

- **Joint tenants** – Married couples, usually buy as joint tenants. This means that if your partner dies, their interest will pass to you (and vice versa).
- **Tenants in common** – Here each of you has a distinct share in the property, perhaps 50/50 or another combination based on how much each contributed to the deposit or mortgage. If you die, your share goes to your estate rather than to your partner.

Parents

If your friends are a bunch of skint no-hopers, or they're saving up to travel the world, or are simply not ready for the responsibility of home-ownership, there may be another option closer to home. Parents who have built up a fair amount of equity in their own homes during the course of various property booms may be willing to help. Parental assistance could take the form of a generous cash sum to use as a deposit. Or perhaps they'd be interested in investing jointly with you, contributing half the mortgage payments, or allowing you to generate income by renting out the spare room. Even parents who don't relish direct involvement may be able to help grease the wheels of your mortgage application as guarantors.

Guarantor mortgages
Though not many parents can afford to suddenly stump up tens of thousands in cash towards your deposit, they may actually be able to help swing things without spending a penny, simply by acting as your guarantor. Here, your parents (or another third party) guarantee that if for some reason you become unable to pay the mortgage in future, they will assume responsibility for paying it.

The attraction of this is that lenders will regard you as much less of a risk, either allowing you to borrow a bigger mortgage than you could on your own, or offering you a more competitive mortgage rate. The reason you can borrow more is because the lender will use the guarantor's income, rather than yours, when calculating how much they'll lend you. So if your Dad earns, say, £55,000 a year, you may be able to borrow up to four times this. The snag is that the lender will also take your Dad's monthly outgoings into account, so the amount you can borrow may shrink drastically if he's already lumbered with a huge mortgage.

It's important to bear in mind that taking on a far larger loan than you can realistically afford to repay each month isn't a smart thing to do. If you overstretch yourself and fail to pay, the buck will stop with your guarantor, who won't exactly be overjoyed at the prospect.

The best arrangement is where the lender only requires that the guarantor covers the shortfall between what you can afford and the full amount of the mortgage. Normal income multiples should apply – so, for example, if you earn £25,000, which qualifies you for a mortgage of £100,000, but the property costs £185,000, the guarantor only needs cover the shortfall of £85,000. The guarantor need only be liable for the early years of your mortgage. Once you've clocked up a couple of decent pay rises you can take full responsibility for your own mortgage.

Your parents need to be aware that if they commit themselves to covering your mortgage it could restrict them from obtaining further loans to do something for themselves – such as buying that holiday home in Tuscany. Being a guarantor is a major responsibility, and won't suit a lot of parents. There can be dire financial repercussions – suppose, for example, that you lost your job and couldn't pay the mortgage. Or what if interest rates skyrocket? What started as a safety net could become a millstone that potentially causes a rift in your family, leading to financial stress and ill-health. So it's important to understand the risks for all concerned.

If things do go wrong, always tell your guarantor as soon as possible so that they have time to prepare. Sit down with them and work out a survival plan. You may be able to get another job within a couple of months, so it needn't be the end of the world.

The ideal guarantor is someone who has already paid off their mortgage and has a good income. Most guarantors are parents, but a relative or even a close friend may be acceptable, although most lenders require that guarantors are not more than 60 years old, which could rule out elderly relatives.

Although most lenders will consider letting you use a guarantor, they may want a larger deposit – say 25 per cent or more – which could defeat the whole point. Instead you might be better off borrowing the deposit direct from parents and paying it back over several years. Or just use the interest on their savings to assist you.

Family offset mortgages

'Family offset' mortgages are similar to the offset mortgages we looked at in the previous chapter, but are particularly useful for first-time buyers. These enable your Mum, Dad, Grandma or other relatives (or friends) to hang on to their precious savings whilst at the same time letting you pay less interest on your mortgage. For example, they may have a few thousand pounds stashed away in some half-forgotten account earning a minuscule rate of interest. If they don't need this interest and want to help you buy a property without losing control of their cash, offsetting can be a good idea.

To do this, they must open savings accounts with a lender offering family offset mortgages. The lender then links their accounts to your mortgage, reducing the interest you're charged on your monthly mortgage payments. The money stays in their name, so they can still withdraw cash as normal. The downside, of course, is that they earn no interest on their savings. Also, the interest rates charged by lenders on offset mortgages may be a little on the high side, which could defeat the point of arranging one. Check price-comparison websites and leading mortgage brokers who publish tables of best buys.

Help for first-time buyers

First-time buyers are a special case. Not only do they underpin the rest of the property market, but they are living proof of the home owning democracy at the heart of our society. Most of us want the security of home ownership, so what can you do if you find yourself priced out of the market?

Experts routinely advise us not to 'borrow more than you can afford', knowing full well that you can't afford to buy anything without getting mortgaged up to the hilt. Fortunately the plight of the first-time buyer has been recognised, and some assistance is available.

Government assistance

Governments are very good at making big announcements in a blaze of publicity, and then not following through. If government were serious about helping first-time buyers, the obvious single action that would help instantly would be to substantially raise the thresholds of stamp duty, the crippling tax burden that spirits away shed-loads of cash from already stretched buyers. But this would be expensive. So instead there are a number of relatively complex schemes in operation to help some buyers get a 'foot on the ladder'.

The most successful of these is the 'Right to Buy' scheme. If you're a council tenant of at least two years' standing you may be able to buy your home at a substantial discount.

Buying with the help of a housing association

Most new housing developments are subject to a planning stipulation that requires a certain percentage to be built as 'affordable housing', including some schemes in posh riverside locations. Once built, these are normally owned and managed by housing associations (HAs).

Shared ownership

In a shared ownership (s/o) scheme you buy a percentage of a property – anything from 25 per cent to 75 per cent – and pay a subsidised rent on the remainder to a housing association. The percentage that you buy depends on the size of mortgage you can raise. So each month you make a mortgage payment to your lender and pay rent to the HA.

The reason this is affordable is because rents are kept artificially low. Over time you can opt to increase the amount you own by 'staircasing' until you eventually own the whole thing. Or instead you can move and sell your share to a new part-owner. Most such schemes are run by HAs, although private developers sometimes offer similar deals.

Priority for s/o schemes is normally given to existing public sector tenants, or those on waiting lists. To join the waiting list you normally need to have lived in the area for at least two years. Up to four people can normally become joint owners, and you need to have a low minimum income.

The first step is to approach local housing associations and complete an application form. If they decide that you qualify and your application is successful, you can look for a suitable property owned by the HA, apply for a s/o mortgage and continue more or less as you would for a conventional house purchase. Some schemes, known as DIY s/o, allow you to find a property on the open market that you like the look of, not just ones owned by the HA.

Shared ownership properties are initially bought under a 99-year lease until you buy the property outright. The HA should be able to suggest lenders who offer shared ownership mortgages.

HomeBuy

HomeBuy is a scheme run by some HAs (and other Registered Social Landlords) that helps 'key workers' and social housing tenants buy a property on the open market. Under the HomeBuy scheme you pay 75 per cent of the property's purchase price using a mortgage and any savings. You apply for a mortgage in

the normal way, but the HA lends you the other 25 per cent (which should cover your deposit) on an interest-free basis, without any payments. Instead, when you come to sell you then have to repay 25 per cent of the market value (which may be more or less than you borrowed, depending on the market). Or you can repay the loan early.

However, eligibility is very tight. You need to be a social housing tenant or on a housing waiting list or 'in housing need'. But you also need to be able to raise a mortgage to cover 75 per cent of the purchase price – which many applicants are going to struggle to achieve. Key workers are eligible for some schemes, and may have more success raising the necessary funding.

The first step is to fill out an application form from a HA in your area, who will check your income and savings. If you qualify you should receive approval to look for a property on the open market within an agreed price range, and within a certain distance of your work. Your choice of mortgage lenders may be limited to those approved by the HA.

HomeBuy Direct is an expansion of the current HomeBuy schemes. It provides five-year taxpayer-backed interest-free loans to help first-time buyers who earn less than £60,000 a year. These loans comprise a 30 per cent deposit on the property you're buying, but only apply to certain newly-built homes, such as city centre flats. However, buyers still need to meet normal lending criteria, so turning up at a bank or building society with a cheque from HomeBuy Direct will not necessarily guarantee that you will be offered a 70 per cent mortgage for the rest of the purchase price.

Key worker assistance

Key Worker Living Programme

The price of the average UK property tripled between 1996 and 2007, whereas average wages rose by only 63 per cent in the same period. As a result, many workers in the public sector have been priced out of the market, causing recruitment problems. The definition of a 'key worker' is generally understood to mean someone who provides a public service – some of whom may be on a relatively low wage, making it virtually impossible to afford a home anywhere near city centres close to their place of work without financial assistance.

Key workers who may eligible for help under these schemes include:

- Nurses and other NHS clinical workers.
- Teachers in schools, further education and sixth form colleges.
- Police officers, and some civilian staff in some police forces.
- Prison and probation service workers.
- Social workers, educational psychologists, planners (in London) and occupational therapists.
- Staff employed by local councils.
- Full-time fire officers, and retained fire fighters.
- Bus drivers.

To keep communities functioning, various government schemes were launched to allow key workers to get onto the first rung of the ladder in areas where they are needed.

To find out whether you qualify for key worker assistance, the normal first point of contact is a local HA (the 'zone agent'). The schemes are administered nationally by the Homes & Communities Agency, and locally by registered social landlords, usually HAs.

Key worker living programme

This is a government initiative that offers financial help to public sector workers to buy or rent a home close to where they work. This may help some nurses, teachers and other key workers who may otherwise struggle to afford accommodation in certain parts of the country. Help is available in different forms:

- HomeBuy scheme (see above) to buy a first home with an interest-free equity loan – provides loans of up to £50,000 towards property purchase.
- Upgrade assistance to facilitate moving to a larger family home – 'Higher HomeBuy' loans of up to £100,000 for 'future potential leaders' of London's education system.
- Shared ownership (typically 50 per cent) for newly-built homes owned by the HA, within travelling distance of your workplace.
- Assistance with renting a home – 'intermediate renting',

where rents are fixed between levels charged for dearer private sector rents and cheaper social housing rents.

The OpenMarket HomeBuy scheme is available to key workers and provides equity loans of up to 50 per cent of a property's purchase price. The loan is only repaid when the property is sold, at 50 per cent of its value at that time. The amount of the loan available to each individual depends on a number of factors, including household income, assets and financial commitments. It is claimed that shared equity schemes will help up to 10,000 first-time buyers earning less than £60,000 annually.

Buying your Council home

Every year around 50,000 public sector tenants apply to become home owners under the Right to Buy scheme. If you currently live in social housing, you may be able to buy your home at a generous discount.

Who can buy?

To qualify to buy your home you need to meet two main criteria:

- You must be a 'secure tenant'. This applies to virtually all council tenants, as well as to many people who rent their homes from other registered social landlords (RSLs) and Housing Action Trusts (HATs). But where tenants of registered social landlords such as housing associations are 'assured tenants' they do not qualify.
- You must have been a tenant with your present landlord for at least five years – unless your tenancy commenced before 18 January 2005, in which case the minimum qualifying period is only two years. During this time, the property you want to buy must have been your only home.

Where former council properties have been transferred to a new landlord, such as to a housing association, the right to buy will normally have been preserved, although in some cases it is subject to a reduced discount.

You won't qualify to buy your home if a court has made a possession order decreeing that you must leave your home. Neither will you qualify if you're an undischarged bankrupt, have a bankruptcy petition pending, or have made an arrangement with creditors and still owe them money.

How big a discount can you get?

The Right to Buy scheme gives tenants a substantial discount on the market value of their homes. The longer you have been a public sector tenant, the more discount you get. Once you have been a tenant for the minimum qualifying period (five years or two years – see above) the discount will be 32 per cent for houses and 44 per cent for flats. This discount becomes even more generous the longer you've been a tenant. For houses you get another 1 per cent discount for each additional full year, up to a maximum 60 per cent. For flats you qualify for a discount of 2 per cent or more for each extra year, up to a maximum of 70 per cent. But all of this is subject to maximum limits depending on where you live, varying from a total of around £16,000 in Wales or London to over £30,000 in the Eastern, South-East and South-West regions. The relevant figures for particular areas can be checked with local councils.

You can buy jointly with family members or with tenants who have lived with you during the past 12 months. If the person you're buying with has clocked up more years than the minimum required, then you should be eligible for the higher rate of discount (subject to the maximum for the area). See **www.dclg.gov**.

In Scotland, the qualifying period of residency is also five years, but with a 20 per cent discount rising by 1 per cent a year for each additional year up to a maximum 35 per cent of the value or £15,000, whichever is the lower. See **www.scottishexecutive.gov.uk**.

Repaying the discount

Having purchased your home, it's important to be aware that if you sell it within the first three years some or all of the discount will have to be repaid. Selling within the first year means you have to repay the entire amount. But selling within the second or third years means you only repay two-thirds or one-third of the discount respectively. There are a few exemptions to this rule, such as where a sale is forced as a result of death or the breakdown of a relationship. But there may be other strings attached, such as conditions requiring you to sell back to the Council, or to someone who works locally in areas where there's a shortage of affordable housing.

Making your application

- Ask your local council/landlord for a free Right to Buy claim form (Form RTB1, or in Scotland Form APP1). There should be no charge for this.
- Complete and return the form. When they receive your application, your landlord should send you confirmation (Form RTB2), normally within four weeks. This will confirm whether you qualify for the Right to Buy.
- Next you should receive an 'offer notice' from your landlord within a further 8–12 weeks. This is known as a 'section 125 notice', and confirms the market value of your property along with the actual price you will have to pay

after the discount has been deducted. It also gives details of any known structural defects with the property. For flats it tells you how much the annual service charge will be.

- If you don't agree with the Council's valuation, you can apply to obtain an independent valuation (a 'determination of value') from the District Valuer – but they may value the property higher.
- Arrange a private survey, to check the condition of the property. In most cases a Homebuyer survey should be sufficient.
- Decide whether you want to proceed and buy the property outright, or just forget the whole thing and withdraw. There is also a third option where you can part-buy under a shared ownership arrangement known as 'Rent to Mortgage' (see below). Whatever you decide, you need to inform your landlord in writing within 12 weeks of receiving the section 125 notice, otherwise they will be entitled to assume you don't want to continue.
- Apply for a mortgage. This is made considerably easier because of the discount. Subject to income and credit references, in most cases it should be possible to borrow up to 100 per cent of the discounted price because of the equity in the property. But the monthly mortgage payments could still end up higher than the old subsidised Council rent.

Once the mortgage funding is sorted, and you have appointed a solicitor and you're happy with the landlord's terms of sale, you should be ready to buy. As always, before signing anything it's important to take independent legal advice.

The above process is sometimes subject to delays. If you can prove this is due to hold-ups receiving forms from your landlord you may be entitled to a reduction in the purchase price.

Rent to Mortgage scheme

Even with the generous discounts available under the Right to Buy scheme, not everyone can afford to buy their home outright. 'Rent to Mortgage' is a shared ownership scheme that lets you buy a share of your home with a Right to Buy discount. Under this scheme, your landlord – usually the Council or a housing association – will keep a share of the property until you're ready to buy the rest.

Watch out!

There are numerous companies that offer assistance in arranging Right to Buy purchases, but they often charge fees for services that should be free, such as obtaining an application form from the Council.

Note also that having bought your home, if you later lose it because you can't afford the mortgage repayments and it's repossessed, there will be no obligation on the Council to rehouse you.

16 FINDING THE RIGHT PROPERTY

Choosing a new home sounds like fun. Snooping around other people's houses promises at the very least to provide hours of cheap entertainment (judging by the number of TV shows devoted to the subject). But the potential for enjoyment is likely to be tempered by the harsh reality of a limited budget, and if your existing property is now under offer the clock will be ticking ominously. Over the coming few weeks, the pressure to make a crucial, life-changing decision costing hundreds of thousands of pounds can reach fever pitch.

In reality, most of us start out with a fairly hazy mental image of the dream-home that we hope to acquire. Then, after viewing a series of

disappointingly shabby and pokey properties in our price range, the truth inevitably dawns that compromises will need to be made. Grand ambitions may have to be scaled down to fit budgets. If you're buying together as a couple, it's sometimes tempting to compromise your partner's requirements rather than your own. The male of the species might, for example, regard a walk-in wardrobe or en-suite bathroom as an unaffordable luxury, but a garage workshop as an essential. Such differences of opinion can easily evolve into smouldering resentments that later flare up in bitter recriminations. So the best approach is to nail down those attributes that you consider to be truly essential before you start. Write out a list of the things you really need, and those that are negotiable. This goes straight to the heart of why you decided to move in the first place.

Listing your criteria

	The ideal property	The minimum acceptable
Location	Backwater Village Views to open land	Not on a main road Edge of small town Near countryside
Schools	Catchment area for church schools	Main reason for moving – essential
Transport	Must be within 30 minutes of office	One hour travelling max
House or flat	House	House
Detached, semi or terrace	Detached	Semi
Modern or period house	Period, ideally Georgian	Victorian to 1930s
Bedrooms	Four	Three large with potential to subdivide
Bathrooms	Two	One, with potential to extend
Living rooms	Two	One large reception
Kitchen size	Large kitchen diner	Potential to 'knock through'
Garage	Detached double	A shed
Garden size	Half an acre	Bigger than present
Condition	Good condition, with modern kitchen and bathrooms	Needing decorative work and some basic DIY. Prepared to fit new kitchen and bathroom, as long as existing are usable for the time being

Deciding what you want

Though it helps to start with a clear picture of what you want, it's also important to be flexible that so you don't miss out on a different type of property that could meet most of your requirements. Suppose, for example, that you've set your heart on a stylish Georgian or Victorian townhouse, but then a spacious Edwardian mansion flat comes up that unexpectedly pushes all the right buttons. Too tight a specification and it could easily have slipped under your radar.

Going through the process of pinpointing your requirements before arranging any viewings should save a lot of time and energy. The key issues can be divided into those that relate to the building itself, and those concerning the area that it's in. You may end up balancing one against the other, because living in a posh, more expensive area usually means having to settle for a smaller property, whereas the same budget would get you a larger flat or house in a cheaper part of town.

The property

Perhaps the most fundamental requirement is size. Often the main reason for moving is the need for more space, so the minimum number of bedrooms is often a key factor.

■ Bedrooms

The number of bedrooms you require often depends on where you happen to be in your life-cycle. Estate agents describe properties by the number of bedrooms, which could be anything from a first-timer bachelor pad with zero bedrooms (a studio flat) up to family-friendly four or more.

Of course, you may be downsizing, perhaps following retirement or divorce, with a reduced appetite for space. But having more than one bedroom makes properties suitable for friends buying together, or where letting a room is part of the plan.

■ House or flat

Flats tend to be lower priced, and appeal to first-time buyers, investors and downsizers. There's often a potential drawback with noise, since you're located closer to your neighbours, but modern flats should have been built to stringent soundproofing standards. Also, leases sometimes include eye-wateringly sizeable charges – see the next chapter.

■ Garden

There are two kinds of people in the world – those with green fingers who love gardening and those who'd rather drink poison than spend hours clipping, snipping and digging. But regardless of your leisure interests, if you have children or pets then a decent garden is normally high on the agenda. Low-maintenance gardens can provide the best of both worlds. In some locations properties with attractive gardens can command a significantly higher price.

■ Parking

No matter how minuscule your carbon footprint, homes without any off-street parking can be a hassle, unless, of course, the street is generously endowed with parking

spaces. This is often a problem even in the most expensive areas, with local councils requiring payment for resident permit-parking schemes. If there's potential to drop the kerb and provide a space or two in the front garden, this could be worth exploring.

■ Garages

Most males harbour certain primitive desires for a garage, a sane place to which to retreat and pimp your ride, or do stuff that less enlightened folk don't fully appreciate. But how many garages today are used for their original purpose of housing vehicles? A garage may be a desirable feature, but it is rarely essential unless your neighbourhood is plagued by joy-riders and 'envy-scratchers'. Off-street parking or an allocated car space is often perfectly sufficient.

Properties with integral garages may have potential to convert into extra living space. Or there may be potential to construct a new garage, subject to planning.

■ Period property

It's a matter of personal taste. Some will pay a premium for a brand spanking new home in perfect condition. Others will gladly pay over the odds for a property radiating centuries of

deeply embedded character, the feel of ingrained history only found in genuinely antique buildings. Somewhere in between these extremes are the majority of properties, although the term 'period property' actually includes anything up to and including the 1930s.

■ High-rise

We're all familiar with the failed architectural dream evident in our cities, strewn with unloved, unkempt tower blocks. But fashions change. With good management and maintenance, some blocks have become desirable residences appealing largely to fashionista singletons, the amazing views perhaps ameliorating the ugliness of the architecture. But mortgage lenders are generally very wary about lending on anything that's more than five storeys high or constructed from reinforced concrete.

■ Property prejudice

Tower blocks aren't the only buildings that worry lenders. Different banks have their own particular 'blacklists' of unsuitable buildings. For example:

- [ ] Pre-1960s timber frame
- [ ] 'Scout hut' timber frame, *ie* those not clad externally with brick, block or stone
- [ ] Flats accessed by 'open deck walkways'
- [ ] Houses with 100 per cent flat roofs
- [ ] Walls built from reinforced concrete
- [ ] Steel-framed houses
- [ ] 'Non-habitable' homes, *eg* without functioning kitchens or bathrooms

Some lenders aren't keen on houses with more than one kitchen, properties built with unusually thin walls (*eg* sub-standard Victorian rear additions), or even thatched cottages. Buildings with a history of subsidence can also prove troublesome.

But if there's one type to be especially wary of, it's post-war Council houses, some of which pioneered new 'non-traditional' types of construction, such as poured concrete, or pre-reinforced concrete (PRC). Some of these are

Unmortgageable. A prefab with asbestos walls and roof

acceptable, especially if they've been upgraded, but many aren't (see Chapter 22).

However, for the vast majority of buildings there shouldn't be a problem – unless, of course, the mortgage surveyor notices that it's visibly collapsing.

■ Condition

To get the home we really want many of us will gladly sacrifice the ideal of a house in pristine decorative condition. Indeed, spurred on by TV property celebs anyone with good DIY skills may relish imprinting their personal mark on their new home with a spot of renovation and improvement.

Most properties you see won't be in too shabby a decorative condition, but then again they won't have the exact kind of kitchen, bathroom or wallpaper that you'd really want. So you could end up refurbishing the whole house – in which case you may as well save some money by buying a really trashy, run-down example in the first place. In a slow market, run-down properties command a lot less money, but conversely in a boom people can be willing to pay almost as much for a wreck as for an equivalent house in good condition.

It's also worth remembering that if your vision involves making structural alterations, these inevitably turn out to be more expensive and messier than you imagined.

The location

Thanks to TV property gurus Phil Spencer and Kirstie Allsop there can hardly be a living man, woman or child in the entire country who is unaware of the fact that *location* is the single most important factor when buying property. In fact deciding *where* you want to live is often the first decision you need to make. Your choice of area will not only depend on commutability to work, but also on your preferred lifestyle – whether you love the vibrancy of the city centre or feel the urge to move out into the country, or perhaps hedge your bets by settling in the suburbs.

Naturally a small Palladian mansion occupying several acres in one of the more leafy counties would suit very nicely, except for one small thing – regrettably, most of us are a few million quid short of the asking price.

A quiet street with speed bumps – indicative of peak hour congestion?

Location – village, town or suburb?

Back in the real world, harsh financial realities can mean having to compromise between property and position. Given the choice of a tiny studio flat in a fabulous area and a period house in a less salubrious district, on balance the temptation may be to opt for the latter, in the hope that the area is 'up and coming'. But it's important to bear in mind that one day it'll be your turn to sell, so it's always best to avoid obvious negatives, such as properties next to 24-hour takeaways, busy pubs, car repair garages, hospitals and fire-stations. Nearby schools and churches can also prove disruptive, with your neighbourhood being regularly invaded by swarms of car-borne parents/worshippers.

Before committing to any one location it's important to consider what you really want from a locality, and it's essential to take a leisurely stroll around the area and thoroughly check it out. Points to consider include:

■ People like us
Despite what we sometimes proclaim, most of us prefer to live in an area well-stocked with people similar to ourselves. Whether we're swinging '24-hour party people', young professionals, students or growing families, it's often the case that like tends to attract like.

■ Transport
Occasionally the papers come up with stories of folk who, for the sake of a glorious home, will endure the most gruelling and expensive commutes to work. Living in

northern France and commuting to London is not unknown. But for most of us, easy access to public transport, or to motorways permitting journey times of an hour or less, are key to the house-buying decision.

Having settled on a viable route to work, it's important to try out the journey at the times of day you will actually be doing it – just to be sure.

■ Local amenities
You know what amenities are important for you. If you're new to the area it's worth spending a little time searching online for the availability of NHS doctors and dentists, hospitals, leisure centres, pools and gyms, churches, libraries, pubs, bars and restaurants.

■ Investment
From an investment viewpoint, property in prime residential areas tends to appreciate in value more quickly over time than the equivalent real estate located in less expensive areas. So opting for a smaller property in a premium area is normally the better buy, pound for pound.

■ Crime
Living in fear every time you pop out to the shops probably isn't a good trade-off for being able to afford an enchanting property. Many buyers will opt for the relative safety of established residential areas rather than risking collateral damage from drive-by gangster shootings and binge-drinking epidemics. This is partly an 'age thing'. One person's perception of a lively vibrant urban area is another's war zone. But for obvious reasons families tend to take a more conservative outlook.

If you're planning to buy in an area you already live in, you will know how safe it feels and have an idea of the relevant crime statistics. Again, bear in mind that the day will come when you'll want to sell, and this will be more difficult in a dodgy area. Check crime statistics online.

Schools

For anyone with a young family, the first question to ask is often about local schools. And as all estate agents know, properties within the catchment area of good schools are easier to sell and command a premium. Parents who are well enough off to pay for a private education for their little darlings may not need to worry about catchment areas. Otherwise there's the dilemma of whether to buy an amazing property in a cheaper area served by a notorious sink-school, and then worrying that your kids will all grow up to be brain-dead glue-sniffers. Like everything else, the fortunes and reputations of schools can change over time, so if you have 'inside information' that a school is on the up, you could be ahead of the market. School league tables can be checked at **www.ofsted.gov.uk**.

Environment

Environmental issues, such as mobile phone masts near a house, can have a significant impact on price. A discount is normally needed to reflect perceived drawbacks. Some of these concerns aren't actually supported by conclusive scientific opinion, and different people will judge them differently. Values can be negatively affected by close proximity to the following:

- ☐ Mobile phone masts
- ☐ Electricity substations and pylons
- ☐ Radon gas
- ☐ Flight paths to airports
- ☐ Main roads and air pollution
- ☐ Railway lines
- ☐ Petrol stations
- ☐ Factories and shops
- ☐ Landfill sites and mines
- ☐ Waste incinerators

On the plus side, you may be able to clinch a bargain and buy a cheaper property in a top postcode area due to its *immediate environment*. Asking prices will be lower for houses next to busy roads or railway lines, or adjoining commercial or retail property.

Intensity of use

Those who bought a house by Stansted Airport in the days when it was a private flying club aerodrome may not have minded the occasional de Havilland Chipmunk droning mellifluously overhead. The trouble is, small aerodromes as well as railways and minor roads have a nasty habit of getting busier over time as intensity of use increases. Even previously undiscovered rural backwaters aren't necessarily safe as thundering convoys of truckers follow implausible satnav short cuts.

Planning changes

Change can create opportunities, as well as threats. It's well known that major infrastructure projects, such as train line extensions, can add tremendous value to areas that were once ignored as being off the beaten track. For example, house prices in parts of South-East London rocketed in anticipation of the East London Line tube extension. Another way the planning environment can sometimes work in your favour is when a major neighbourhood detraction is due to be taken out – such as where a polluting old eyesore cement works is scheduled to close. But of course, such events can be a double-edged sword because of local job losses.

Flooding

Once upon a time, public enemy number one for insurers was 'subsidence'. But as climate change has evolved, the risk of flooding has suddenly taken on the role of chief bogey-man. Fortunately, before buying you can easily check whether your house is located in a flood plain by searching

by postcode on **www.environment-agency.gov.uk**. If it is, don't be too downhearted – the whole of Central London is sitting on a flood plain. What really matters is whether there has been recent flooding and the chance of it recurring.

How good is an area?

If you're not familiar with the area you're thinking of buying in, it's essential to do your homework. A little online research should tell you enough to be alert to the downside of an unfamiliar area. You can check out schools, crime and Council Tax rates etc on **upmystreet.com** or **yell.com**. But there's nothing like judging it for yourself. First impressions can be important, but may not tell the full story. One thing's for sure, the charming estate agent selling you the property won't be overly keen to divulge details of the local mafia turf wars or marauding girl gangs.

To accurately assess an area, it needs to be checked out at different times – at the weekend, at night, and during the week. Quiet suburbs can suddenly be transformed into 'rat run' racetracks, choked with gridlocked traffic at peak hours. Nearby schools may attract Mums double-parking and blocking narrow streets with SUV uber-wagons. A nearby pub could be a tremendous boon, but could also be a mecca for armies of teenage binge-drinkers after dark. Nightlife is great when you want it, but not when you've got to get up at 6:30am the next morning.

Handy tips for assessing an area include:

- Do local shops sell the kind of stuff you would buy?
- Does the local pub feel reasonably welcoming?
- Are gardens well-maintained or strewn with rubbish?
- Are any houses boarded up after being fire-bombed?
- Count the number of bells on each door – lots of flat conversions can mean parking and noise issues.
- Do many houses have commercial vehicles parked outside?
- Be nosy – peer through windows (you might be invited in for a cup of tea!).

Up and coming areas

In a buoyant property market, stories proliferate in the media about spotting 'up and coming' areas. Buying ahead of the game is a tempting short cut to riches. Being smart enough to get in before the herd can earn you a small fortune as prices rise at above-average rates. Chelsea, for instance, was once a down at heel quarter inhabited by penniless artists. But areas can also go the other way and rapidly lose value.

Of course, spotting the next big thing is not as easy as the media sometimes suggest. Some up and coming areas never seem to actually happen, for example London's Kings Cross, which has resisted what used to be called 'gentrification' (then 'yuppification' and now 'colonisation') despite boasting a gleaming new Eurorail terminal.

It tends to be young professionals who are prepared to gamble on a postcode area, rather than young families who are safer sticking to established areas.

Websites such as **upmystreet.com** sometimes announce the latest property hotspots, often based on plans for infrastructure investment. For example, some towns in Kent have benefited from new Eurostar rail links, whereas parts of Dorset and East London have been touched by Olympic magic. But you need to be selective – an additional runway at Heathrow is unlikely to bring much joy to surrounding areas.

Such predictions are at best only an educated guess, and tough market conditions can torpedo 'growth plans'. However, there does tend to be a 'ripple effect' in a rising market, as people who can't quite afford to live in the best neighbourhood often buy just outside it. Then it's only a matter of time before the gastro-pubs and bistros appear, trees are planted and green spaces blossom. This happened recently when London's East Dulwich became home for young professionals, actors and media people who couldn't afford traditionally upmarket West Dulwich. Similarly, a major new housing development can affect the balance of a formerly unexciting quarter, adding new momentum as fashionable buyers pour in and rediscover an area's hidden charms.

Herd instinct, egged on by media hyperbole, is the main driver of property booms and busts, so areas can change one way or the other surprisingly swiftly.

Fringe areas

In a depressed market 'up and coming' areas suddenly become known as 'fringe areas', and there is a tendency for values to drop quicker than in better-quality, well-established postcodes. But then choosing pretty much any property means gambling big sums of money on how the market will view the area in future. So what can push a formerly buoyant locality into reverse gear?

An area is a function of the population who choose to live there, and their spending power. If a major local employer folds, local shops may close as spending is reduced. Fashionable areas may suddenly become terminally uncool. Even depressingly monolithic new architecture can play a part in the downward spiral. Some areas have started to decline when problem tenants have been moved in, or perhaps a mini crime wave gets out of hand. Eventually, if enough local residents react to persistent noise and disturbance by selling up, a 'down and going' momentum can develop where more owners move away, increasing the supply of properties on the market. This causes prices to fall, making them more attractive to social landlords, who buy up more properties.

Conventional wisdom has it that owning a less good property in a nice location is better than owning the best property in a naff area. But you have to be careful when following this advice. An area may be delightful, but living in the wrong house can drive you mad. Too many kids crammed into too few bedrooms while you try to work from home is a recipe for trouble. To get the balance right, it might be better to settle for a reasonable location with affordable property, perhaps one with potential for a loft conversion. You shouldn't have to live in a mugger's paradise to buy a nice house.

True story

Duncan and Helen fell in love with a handsome five-bedroom Georgian semi-detached house in an 'undiscovered' part of Saint Paul's, Bristol. It had previously been let as an HMO ('house in multiple occupation') and had great potential. But as soon as they moved in, they noticed a posse of local youths congregated most evenings on their front garden wall, drinking and smoking until late. The local school was dire and there were no other children locally for their kids to play with. After a couple of weeks, Duncan's car was deliberately scratched. One day when they were out at work there was a break-in, and the police were not too optimistic about catching the criminals. Ultimately, as the stress began to affect their relationship, it seemed that the best course of action was to sell up, even at a loss.

Starting your search

It has never been easier to search for property. The estate agents' website RightMove.co.uk have a virtual online monopoly, claiming that as many as 90 per cent of estate agents list their offerings with them. But there are several other sites such as PrimeLocation.co.uk etc that are also worth checking.

It's very easy to overlook the fact that a significant number of properties aren't sold conventionally through

estate agents. It is often simpler and easier to buy a newly built property, and some developers prefer to deal direct with the public. If you're looking at the other end of the spectrum, for less mainstream properties – such as those in need of renovation or for investment – buying at auction can be an excellent alternative. But perhaps the strongest trend is for an increasing number of home owners to 'cut out the middleman' and sell privately.

But regardless of where you search, after you've been house-hunting for a while a strange thing seems to happen. The property that your heart becomes set on, the one that you really want, always seems to be priced tantalisingly above your absolute maximum budget. It's out of reach and financially suicidal. But you still desperately want it.

Buying through estate agents

The overwhelming majority of UK properties still sell the traditional way, via estate agents, so the chances are that this is how you will find your new home. But because of the sheer number of competing agents you may have to draw up a shortlist of the ones that are worth approaching. By searching online, or looking at their ads in local papers, you can get a feel for which agents specialise in your kind of property. Although 'posh' agents occasionally sell standard properties, and vice versa, most have a 'market sector' that they know best.

Registering with agents
You want to be the first person the agent thinks of as soon as they get a new instruction to sell the type of property you're after. With this in mind, it's worth popping in and registering in person so that they can see you're a serious buyer (or a potential seller). You can't beat a face-to-face rapport. To help underline your status as a keen buyer, you need to be ready to start viewing suitable properties.

Traditionally, within a few days of registering, your postman would stagger up to your front door weighed down with reams of sales particulars. Today, although some agents still routinely post out details, email and phone contact is the norm – so be sure to regularly check your emails. Even in quiet markets, the best properties can be snapped up before the details have been finalised or posted on the web. So it's essential to provide a phone number where you can be contacted throughout the day. It also pays to keep yourself at the forefront of your agent's memory by frequent calls and emails. To keep ahead of the game, register for SMS text alerts and email updates as soon as new homes are listed.

One of the great mysteries of buying houses is why, having registered a specific interest in detached houses in village locations, for example, you are then bombarded with details of flats, bungalows and properties in wildly

varying locations and price ranges. Irritating though this is, agents know from bitter experience that despite what buyers tell them, many will end up making offers on remarkably different types of property.

To get the best out of estate agents, it helps to know how they operate. What they like most are serious buyers who know what they can realistically afford – or, even better, don't have a property to sell, or at least have an offer proceeding on their present home. So as a buyer, you need to have a clear idea about what you want before starting and have got your finances sorted before viewing properties. What they like even more is 'cash buyers' with funds available to spend right away.

It's always best to be straight about how much you can afford, even if the agent can't quite succeed in disguising a mildly contemptuous sneer. Pretending you can afford more just wastes everyone's time and ultimately looks a bit silly – plus you end up viewing lots of houses that you won't be able to buy, which can prove disheartening. But if you like the look of a property, be ready to instantly spring into action and book a viewing.

How estate agents assess buyers
As soon as you stroll into the agent's office they will want to assess you. In the course of a typical day, agents have to deal with a fair number of timewasters and nosey-parkers, so having announced your interest as a potential buyer you will then be graded. A good agent will make this a painless experience so you may not even be aware of. Whether you're classified as 'hot' or not, will largely depend on the following:

■ Hot buyers
To qualify as a 'hot buyer' and go to the head of the queue you must be 'proceedable'. This means you have funds to spend, or at least will have in the immediate future. 'Hot buyers' include cash buyers, people who've already sold

their current property (*ie* have it under offer), people living in rented accommodation, first-time buyers and investors with mortgages approved in principle. Indeed, anyone who can lay their hands on sufficient funds to proceed without selling their own house. The estate agent's smile will broaden directly in relation to how much ready cash they think you have to spend.

■ Hot sellers

If you haven't sold already, don't despair. The agent may still muster a faint smile because they sense a business opportunity. If you live locally, they will promptly switch into sales mode to persuade you to instruct them to sell your present property, even if it's currently on the market with another agent.

■ Others

You may only qualify for a frown if you currently live outside the area and haven't yet sold your present dwelling. Agents know that statistically over 90 per cent of enquiries from buyers based out of the local area will not result in a sale.

It's important to remember that the estate agent's job is to get the best price for their client, the seller. This has to be said because a good sales negotiator can charm buyers into a sense of 'we're on your side'. Agents know that a certain amount of 'best buddy' schmoozing of prospective buyers can maximise the number of viewings to a property, and hence boost the chances of receiving an offer. It also greases the wheels of negotiation should you decide to put in an offer.

Accuracy of descriptions

Tony Blair was once described as 'the ultimate estate agent', an accolade that was not intended as a complement. But this is perhaps a little unfair on estate agents. MPs have considerably more scope for lies, spin

Photos: PAphotos

Above: Loadsaroom! – Estate agent demonstrates advantages of a 'cupboard kitchen'

and downright dishonesty than agents, who are bound by the terms of the Property Misdescriptions Act. It is a criminal offence for inaccurate information to be published, which is why 'draft details' are always subject to the seller's approval. Property details today are often very brief and tend to avoid mentioning anything beyond the blindingly obvious. However, agents are skilled at producing details that bring out the property's positive attributes – not least by employing professionally photograhed wide-angle filtered shots that cast run-of-the-mill suburban semis against balmy blue-sky backdrops.

Property particulars

The time-honoured way for agents to sell a property was to first draft a description of it, then add a photo, and finally stick it in their shop window. Once copies had been posted out to potential buyers registered with them, they could sit back and wait for the phone to ring.

Spot the difference: Contemporary property particulars, and details circa 1987

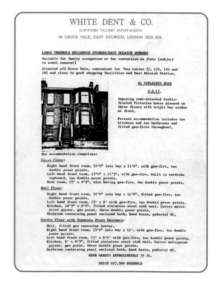

Left and above: An inconvenient truth. Whatever happened to the busy road, the 24/7 store next door, and the factory to the rear?

Scan forward a few years to the age of websites and virtual tours, and, the ability to write good quality property particulars is still a key part of the sales process. Apart from vastly improved print quality, one major change is the ditching of excessively flowery language. The Property Misdescriptions Act 1991 saw to that by outlawing 'false or misleading' statements.

But despite the legislation succeeding in curtailing the worst abuses, most of the complaints received by the Estate Agent Ombudsman still concern inaccurate sales literature. Often this is just down to carelessness (although errors somehow always seem to flatter the property in question). Typically this relates to daft things like saying there's a garage when there isn't, or describing terraced houses as semi-detached. The best advice is to take what you read with a pinch of salt, and check it with the seller. As a buyer, if you don't understand something ask the agent, otherwise you could waste a lot of time, or risk making an expensive mistake.

Some tricks of the trade are simply designed to present the 'product' in the best light:

- Photos shot with wide-angle lenses, making small rooms appear larger.
- Basements and rooms without windows that appear bright because the lights are on.
- Photos that are tightly cropped, to cut out ugly neighbouring buildings.
- Computer images of new developments, showing mature trees, traffic-free streets, and immaculately dressed 'shiny, smiley people'.
- Skies that have been artificially 'blued' and grass that has been 'greened'.

Of course, there will always be a fine line between making a house appear better than it is and setting out to be deliberately 'misleading'. And you have to pity the agent trying to favourably describe some horrible rat-infested dump into which no one in their right mind would want to set foot. Some of the more colourful euphemisms agents employ are well known:

'With great potential'	= Not much to look at
'With potential building plot'	= If it was that easy to get planning permission the present owner would have already done so
'Convenient for Motorway'	= Sorry, I can't hear you for the traffic noise
'Vibrant city centre location'	= Vomiting binge-drinking neighbours
'Convenient for shops and restaurants'	= It's above the chip shop
'Would suit DIY enthusiast'	= Visibly subsiding
'Traditional'	= Dated, in need of renovation
'Period property'	= Anything older than the estate agent
'Cosy'	= Cramped and pokey
'Landscaped garden'	= A few shrubs
'Contemporary'	= A bland 1960s or 1970s box, or something a bit odd-looking

Estate agent law

Despite the fact that as a buyer you're not actually their client, estate agents still have a legal duty to treat you 'fairly', under the terms of the Estate Agents Act 1979. But what if you suspect that something fishy's going on? Suppose you make an offer and the agent claims to have already received a higher offer from a cash buyer? You may well believe that this is simply a ruse to get you to part with more money by increasing your offer.

According to the Office of Fair Trading (OFT), agents must not state that they have already received offers or claim that other potential buyers are waiting in the wings unless true. Nor must they invent rival bids. The OFT suggests that people should demand to see evidence if they have suspicions. Which is all very well in theory, but can be difficult in practice, particularly if you want to keep on good terms with the agent. Agents are under no legal duty to

Estate Agent scams

Most agents play strictly by the rules. But occasionally reports surface of underhand activities and illegal practices:

■ Bumping up the price

The agent tells you there's another (non-existent) offer on the table for the property you want to buy, in an attempt to get you to make a higher offer, thereby raising the price paid.

■ Lying about the property

The agent assures you that planning permission for the swimming pool or extension (depicted in the brochure) was obtained. But if this information turns out to be wrong, once you've exchanged contracts it's too late. It's up to you and your solicitor to verify any such claims and spot any non-compliance. Don't take the agent's word because what they tell you verbally is largely irrelevant, as it's your word against theirs. By all means ask for written proof, but watch out for caveats like 'to the best of my knowledge'.

■ Not passing on all offers

Agents have a duty to pass on all offers to their client. If you suspect this isn't happening one solution is to approach the seller directly, putting a note through the door saying 'I was just looking at your house again and really love it. I do hope you're interested in our offer. We look forward to hearing from [their agent].' That way the agent is boxed in, as you're not trying to cut them out, just being keen. Put your phone number on the note, just in case.

■ Encouraging gazumping

Not withdrawing the property from the market when your offer has already been accepted, thereby encouraging 'gazumping' – a higher offer from a rival buyer.

■ Binning bids

Several buyers want the same property and it goes to 'sealed bids'. The agent bins the ones that are higher than the bid of his friend. An agent working for a well-known national chain recently admitted that after opening all the buyers' offers he illegally added his own extra bid, a measly £5 higher, thus becoming the successful and highest bidder.

reveal details of other offers they have (genuinely) received on a property, which as a buyer can be a trifle niggling.

Although it would be an unusual request today, an estate agent can, if they wish, demand a deposit from a buyer. However, all clients' money must be held in separate client

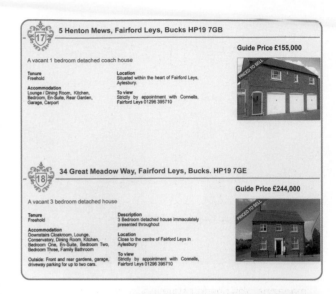

5 Henton Mews, Fairford Leys, Bucks HP19 7GB

Guide Price £155,000

A vacant 1 bedroom detached coach house

Tenure
Freehold

Accommodation
Lounge / Dining Room, Kitchen, Bedroom, En-Suite, Rear Garden, Garage, Carport

Location
Situated within the heart of Fairford Leys, Aylesbury.

To view
Strictly by appointment with Connells, Fairford Leys 01296 395710

34 Great Meadow Way, Fairford Leys, Bucks. HP19 7GE

Guide Price £244,000

A vacant 3 bedroom detached house

Tenure
Freehold

Accommodation
Downstairs Cloakroom, Lounge, Conservatory, Dining Room, Kitchen, Bedroom One, En-Suite, Bedroom Two, Bedroom Three, Family Bathroom

Outside: Front and rear gardens, garage, driveway parking for up to two cars.

Description
3 Bedroom detached house immaculately presented throughout

Location
Close to the centre of Fairford Leys in Aylesbury

To view
Strictly by appointment with Connells, Fairford Leys 01296 395710

Tempted by low 'guide prices' to submit an offer ?- see chapter 19 bank accounts, and covered by adequate insurance, as set out in the Estate Agents (Accounts) Regulations. Receipts for deposits must be provided.

Agents must also not discriminate against buyers. So-called 'preferential listing' is not permitted. This is when buyers are told they will be given priority or preferential service if they buy financial services, such as insurance or a mortgage, offered by the estate agent. In practice, with limited sanctions in place, it can be difficult for consumers to challenge these sorts of practices.

Buying privately

To get the house you really want means trying every angle. A small but significant number of properties are advertised privately. To save a lot of hunting around, all the main private seller websites can be found at **SellersNET.co.uk**.

As well as searching online, the following can elicit a surprising amount of fruitful information, possibly unearthing a house that no one else was aware of:

■ **Place a 'wanted' ad** in your local papers or parish

magazine. You needn't state a price range or be too specific, just list the essential criteria. Both you and the seller will know roughly what that type of property sells for.

- **Place a 'wanted' ad** with an online listing service – see website.
- **Read ads from private sellers** in local papers and in LOOT, Gumtree, etc.
- **Leaflet drop** – you may already know the ideal type of house that you'd like to buy. It's just that they're not currently for sale. It's sometimes worth popping a 'wanted' leaflet through the door. By stressing savings on agents' fees it may prompt a response, reaping big dividends.

True story

Greg and Ann wanted a detached house in a local village, and could afford up to about £550,000. The condition didn't matter, but they wanted a good-sized plot, ideally adjoining open land. They drafted a 'wanted' advert, which was duly placed in the local parish magazine to run for three months. They received a handful of enquiries by email and phone. Some properties were worth viewing.

They also took photocopies of the advert from the magazine and used these as leaflets to put through doors of suitable properties. Next day the phone rang and a viewing was arranged. They loved the property and were willing to make an offer. However, it turned out the house was already on the market with a local agent. So before accepting a private offer the sellers first checked their position with the agent. They had a standard 'sole agency agreement' and the agent confirmed that Greg and Ann were not registered with them, so no commission would be chargeable in the event of a private sale. The property was duly purchased at a price that split the saved commission fee between buyer and seller.

- **Knocking on doors** – as above, but this direct approach may elicit information from someone who knows someone else who is thinking of selling.

One obstacle to buying privately can be tradition. Sellers sometimes assume they're not allowed to sell privately if they're using an agent at the same time. But the Internet is changing this. (See Chapter 9.)

Search agents

For the wealthy few with hectic lifestyles and plenty of spare cash, employing a specialist property search agent to help track down the home of your dreams can take the slog out of house finding. These expert house-hunters will identify properties that fulfil your criteria and conduct the first viewings. They will also advise you on what price to pay, and what the best areas are for local schools and amenities. They will negotiate the deal on your behalf and see the purchase through to completion. The fees charged are comparable to those charged by estate agents to sell a property, but normally require a deposit at the outset.

Buying a new property

Busy people don't want a home that's going to require updating. They don't want to waste precious time doing home improvements, clearing out gutters or grouting bathroom tiles. So the promise of a repair-free existence can be a very attractive proposition, safe in the knowledge that if anything does go wrong it will automatically be covered. The icing on the cake is that buying from a

developer means you're most unlikely to be messed about, with a capricious seller changing their mind or pulling out.

Just like buying a new car under warranty from a dealer, buying a brand new home can cut out a huge amount of hassle. But of course, you pay more for the privilege. There tends to be a price premium of at least a ten per cent on new homes, which evaporates after a few years as values tend to move into line with the local second-hand market. But unlike a car, the value of a house doesn't drop like a stone from the minute you open the door (subject to market conditions!).

According to the Office of Fair Trading, seven out of ten buyers of newly-built homes notice faults after moving in, although these are mostly minor issues to do with decorating, glazing, plasterwork or fitted appliances and don't cost the buyer anything to fix. Nevertheless, as occasional 'new homes from hell' stories remind us, buying from a developer isn't always plain sailing. Here are a number of tips to getting the best deal and reducing the risk of problems when buying new:

- Buy from a developer with a good reputation for quality.
- Don't just view the show home – check the quality of finish in the 'real' houses.
- Talk to other people who've already moved in. Ask about teething problems, and how willingly (or not) they were dealt with.
- Visit previous developments built by the same firm locally – do they still look in good condition, or has the glazing misted up and the walls stained from leakage and deterioration?

It's often best to buy one of the last houses to be completed on a large development since major home-builder companies are more likely to be willing to negotiate a good deal, being keen to move on to the next project. You may even get show-home carpets and curtains thrown in. Buying towards the end of the firm's financial year can also be a good time to do a deal, as they'll want to maximise their sales results. Where there's a surplus of new flats in a slow market, first-time buyers can sometimes benefit from incentives as house-builders try to offload remaining stock. For example, some developers require no deposit and will let you pay 85 per cent of the purchase price, with the remaining 15 per cent offered as an interest-free loan by the developer. The deferred amount is paid back later as 15 per cent of the property's open-market value within ten years of purchase, or at the time of any earlier resale.

Buying 'off-plan' (*ie* buying a property on the basis of the developer's plans) can be risky. Committing to buying something you haven't seen, or that doesn't yet exist, isn't normally a great idea, especially one that costs hundreds of thousands of pounds. Of course, developers love nothing better than getting 'money up front'. So in a boom market there may be pressure to buy before building has even started for fear that prices will rise even higher by waiting for it to be built. But if you look beyond the computer-generated images of contented futuristic people on digitally enhanced brochures of the proposed development, you may spot some nasties nestling in the small print. For example, the developer may reserve the right to change the design and materials. If you do buy off-plan, always tie the builder down to a firm completion date.

NHBC

These are four letters that the buyers of new houses will want to see on the paperwork. The NHBC 'Buildmark' warranty is the best-known newbuild scheme, but there are other equivalent products recognised by the Council of Mortgage Lenders (CML), such as Zurich, which are also acceptable to lenders. See **cml.org**.

Buying new – extra checks that your solicitor will need to make

- Has the house been built on contaminated or filled land? If it has, you will need valid certificates to show that the land was properly treated, which may prove crucial when it comes to arranging buildings insurance.
- Have the roads and sewers been 'adopted' by the local authority? Otherwise, who pays for their upkeep?
- The extent of any social housing within a development.
- Any restrictions on extending the house in future.
- Test certificates for any electrical or gas appliances.
- A suitable ten-year warranty.

On new construction, NHBC may also act as the Building Control authority instead of the local council, so they take the rap should the builders not have complied with the building regulations (e.g. perhaps forgetting to install loft insulation). Lenders will not release mortgage funds until the buyer's conveyancer has confirmation that a final NHBC inspection has been carried out and that the NHBC warranty will be in place before legal completion. The NHBC warranty also covers you should the builder become insolvent between exchange and completion in which case your deposit should be safeguarded and any repairs that the builder would have been required to do in the first two years will still be carried out.

However, it's a common misconception that buying a new house means you can totally forget about repairs and maintenance during the first ten years. For a start, normal wear and tear isn't covered. Nor are things like fences or white goods (which have a manufacturer's warranty). Indeed, after the first two years the extent of cover is surprisingly sparse.

NHBC protection is in two parts:

Years one and two – During the first couple of years, the builder has to put right at their own expense defects that arise due to failure to comply with NHBC minimum standards. The cover includes minor defects such as shrinkage cracking, dampness and condensation – as long they were caused by defective workmanship or materials at the time of construction rather than as the result of an extension or alterations that the owner has carried out since moving in. There is, however, one sneaky get-out clause to watch out for: you're not covered for 'wear and tear or deterioration caused by neglect or failure to carry out maintenance'. That seems a bit rich, because a properly built house shouldn't require any particular maintenance by the owner during the first year or two beyond the routine servicing of boilers and hot water and central heating systems.

Years three to ten – From year three to year ten you are covered only for more serious repairs that arise under NHBC's insurance policy for defects such as subsidence and structural failure. Minor defects are excluded.

In most cases, any major defects are likely to have materialised once a property is about five or six years old. But if you buy a house that's less than ten years old from the original owners, there's a potential trap – you can't claim for any defects that the first owner has already reported, or, indeed, for defects that were visible at the time of purchase, upon 'reasonable inspection' (whatever that may mean).

Nonetheless, when buying a pre-owned 'nearly new' house that's less than ten years old, it's important to check that it still has a valid NHBC certificate or an acceptable equivalent. However, different mortgage lenders have different rules on this. Some won't lend on properties less than ten years old without a warranty, whereas others only insist on this for the first two years.

Buying at auction

If you believe the hype, property auctions are crammed with amazing deals. Unfortunately, being a bit good at eBay doesn't automatically qualify you to pick the bargain of the century. It's easy to forget that the people selling are equally convinced they will achieve a great result, hoping that punters with more optimism than experience will succumb to 'auction fever' and wildly overbid.

Around 30,000 properties are sold each year at auction, but these tend to be ones that are quirky and hard to value, such as those with obscure development potential or with dodgy leases, income-generating investments and odd pockets of land. Auctioneers often end up disposing of the stuff that estate agents have conspicuously failed to sell. Mortgage lenders sometimes offload repossessions at auction, as this is a swift way to fulfil their legal duty by selling at 'market value', with the reserve price set in advance by a qualified valuer. Councils and housing associations dispose of large lots of properties at auction for similar reasons.

For buyers, auctions have the major attraction that when the auctioneer's gavel falls, the deal is done, and the property is theirs upon completion. This gets around the problem of lengthy, slow-moving chains, which are the curse of the traditional house-buying process. However, uncertainty isn't entirely eradicated. Properties are sometimes mysteriously withdrawn prior to auction or you may get outbid, so all the money spent on surveys and legal fees may be wasted. But these are risks that you also face with conventional property transactions.

Before wading in and bidding, it's advisable to first do a dry run and sit through an auction to 'get the feel of it'.

Start by contacting auction houses to request catalogues, which sometimes need to be ordered via premium rate phone numbers. Subscribing to mailing lists can cost from about £15 per annum, but because there are nearly 200 firms that hold property auctions around the country it may be simpler to subscribe to online listings that allow you to 'view properties for sale at every auction in the UK' for an annual fee of between £50 and £100. (See website.)

Before you buy

To prepare for buying at auction you need to arrange all the things that house buyers normally do – just a lot quicker. Time is short. There may be only three weeks between the catalogue appearing and auction day, so it is essential to receive catalogues hot off the press, and to move quickly. Be prepared to chase solicitors and lenders. If you do decide to take a punt on a suitable property,

notify the auctioneers in advance that you're serious about specific lots, and request that they keep you informed of any developments.

■ Arranging funding

You must have a ten per cent deposit ready on auction day (payment by banker's draft is acceptable, and sometimes debit cards, but not usually cash or credit cards). The remaining 90 per cent of the sale price must be in place by completion four weeks later. Auctioneers also charge a 'buyers' premium' which can be anything from about £250 to 1.5 per cent of the selling price. You will, of course, have to budget for stamp duty and all the usual legal, survey and mortgage fees.

Don't buy at auction if you first need to sell your own house to finance the new one, unless you've already exchanged on the sale and can co-ordinate the move. Organising a mortgage is not very different from a conventional purchase, but because of the time pressure the wheels must be put in motion as early as possible, since if you fail to complete you could lose your ten per cent deposit. Ideally it is best to obtain ready funds by remortgaging an existing property. Bridging loans or buy-to-let mortgages can be a useful method of arranging short term funding. To save time, mortgages can be agreed in principle with your lender even before the catalogue is published.

■ Valuing

Once you have identified a target lot, if you need mortgage funding the lender's valuer will need to carry out an inspection, allowing sufficient time for the mortgage offer to be processed and confirmed in writing. But it's also

essential to satisfy yourself what the property is really worth and how high you are prepared to bid. To discover what similar nearby properties have sold for recently, check with local estate agents, or view Land Registry sales prices online. Talk to Council planners to see if there's any history of planning applications that could add value.

■ Legals

HIPs are still required for property sold at auction, so some of the necessary legal information should already be available. Your solicitor must carefully inspect the 'general conditions of sale' (along with any 'special conditions') published in the catalogue. Legal packs held by the auctioneer should contain all necessary searches, Land Registry office copies and details of leases etc. Always scrutinise the 'addendum' in the catalogue, which will contain amendments to any descriptive errors as well as important additional legal information. It's possible that some killer fact that significantly affects the value could be buried here. As per normal, your solicitor will need to check the contract and get answers to enquiries.

■ Survey

Defects such as serious damp, dry rot and structural problems won't be advertised. It is very much a case of *caveat emptor*, so it is essential to arrange a private survey – or at least a take a 'walk around' accompanied by a

knowledgeable professional, who may also be able to provide a ballpark figure for 'refurb' costs, upon which you can base your maximum bid.

■ Viewing

Group viewings are normally prearranged at fixed times, perhaps on three

or four separate days, details of which are listed in the catalogue. It's normally a good idea to phone before leaving home to check that your lot hasn't been 'sold prior' or 'withdrawn prior'. It may not always be possible to view tenanted properties. Check that the boundaries on site correspond to those shown in the documentation.

Bidding

Never bid on a property unless you have already viewed it, surveyed it, checked the legals and sorted the funding. On the morning of the auction, phone to confirm that your chosen lots are still available. Always set yourself a maximum price and stick to it (the lender's loan-to-value lending ratio may limit how high you can afford to go).

Properties are marketed with 'guide prices' which are supposedly 'an indication of the price the seller is hoping to achieve'. In reality they are often pitched significantly below the likely final sale price to cunningly entice wide-eyed buyers. There will also be a secret 'reserve price' which is the minimum the seller will accept. Although reserves are never disclosed, once the bidding exceeds this figure the seller is then legally obliged to sell the property to the highest bidder.

Don't worry about a bit of involuntary nose-scratching – the auctioneer can spot the difference between a serious bidder and a nervous twitch. By sitting sideways on you can observe the auctioneer and notice whether they're taking genuine bids or artificially boosting the price by 'taking bids off the chandeliers'.

Auctioneers are known for their ability to slowly 'charm the price' upwards, in smaller and smaller jumps, squeezing out every last penny. If you think your nerves could become a bit jangled, you don't actually have to be present to bid in person. You can appoint a colleague to bid for you (with written authorisation), or you may prefer to bid over the phone. Alternatively, you can choose to bid by 'proxy' – similarly to the process on eBay – where you submit a maximum price you are prepared to pay, and a staff member will bid on your behalf up to that figure. If bidding is light, the property could end up being purchased for you at a lower figure. A binding contract is entered into upon the fall of the auctioneer's gavel, at which point your ten per cent deposit will need to be paid. If a property remains unsold, sellers are often receptive to negotiating an offer after the auction. If your bid is successful, you must be ready to immediately arrange buildings insurance on property.

In a market downturn, some auction houses may relax the rules to make it easier for buyers. Some will accept smaller deposits and allow six to eight weeks to complete, rather than the standard 28 days. 'Conditional auctions' are a recent innovation, where the agreed sale is conditional upon buyers arranging finance after the auction, cutting wasted up-front costs in the event of an unsuccessful bid.

See website for links to forthcoming auctions.

17 | FLATS/LEASEHOLD PROPERTY

It's well known that buying a flat is generally a more complex operation than buying the equivalent house. At least, that's what the solicitors tell you to justify higher fees as soon as you utter the dreaded word 'leasehold'. So what exactly is all the fuss about?

Generally speaking, houses are sold *freehold*, which means that they belong to the owner forever (or until the house is sold). Flats, on the other hand, are normally

leasehold, which means you effectively have part ownership as the property will only be yours for a period of years. Fortunately, this period of years is likely to be a lot longer than most of us are likely to live. In practice this shouldn't be enormously different to owning freehold, but it does add to the conveyancing work, which is why it's the first question solicitors ask when you phone for a quote.

Flat or maisonette?

At this point it might be worth nailing one fundamental question that sometimes sparks furious debate – what exactly is the difference between a flat and a maisonette? To some, a maisonette is just a posh word for a flat, a term estate agents might employ in an attempt to bump up the value. But the general view is that a maisonette is a flat with its own front door opening out directly onto the big wide world. There may be some external steps, but there are no shared entrance lobbies or long communal corridors. Maisonettes also typically comprise separate ground floor and first floor apartments in a two-storey building - *ie* 'two units in one house'. Arguably the enhanced privacy of maisonette-living should stimulate their value. But at the end of the day both flats and maisonettes are normally leasehold and subject to the same concerns when it comes to management and maintenance.

Freeholders and leaseholders

Imagine a block of flats. The overall building will actually be owned by a freeholder who has leased out each flat for an extremely long time. New leases are typically drawn up for 99 years, 125 years or an impressive 999 years (very common in Northern Ireland). So when you buy a 'second-hand' flat the remaining length of the lease (known as the 'term') will normally be the original lease term, less the number of years old that it is.

The fortune of one of Britain's richest men, The Duke of Westminster was originally based on the premise that if a freeholder waits long enough, leases granted yonks ago will eventually revert to them – or more likely to one of their heirs. This way you effectively get back something that you've already sold – the ultimate 'having your cake and eating it too' windfall. Without leaseholds through the centuries, perhaps some of today's aristocracy would be driving buses for a living.

But today's leaseholders have other options. Rather than watching your lease shrivel pathetically over the years to nothing, most will at some point apply to extend their lease, or may jointly buy shared-ownership of the freehold along with the other leaseholders in the block (see below). Freeholds themselves are not generally worth a massive amount of money, and are bought and sold at auction as income-generating 'Freehold Ground Rents'. The price depends mainly on the annual income derived from all the small ground rents combined. But there is another potential source of income. Wily investors also know that flats with shorter remaining lease terms become harder to sell, and leaseholders wanting to extend their leases can be charged substantial sums for the privilege.

Ground rent

A lease is basically an extremely long-term letting agreement, with the rent already paid up front as the purchase price. So the 'ground rent' is simply a token gesture, a distant relative of the rent that you'd pay when renting a flat. Usually it's a small amount, such as £100 to £200 per year, perhaps paid in two lots of six-monthly instalments to the freeholder.

Service charge

The vast majority of flats are managed by either the freeholder-landlord or a management company responsible for repairs and maintenance. However, managing agents are often employed to physically carry out the day-to-day works at the property. This, of course, isn't done out of the goodness of their hearts. The owners of the individual flats, the leaseholders, have to pay a service charge (or maintenance charge), which unlike

ground rents can involve serious money, often totalling several thousand pounds per year.

The service charge should cover maintenance of the external fabric of the building as well as the upkeep of communal areas, such as cleaning entrance lobbies, stairs and corridors, plus taking care of any lifts. One of the ironies of buying flats is that modern blocks requiring relatively little maintenance often have far higher charges than rambling old mansion blocks in need of extensive care (see section on 'Sinking funds', below). Costs incurred by the freeholder-landlord for arranging buildings insurance are sometimes included or may be invoiced separately.

Things to watch out for

Purchasers of flats need their wits about them. There are a number of key points to watch out for when buying leasehold property. These are discussed in more detail later, but briefly they include:

■ The lease term
If the remaining lease term is currently much less than about 70 years it could mean that when you come to sell in future, it could be too short for your buyer's mortgage lender, who may refuse to lend. This in turn can reduce the value of the flat, because of the potential cost of getting the lease extended. (See boxout on page 132.)

■ Charges
It's essential for solicitors to obtain written confirmation that all the charges due, such as ground rent and service charges, have been fully paid up to date.

■ Repairs
Is there any backlog of outstanding works, especially big-ticket items like windows and roofs? Check whether the freeholder has accumulated some reserve 'sinking fund' money to cover any big future repair bills. Otherwise you could get hit with some nasty bills in future.

How to extend your lease

Once your remaining lease term has withered to 70 years or less, mortgage lenders can get a bit sniffy because they know that properties with shorter leases can start to reduce more swiftly in value. So it makes sense to apply to extend your lease. This will be a lot easier where the Freehold is already owned by all the individual leaseholders (see below).

The first step is to find out how much extending your lease is likely to cost, which unfortunately isn't always as easy as it sounds. To start the ball rolling, a suitably experienced local surveyor should be appointed to come up with a professional opinion of value.

However, valuing a leasehold extension is a complex business. It depends on a number of variables, including the market value of the flat, the length of time left on the lease, and the value of the landlord's interest (ie how much ground rent income the property generates each year, and how much the flat is likely to be worth many years in the future at the end of the lease).

You can then either serve the freeholder with a formal notice of your intention to extend your lease, or open informal talks with them, based on the figure stated in your independent professional valuation.

The problem with this system is that, at the end of the day, the cost of an extension is still a matter for negotiation, and some freeholders can be very good at exploiting their position by demanding awesome sums of money. If you and the freeholder cannot agree a price, you need to take the case to the Leasehold Valuation Tribunal.

Approximate costs

- Valuation: for a property worth less than £300,000, a typical valuation will cost around £500, rising to around £700 for a £500,000 property.
- Serving notice: from £275.
- Legal fees: from £500 to £1,000.
- Application to the Leasehold Valuation Tribunal: £400.

■ Rules

Does the lease contain any petty restrictions that could unreasonably cramp your lifestyle – are pets banned, for instance?

■ Who's who?

Simple question: who exactly is your freeholder? Some may have disappeared without trace and are impossible to contact. Perhaps there's a managing agent? If so, are they doing their job properly? If it ultimately turns out to be impossible to make contact with your freeholder, then they can be designated an 'absentee landlord'. If a leaseholder can prove this, then it should be possible to take legal action to acquire the 'right to manage' your property.

Legal work

This is where you begin to appreciate the extra work that solicitors have to struggle with when purchasing leasehold properties. Whereas a conveyancing job on an average freehold house could be done by Freddy the hamster without the need for too much extra tuition, there are a lot of questions to ask with flats, not least how many there are. Of course, in some buildings there may just be two flats, perhaps where the original upstairs and downstairs of a house have been converted. At the other extreme, architects have succeeded in cramming hundreds of flats into monumental tower block megastructures, to create complex cities in the sky.

Legally, however, there's not a lot of difference. In both cases the individual flats form part of a larger building, so it's necessary to decide who exactly is going to be responsible for maintenance, and how the cost of repairs should be shared. After all, if the roof were to one day need replacing, it would be a trifle unfair for the person dwelling on the top floor to be lumbered with the bill. And what if the bloke in the ground floor flat decides to remove a structural wall, perhaps forgetting that all the flats above rely on it for support? Clearly there needs to be some sort of restriction on owners chopping out bits of the structure and making major alterations willy-nilly.

Such problems are solved by giving each owner a lease, a legal contract that clarifies who is responsible for what. The lease should list all the important obligations, such as repairing the exterior and maintaining common parts, gardens and garages. It should also confirm shared rights of support, thereby limiting what owners can do. At least, it should. Some older leases were badly drafted and may not be at all clear, or they completely omit important information. Others may contain punitive charges imposed by greedy freeholders intent on behaving like feudal landlords taxing the urban poor. So it's basically up to your solicitor to be sharp-eyed enough to spot such concerns before you sign on the dotted line.

What's in a lease?

The lease governs your relationship with the freeholder and with other leasehold flat owners in the block. The lease is a long contract between the leaseholder and freeholder, setting out all the rights and duties of each party, such as who is responsible for maintaining and insuring the building, and paying the ground rent and service charges. Although leases follow a standard format some older ones may not be clear and can contain weird stipulations or hidden nasties. So your solicitor will need to carefully check the lease for any clauses that are unreasonable or 'onerous'.

The basic structure of all leases is similar. They start with the names of the parties, the length or 'term' of the lease and the amount of ground rent. Then there are the various obligations for the flat owner (the 'leaseholder' or 'tenant'), and for the freeholder ('landlord'). For example, 'the landlord is to maintain the property's exterior and common parts, and the tenant is to pay a proportion of the cost of maintenance & repairs as a service charge'.

H.M. LAND REGISTRY

County: Greater London

District: Southwark

Title Number:
Property: 9 Ropleston Road London SE 155 AH

THIS LEASE is made on the 29ᵗʰ day of August 2003

BETWEEN
(1)   **THE LESSOR** as described in Schedule I of this Lease ("the Lessor" which expression shall where the context so admits include the reversioner for the time being immediately expectant upon the determination of the term hereby created)
(2)   **THE LESSEE** as described in Schedule I of this Lease ("the Lessee" which expression shall include the person or persons in whom the term hereby created is from time to time vested by assignment devolution of law or otherwise)

WHEREAS:-

1.   The Lessor is registered with freehold title absolute under the above title number of the property as described in Schedule I of this Lease ("the Property") which consists (inter alia) of two self contained flats and has previously granted a lease or intends to grant a lease of the other flat at the property and such leases impose or intends in every future lease to impose covenants and regulations similar in all respects to those contained herein
2.   The Lessor has agreed with the Lessee for the grant to him of a lease of the premises described in Schedule I hereto ("the premises") for the consideration and at the rents and on the terms and conditions hereinafter appearing

NOW THIS DEED WITNESSETH as follows:-
1.   In consideration of the sum of TWO HUNDRED AND TWENTY FOUR FIVE HUNDRED POUNDS (£ 224,500.00) now paid by the Lessee to the Lessor (the receipt whereof the Lessor hereby acknowledges) and in further consideration of the rents and covenants on the part of the Lessee hereinafter contained and reserved the Lessor HEREBY DEMISES unto the Lessee ALL THAT the premises
TOGETHER WITH the Rights more particularly detailed in Schedule 2 hereto but EXCEPTING AND RESERVING the rights and matters more particularly detailed in Schedule 3 hereto
TO HOLD unto the Lessee for the term of years more particularly detailed in Schedule 1 hereto from the commencement date more particularly detailed in the Schedule I hereto YIELDING AND PAYING THEREFOR during the said term the yearly rents detailed in Schedule 1 hereto by equal half yearly payments in advance without deductions on the Twenty Fourth of June and the Twenty Fifth of December in every year the first of such payments or a proportionate part thereof to be made on the execution hereof and to be in respect of the date hereof to the next Payment day [such rents to be paid by Bankers Standing Order if the Lessor so directs.]

First page of a typical lease

Assessing the service charge

When buying a flat, one of the key questions is how big the service charge is. Needless to say, these can sometimes be very high indeed, notably where there's a serious backlog of repair works. But service charges may be very high for other reasons, perhaps because the building is being badly managed and the freeholder is busy siphoning off funds. So it's important to ask for copies of the service charge accounts over a few years to see how consistently the building's maintenance regime has been applied. Although leaseholders are protected by law from excessive charges for shoddy work, it's best to avoid potential worries in the first place. A badly-managed block should normally be evident from the visible lack of maintenance, often combined with high charges. Legally, a service charge is only payable if it's 'reasonable', so it's important to ask the seller if there are any disputes with the landlord about the level of charges. You don't want to step into an ongoing legal battle. Also, check the lease to see when the service charge is payable, normally annually, six-monthly or quarterly.

In reality, accurate figures aren't always available at the time you need them. At completion, very often the accounts showing the true sums for the year that you're buying will not yet have been prepared. Although freeholder-landlords are now under a legal obligation to issue leaseholders with annual itemised service charge statements, in some cases even the previous year's costs

may not yet have been finalised. If accurate figures are not available at completion then 'assessments' and 'apportionments' are made instead – in other words, only educated guesses. The problem is, as soon as you become the owner of a leasehold flat you will suddenly be liable for all expenses – even those that accrued before you bought.

Sinking funds

As well as charging for works scheduled for the current year, most leases allow for a 'sinking fund'. This is a 'war chest' of cash, built up over time so that leaseholders aren't stung with a massive bill when the roof needs replacing or expensive works to windows or lifts are needed for the entire block. So it's a good sign if there's already a sizeable amount of cash in the kitty.

Repairs

Ask the seller whether there are any scheduled major works, typically ones that would require payment from you of £300 or more for a single job. Legally, all such works must be notified to the leaseholders before being carried out. The frequency of larger maintenance works is normally specified in the lease, so, for example, external decorations are often stated as needing to be done every five years. This information will help you budget accordingly.

Subletting

Leases often state that you are not permitted to sublet a flat, or to assign (pass on) the lease to someone else *without the landlord's consent* – which normally means that you *can* sublet it because legally the landlord's consent 'must not be unreasonably withheld' (although they may want to charge a small fee to confirm this). But in other cases there may be an absolute ban. Any such restrictions against subletting could be crucial if for example you're a buy-to-let investor. So if you're planning to rent out your flat, this must be checked.

Breaches of covenant

Another important thing to check whilst delving into the (possibly murky) history of your lease, is whether there have been any breaches. If a previous leaseholder has done any serious stuff that's not permitted, violating the conditions of the lease, there could be trouble ahead. For example, any unauthorised structural alterations, like internal walls removed and chimney breasts removed, would have required consent from the freeholder (and Building Control).

A more common breach is where ground rent or service charges haven't been fully paid. This is crucial to check because, strictly speaking, any breach of covenant could allow the landlord to terminate your lease and repossess the property (with a court order). Mortgage lenders are aware of this risk and will lean heavily on the leaseholders to encourage them to cough up. So before buying, you need to get the freeholder-landlord to confirm that there have been no breaches of covenant, and especially that all charges have been paid.

Share of freehold

Estate agents often trumpet the fact a flat is being sold with 'a share of the freehold'. This doesn't mean the flat itself is

freehold – that would be bad news, as mortgage lenders won't lend on freehold flats. What it usually means is that the freehold of the block is owned by a limited company which, in turn, is jointly owned by the leaseholders in the block, as shareholders (or members). This is now a

fairly common set-up. As a buyer you need to ensure that the seller transfers their shares in the company to you upon completion, or that you're registered as a new member of the company. A search on the Companies House website (**www.companieshouse.gov.uk**) will confirm whether the company is up-to-date with the necessary filing of its annual returns.

The attraction of this arrangement is that it gives leaseholders more control over the management of their property, rather than the freehold being owned by some shady operator who picked it up cheap at auction as an exercise in profiteering. It also means the terms of the lease can be changed if required to suit the leaseholders, if they agree it amongst themselves. This is especially important where lease terms have shrunk dramatically, and you want to extend the lease. Otherwise, landlords can charge several thousand pounds for a lease extension. On the debit side, owning a share of the freehold can mean sacrificing some of your time to attend meetings and suchlike. But at least you'll get to know who lives on the other side of your ceiling and/or floor.

Buying your freehold

Leaseholders are entitled to jointly purchase the freehold of their block. The right to compulsorily buy out your landlord's freehold interest is known as 'enfranchisement'. As noted above, the main reason for doing this is to gain direct control on the management and maintenance of the building. It should also make obtaining a lease extension considerably easier and cheaper and should add to the value of your property.

The good news is that to qualify there is no minimum period that you need to have owned the flat, indeed you don't even have to live there yourself. But there are some (not too demanding) criteria that have to be met before you can apply – see the boxout.

Do you qualify to buy your freehold?

- At least half the total number of leaseholders must want to apply – *ie* representing at least 50 per cent of the number of flats in the building. Where there are only two flats in the building both leaseholders must participate.
- If the building was originally a house (since converted) and there are now less than five flats, the leaseholders won't qualify if the freeholder who carried out the original conversion still lives in the building.
- The leases of those who wish to participate must have originally been granted for at least 21 years.
- No more than a quarter of the total internal floor area of the building can be in non-residential use, such as shops or offices.

Steps to buying your freehold

1. Start by discussing the idea with the other leaseholders in the building to see whether they want to participate, and check whether you qualify.
2. To formally exercise your right to buy the freehold you must then serve notice on your landlord/freeholder of your intention to buy. This is done in the name of a 'nominee purchaser', which normally takes the form of a limited company set up by the leaseholders.
3. The next step is to appoint a valuer to determine the likely cost of buying the freehold. Surveyors specialising in 'enfranchisement' valuations can provide a professional report and opinion of value to use in negotiations with the landlord.
4. Obtain quotes from solicitors for the necessary legal work.
5. The landlord must then come back with a counter-notice, and negotiations to agree the right price will follow. If you cannot agree a price with the freeholder, you will need to refer the case to the Leasehold Valuation Tribunal to have the matter settled. But in addition to this cost, you may also have to pay the landlord's legal fees.
6. Once the price has been agreed, a solicitor experienced in such matters can be appointed and a suitable management company set up, with directors, a treasurer and a company secretary duly appointed from within the massed ranks of the leaseholders (see below). As shareholder/directors, regular meetings can be arranged and agendas drawn up. Then all that remains is to return to your flat and prepare for government.

Approximate costs

- Valuation: anything from £600 upwards depending on the number of flats in the building and their value.
- Serving notice: from £275.
- Setting up a freehold company: £175.
- Legal fees: around £1,000.
- Application to the Leasehold Valuation Tribunal: £400.

How much is the freehold worth?

The present owners are obviously not going to give their freehold away for nothing. The trouble is, putting a value on freeholds can be something of a dark art. Valuation of freeholds is based on a mix of the following:

- The annual income from ground rents from the flats.
- The likely value of the building when it eventually reverts to the freeholder in the distant future, at the end of the existing leases.
- 50 per cent of the 'marriage value' i.e. half the likely increase in value of the property if the leasehold and freehold interests are combined (not payable when the remaining lease term is 80 years or more).

Limited companies

When flat owners want to buy the freehold of their building, they normally do so by setting up a limited company. This requires a small number of directors to be appointed to run the company, chosen by the residents from among their number. Being a director means devoting a certain amount of your time to the company's affairs, even if you have appointed managing agents to run things day to day.

One reason for jointly owning the freehold via a limited company is that it makes things a lot easier when it comes to selling individual flats in the block. The alternative is for the freehold of the building to be purchased, without forming a limited company, in the names of all the individual leasehold flat owners. But then every time someone wanted to sell their flat, the freehold would also have to be transferred – at great expense and inconvenience.

The company owning the freehold can be set up in one of two ways. The more common and simpler method is to form a company 'limited by guarantee', where the current owners of any flat automatically become members of the company. Alternatively it can be 'limited by shares', where each owner's share has to be transferred when their flat is

Jargon-buster

- **Marriage value**: is the increase in the value of a flat following the purchase of a share of the freehold or of an extension to the lease.
- **Peppercorn rent**: is a very low basic ground rent which the freeholder charges the leaseholder.
- **Right to manage**: is the right of the leaseholders to take over the management of their property from the freeholder or managing agent.

sold. This method is used where you want some flats to have a bigger 'say' in the management than others, perhaps with a larger number of shares allocated to owners of larger flats than to smaller ones.

There are actually four types of home ownership or 'tenure'. The main ones, of course, are freehold and leasehold, but there is also commonhold (see below), and shared ownership, where you part-buy and part-rent, paying a mixture of mortgage and subsidised rent (see Chapter 15).

Commonhold

It's well known that people prefer freehold ownership. Although leases should last a lifetime or more, you have less control, plus there's something unnerving about your home being held on a lease that will ultimately vanish, albeit extremely slowly, unless extended – which can, of course, prove expensive.

As a result of such concerns, a new form of ownership was launched in 2002, so that properties with common parts such as flats could be owned as 'commonhold' with shared maintenance obligations. Leaseholders have the right to convert to this new type of tenure if they buy out the landlord.

Like freeholds, commonholds have unlimited duration. The common parts of the building are owned by a commonhold association, in which the flat owners have a share. Instead of a lease, there is a commonhold 'community statement' that defines the relationship between individual flat owners ('unit holders') and their rights and responsibilities.

So far this new form of ownership has applied mainly to newly built blocks of flats. In effect the arrangement is similar to a 'shared freehold'. Buyers need to carry out searches in relation to the flat and the common parts held by the commonhold association, each of which has its own Land Registry title number. When buying a commonhold property you will be bound by the terms of both the *community statement* and the *articles of association* (for the common parts), so these must be checked carefully. See **www.landregistry.gov.uk**.

Living over the shop

If you're on a tight budget, buying a flat above a parade of shops should make your money go further. Depending on the type of business underneath, you can save between 10 and 20 per cent of the price of an equivalent property on a local residential street. You're likely to get a lot more property for your money as well, as such flats are often generously proportioned and spacious, perhaps extending over first and second floors.

Flats above shops are popular with investors because, although cheaper to buy, being located above a business should not significantly lower the rental value. Tenants on six-monthly or yearly contracts are not likely to be as bothered as owner-occupiers about what lies beneath them.

One thing to bear in mind is that service charges cover the whole building, shops and all, and are normally much higher than on a purely residential property, so you would hope that the leaseholder of the shop would contribute a larger share. In reality there is no standard rule as to who pays what, and you could get lumbered for big maintenance bills for large flat roofs and shared open walkways etc.

What's the use?

Obviously, one of the first questions to ask is 'What's downstairs?' A property above a bookshop would be more acceptable than living over a restaurant or bar, and prices reflect this.

But uses can change, so it's essential to check with the local authority planners and the freeholder that there are no plans for the business to change.

Having a bar or restaurant down below can incur much higher building insurance because of fire and security risks, which means your premium may be higher. Often the quality of sound and fire insulation separating the residential area from the shop below can be poor, making some types of activities particularly intrusive.

Some mortgage lenders won't consider properties located above a business. Others will pay careful attention

True story

Two young men bought a flat above a fried chicken takeaway shop in Peckham, South London. As first-time buyers they thought they'd picked up a bargain. The estate agent who sold it to them says that 'Initially they were quite blasé about it.' But later they came to regret their purchase: 'Their floors would heat up every day because of the cooking downstairs and the smell of chicken filled their home. They got the flat cheap, but had had enough after six months and sold up.'

to the mortgage valuer's report, and will draw the line at some shop uses; things like dry-cleaners, takeaways and bars are not popular – in fact anything with fumes, smells and the risk of disturbance. It's also common for the buyer to be asked for a larger deposit, as much as 30 per cent.

The other downside is that, unlike conventional flats, you may not qualify to buy the freehold (under enfranchisement legislation). On a mixed residential and retail/commercial building, a third-party investor usually owns the freehold.

Things to check

Your solicitors may be having a field day pondering over lengthy legal documents, but there's more to buying a flat than perusing ancient leases. If you're having a survey, the following points should be checked and reported on. If you risk buying without a survey, you could be in for some nasty surprises.

■ Purpose-built or conversion?
Mortgage lenders always seem to be keen to distinguish between flats that were designed and built as such, and those that have been subsequently converted. Many grand old houses have been divided up

Above: Victorian mill converted into flats

Left: Edwardian maisonettes built to resemble houses

Change of use

Changing the use of a building from one category to another usually requires planning permission.

There are different 'use classes' covering Shops, Food and Drink, Financial and Professional Services, Business, General Industry, Storage and Distribution, Dwelling Houses, Residential Institutions, Hotels, Non-residential Institutions, Assembly and Leisure.

Examples of *permitted* changes of use include:

■ Post office to hairdressers *does not require* planning permission
■ Restaurant to supermarket *does not require* planning permission
■ Wholesale warehouse to sewing factory *does not require* planning permission

Examples of *non-permitted* changes of use include:

■ Estate agent to tanning salon *requires* planning permission
■ Dwelling to guest house *requires* planning permission
■ Newsagent to hot food takeaway *requires* planning permission
■ Dwelling to flats *requires* planning permission
■ Petrol filling station to car sales lot *requires* planning permission

You can change from one use to another within the same 'use class' without planning permission. In a few cases you can even change to a different class without permission. For example, planning permission is required to change from an A1 shop to an A3 'Food and Drink' class, but isn't required the other way round, *ie* from A3 to A1.

A1 (shops)
This is the use-class for things like newsagents, hairdressers, post offices, pet shops, supermarkets, sandwich bars (which don't predominately sell hot food), florists, greengrocers and off-licences. Therefore the use can be changed *from* any of the above *to* any of the above without requiring planning permission, as they are all in the same use class.

A3 (Food and Drink)
This is the use-class for hot food takeaways, restaurants, pubs and cafes.

into self-contained apartments for this purpose, and more recently flats have been hewn out of old warehouses or even office blocks. Why do lenders need to know this? Possibly because in the 1970s and 1980s a lot of dodgy conversions were carried out, with minimal attention to such matters as sound insulation and fire safety. Purpose-built blocks are also more likely to be better run and maintained and have correctly drafted leases (but not always).

■ Sound and fire

Sound insulation between flats has been a requirement since the 1980s, and today is taken very seriously indeed, being subject to scrupulous inspection and even requiring pressure testing. But as noted above, older converted flats often managed to bypass the rules, and may have a perilous lack of insulation, in which case some expensive upgrading work may be necessary.

Sound insulation to an existing building can be applied in two main ways. A new 'suspended ceiling' is often constructed about 150–200mm below the original ceiling. This can be a timber framework employing new joists run from the walls, leaving a clear void between the old and new ceilings, which is stuffed with sound deadening mineral wool insulation. A thick new double layer of skimmed plasterboard creates a fresh and fire-resistant new ceiling. Recessed lights should be avoided, as cutting holes obviously won't do a lot for insulation performance. The purpose of the air gap is to cut 'impact sound' – ie people knocking, banging or just walking directly on the floor surface.

Meanwhile, more insulation is stuffed between the original floor joists above. Finally assuming you can arrange access, a 'floating floor' can be laid over the floor above, with layers of special acoustic boarding sealed at the edges. This helps absorb vibration and airborne sound, such as shouting and music. Of course, it helps no end if the upstairs flat dwellers have carpeted floors rather than laminate or stripped wood, and don trainers rather than stiletto heels – or if they've taken a vow of silence. Partition walls don't normally have to cope with impact sound, just airborne noise, and can be lined with insulated plasterboard.

Fortunately, the necessary fire separation may already have been achieved as a result of the double plasterboarding used to create the sound barrier. Otherwise, lining a wall or ceiling with a single layer of pink 12.5mm fireboard should do the trick.

All flats above ground level should have fire doors – ie special doors with 30 minutes' fire resistance. The exception is to bathrooms, unless they contain a boiler. Self-closers are also technically required, but they're a pain to live with and may have been removed or disabled long ago. But it's a wise precaution to make a habit of keeping kitchen and living room doors closed at night, as these are the two areas where fires most commonly break out.

Perhaps most important of all, invest in some decent smoke alarms – they should be wired into the mains and have a battery backup. Be sure to buy those with a cut-out switch in case of false alarms. Position them correctly and they can be a real life-saver.

Lastly, plan your escape route in an emergency. Decide which windows you could safely squeeze through without plummeting to your doom, and keep them unlocked. Consider keeping a foldable escape ladder or rope handy.

■ Consents

Solicitors always need to check that planning consent for 'change of use' was obtained for conversion flats. Even more important, you need to check that building regulations were also complied with – and see a completion certificate obtained by the developer to prove compliance. If consents were not fully complied with, a retrospective application can be made, but this is time-consuming and could reveal problems – such as inadequate sound and fire insulation – or could be refused. Either way, solicitors must check this as early in the process as possible, hopefully finding the correct information is already available in the seller's HIP.

■ Position

Depending on the size of block and how busy it is, sleeping with your head a few inches away from the main entrance door isn't necessarily conducive to a good night's contented snoozing. In other words, if you buy a ground

floor flat adjoining the communal entrance lobby, the noise from people coming and going and doors slamming can drive you mad. Conversion flats with thin timber stud partition walls are especially prone to such problems.

On the other hand, well designed ground-floor flats with private gardens can command a premium, although occupants need to be aware of the enhanced risk of security problems and break-ins. At least there will be no noise from the people downstairs (unless there's someone in a basement).

Top-floor flats aren't necessarily all plain sailing either. Without a lift, you could risk becoming extremely fit, traipsing up and down the communal stairs each day. And you need to be very sure where your options lie in relation to escape from fire in an emergency. Check also the quality of insulation in the loft. One good thing is that if there's a leak from a bathroom, it won't be you who has to erect an umbrella.

Evidence of leakage is something surveyors check for. Because flats are often designed on a modular basis, with all the flats above and below having their bathrooms and kitchens stacked one above the other, one person's exuberant bathroom antics can cause a cascade of problems for everyone living underneath.

■ Occupation

Are there many rented flats in the block? It's well known that tenants are sometimes less careful occupiers than owners, and there can be more risk of hazards such as overflowing baths and noise. Students and rock stars have a certain reputation for unneighbourliness. Other flat dwellers may have jobs that demand working unsocial hours, so they may want to get some shut-eye when you want to party and vice-versa.

■ Services

Check that your flat has its own electricity, gas and water meters. Check where the stopcock is that controls your cold water supply. It's also worth checking whether there's a communal lobby with access to the main water pipes that supply the flats upstairs (just in case the occupants disappear off on holiday and leave the bath running!). These days, shared services are rare, but some blocks have old-fashioned communal boilers, and may have water tanks situated remotely from your flat.

■ Parking

Here we come to a potentially highly contentious subject. How many allocated car spaces does your flat have, if any? What if you hold a party and have lots of visitors? Is there a problem with local shoppers or commuters parking there? Are there any extra charges to pay? Older purpose-built flats often have large blocks or 'batteries' of garages, usually of poor-quality construction, with thin brick walls and decrepit flat felt or corrugated asbestos cement roofs. Maintenance is frequently overlooked. Do the garages have an electricity supply?

■ Communal gardens

You normally expect to pay towards the upkeep of communal areas and gardens in your service charge. But are the communal gardens well maintained? Have any of the ground-floor flat owners illegally fenced-off part of the gardens for their exclusive personal use? Maybe you have your own private garden with the flat, which may be 'non-contiguous', *ie* on a separate plot some way away.

18 | GOING VIEWING

their photography sometimes deserves awards for creativity. Images are often professionally enhanced thanks to the use of wide-angle lenses and coloured filters. It's rumoured that some agents even go so far as to 'photoshop out' inconvenient electrical substations and telegraph poles. Even glorious blue skies may have been digitally reproduced. So the impression of charming bucolic open space worthy of Constable's brush may lack something in gritty realism, perhaps having chosen to exclude the bus depot next door. The properties you like the look of may turn out to be massively over-hyped as well as overpriced, shattering carefully raised expectations.

Stretching the truth – wide angle shot

You may like the look of a property on paper, but estate agents' particulars and brochures naturally don't tell the full story. Even online virtual tours won't give an honest 'warts and all' picture, so it's essential to discover what a place is like in the flesh. There's no substitute for seeing it with your own eyes.

House-hunting can be an exhausting business. Unless you're a serial nosy-parker, a lot of time can be wasted viewing unsuitable properties. The trick is to manage your time by ruling out inappropriate properties before arranging viewings. The majority can be crossed off your list simply by taking a quick preliminary drive-past.

If you think agents' descriptions are wide of the mark,

Making appointments

If at this stage your present home is already under offer, you're likely to be under pressure to find the best available property within the space of a few short weeks. In a strong market you'll need to get in before rival house-hunters, so it can pay to start early in the day. However, with the best will in the world you're unlikely to manage more than about five viewings in a day before collapsing from exhaustion, even if they're all conveniently located in the same area. Most people view properties at weekends or in the evening after work.

Unless the sellers have chosen to sell privately, appointments to view are usually made via the estate agent. However, that doesn't mean the agent will be present when you turn up. Some home owners prefer to show you round personally. This may be a blessing in disguise as at least you'll be spared the incessant stream of sales banter. Alternatively, if times are hard a junior negotiator may be volunteered to

Below: Nice entrance hall, shame about the stairs

drive you round a number of properties. But watch out for 'tactical viewing' where you're deliberately shown some overpriced dumps before being shown around the place they really want to shift, so that it appears more desirable.

Less common are group viewings, where agents book all interested parties to look round together, perhaps on a Saturday morning. This makes life considerably easier for the agent and minimises periods of disturbance for sellers. The idea behind such mass viewings (or 'open house events' as they are sometimes grandly billed) is to play one buyer off against another by creating the impression of demand. The hope is for a competitive frenzy to develop, eliciting ever-higher offers from rival buyers. But in a quiet market the opposite can happen as embarrassed strangers stand around looking awkwardly at each other, wondering why there is so little interest.

If the seller is particularly difficult about agreeing times of viewings, it's not usually a good sign. Uncompromising people can be hard to do business with, or they may be strategically timing appointments to spare your ears from next door's drum rehearsals.

How to view

Most of us have a gut instinct whether a place is the right one for us within a few minutes of walking through the front door. But leaving your biggest investment purely down to instinct isn't always wise, plus there's an awful lot of information to take in, so it's always best to bring someone with you for a second opinion. It's sometimes easy to get carried away during viewings, so a friend or partner can help you remain objective, perhaps stopping you making a wild offer in the heat of the moment. They may also see problems where you don't or see opportunities that you've missed. Having a comrade at hand is also important for safety reasons. However, kids and dogs tend to get in the way and distract you, so if possible leave them at home.

Don't let the home owner or agent rush you. You're entitled to take all the time you need to make a major decision involving enormous sums of money. Even so, on your first viewing all you can realistically expect to achieve is to get an overall feel for the property. It's totally impossible to take everything in all in one go – deciding which rooms would suit whom, sizing up where your furniture could go and judging the colour of the decorations – whilst trying to make small talk and simultaneously surveying the condition of the building.

Try to look beyond the surface. By relying on first impressions you could end up rejecting an otherwise sound property at a bargain price, purely on the basis of off-putting woodchip wallpaper and malodorous doggy smells. You may have to use your imagination to see beyond the encrusted shag pile carpets and avocado bathroom suite. Try to visualise the potential for rooms to be enlarged or subdivided to suit your requirements.

During viewings it's best not to say too much. Laughing openly at the sellers' appalling taste in wallpaper and furnishings could antagonise them, so they make a mental note not to sell to you. Alternatively, appearing obviously super-keen at this stage could weaken your negotiating position if you later come to make an offer.

Checklist

To properly assess a house, take a list of important points to check. This will be based on the essential qualities we sketched out back in Chapter 16. A camera, a tape measure and binoculars can come in very useful, along with a notebook to jot down details so at the end of the day you'll have something tangible to jog the memory.

There's a lot you can check before even going inside. Just observing the immediate environment can reveal a lot of important stuff. For example:

- How safe does the street appear, and is it safe for children?
- Are the neighbouring flats or houses well cared for?
- Do the neighbours run a business with vans parked outside?
- Are there any electric pylons or mobile phone masts nearby?
- What are the parking arrangements?
- Is there much road noise?

Original feature: Victorian 'rear parlour' with double doors leading to 'front parlour'

It's worth noting whether any big-ticket items are getting on a bit and likely to need expensive replacing in the near future. So if possible take a quick butchers at the outside of the property and note the general condition of the brickwork, roof tiles, paintwork and windows. Internally, things like kitchen and bathroom fittings, the electrics and the heating system may be crying out for expensive replacement. Spotting any obvious defects can help you justify a lower price if it later comes to making an offer. Obvious issues to look for include signs of damp such as bubbling paint or peeling wallpaper, and musty smells. Fresh paint may have been applied to hide a damp patch. Look for evidence of leaks, especially to ceilings below bathrooms.

It's worth bearing in mind that no property is going to be 100 per cent right, but many will have the scope to be adapted to your requirements. So once inside, look for potential to extend or convert the loft. There may be outbuildings with potential for conversion into office space, or a surplus utility room that could be knocked-through to create an attractive kitchen/diner.

Follow-up viewings

If you like a property, you'll probably want to arrange a second viewing. If the market's slow you can afford the luxury of taking your time, even going back a third or fourth time. You don't want to rush such an important decision, but neither do you want to dither while someone else snatches the prize from under your nose.

Having toured a fair number of properties by now, the reality of what's available on the market means you may have to compromise on some of your original ideals. At least a quarter of buyers admit to having changed their minds about what they wanted once they started viewing seriously.

On second viewings you notice a lot more. If you haven't yet seen the place in daylight, it will now be clear how much, or how little, light gets in. Hallways can sometimes appear depressingly gloomy, and dining rooms may suffer from being marooned in semi-darkness where a rear extension has been added. Having seen the place before, you'll have a list of points you want to clarify – the size of the third bedroom, whether the kitchen had a gas cooker, was there a shed in the garden?

Now you can really get busy taking snaps or videos to study later at your leisure. You can also check that basics such as taps, showers and light switches are all in working order, and find out when boilers and consumer units were last tested.

A lot of owners and agents feel obliged to stick to you like glue, droning on and pointing out the bleedin' obvious. This is usually down to nerves on their part, but can distract you from the important things that need to be checked. If the running commentary begins to sap your will to live you might want to make a suggestion 'Would it be OK if we just had a couple of minutes to discuss it between ourselves and to get a feel for the place?'

To see more of the neighbourhood, park some distance away and take a good walk around. If there are lots of giant aerials and dishes sprouting everywhere it may be a clue to the quality of TV reception in the area. It's always wise to make additional visits to the immediate area at different times of day to nose out potential issues in the locality – the usual suspects are listed below. But even the most innocent looking green field could morph into a rock festival for a couple of weeks a year or play host to the occasional Civil War re-enactment.

■ **Roads**

Noise from main roads can mean having to keep windows closed in summer, and can be a worry if you have children and pets. Even backwaters can suddenly become 'rat runs'. Be sure to visit during the morning and evening rush hours.

■ **Schools**

School traffic can transform an otherwise lazy lane into congested double-parked gridlock. Busy periods are 8:30–9:15am and 3:00–3:45pm. This may not be an issue for those who are out at work every day, but bear in mind that schools occasionally host weekend events too. Also, playground noise can travel a surprising distance.

Photo: wikimedia

■ Railway lines and stations
Early morning commuters like to save on car parking charges by parking down the road from the station and in side roads. If the house is near the railway line, it's obviously worth checking how frequent and noisy the trains are, especially at night. Likewise flight paths.

■ Shops and parks
Open-all-hours corner shops may have a loyal teenage following, perhaps congregating en masse and alarming the gentle citizens of the borough with exuberant booze-fuelled antics. Local parks may provide a haven for connoisseurs of Special Brew and full strength scrumpy.

■ Pubs
What could be more enticing than a charming 'Inspector Morse' country retreat within walking distance? A positive boon to the thirsty lady or gent. But pubs can be a mixed blessing. A local 24-hour hard-drinking establishment with a profitable sideline in drug dealing and drive-by shootings

True story
The Romans had a phrase for it – *caveat emptor*. Caligula would doubtless have blushed at the prices of some over-hyped villas on the first-century housing market. But whilst neighbourhood chariot races may be a thing of the past, the advice 'buyer beware' is just as relevant today when it comes to buying property. However, buyers sometimes go to the other extreme and become overly suspicious – even downright paranoid.

Upon spotting a low-flying helicopter during a recent viewing, one apparently keen prospective buyer convinced himself that the peaceful village residence in question must be blighted by noise from regular airborne military activities. Of course, the more the seller gave assurances to the contrary, the more convinced the buyer became that there must be something to hide, picturing squadrons of *Apocalypse Now* choppers buzzing the property day and night.

may not be such good news. Pubs and nightclubs tend to show their true colours come 'chucking-out time'. Even quaint village pubs might hold the occasional event enticing swarms of balding, paunchy Harley-Davidson riders to descend and devour pig roasts. Lock up your daughters.

We ask the questions

Sooner or later you will find a property that appears to fit the bill. A second viewing confirms that it does indeed tick all the right boxes, perhaps subject to a spot of updating here and there. But before making an offer there are a number of key questions that need to be asked, some of which can be casually dropped into the conversation as you tour the property. Some of this information may already have been volunteered by the owner or the agent, and most should in any case be covered by your solicitor or surveyor. But it makes sense to satisfy yourself now, rather than find out in a couple of months that the house is prone to flooding every spring, or perhaps that the present owner originally picked it up cheap on account of a gruesome murder.

So before going any further, look the seller in the eye and politely ask the following:

■ Questions about themselves

How long have you lived here?
This is an easy, icebreaker question. But if the answer is in months rather than years, perhaps it's because buying the property turned out to be a major blunder.

Why are you moving?

They may have a young family who have outgrown the available space. Or perhaps they need to relocate for their work, or urgently desire a lifestyle change by moving to the mountains of Patagonia. The one thing you can certain about is that they won't tell you it's because they've got neighbours from hell, or that the local school is Britain's worst. Play detective to see if you think their reason is genuine.

■ Questions about the sale

How long has the property been on the market?

This will normally depend on the state of the property market. If it's been on for ages, it may be that the sellers have been let down or had sales fall through due to problems elsewhere in the chain. Perhaps their previous buyer panicked and pulled out because of matters raised in the survey or the searches. The good news is that you should be able to drive a hard bargain if the owners are fed up to the back teeth and just want to get on with their move. But think carefully about buying a quirky property, as you may experience the same difficulties when you come to sell.

Have you had many viewings/offers?

If the answer's 'No' then it may be down to a duff estate agent, or overpricing. Watch out for agents who exaggerate interest or invent other offers to panic you into buying.

Are you in a chain?

Most sellers will be simultaneously buying another house to move to. The longer the chain the more chance there will be of a problem with another property causing it to break.

What's included in the sale?

Many sellers can't face the hassle of removing all the old carpets and curtains, which in any case probably won't be the right size for their new house. But it's important to be clear about what is and isn't included, to avoid silly disputes arising later.

■ Questions about the local environment

What are the neighbours like?

If you can't hear their reply because of the deafening argument raging next door, it might not be worth pursuing this line of questioning. No one wants to live next to a Fred West, so it's worth asking for a few details about the neighbours. Do they sound like your kind of people? Do they work unsocial hours? Your solicitor will later ask for confirmation that there have been no disputes or complaints made about neighbours (see Chapter 7).

Where's the nearest shops, schools, surgery etc?

You probably already have a pretty fair idea about the local amenities, but the sellers may well be able to offer some handy tips about what's hot and what's not.

Have there been any burglaries or car break-ins or thefts?

A tough question to which, regrettably, a lot of us would have to hold our hand up. But this should be considered in perspective – in many cases it will have been a one-off isolated incident.

■ Questions about the property

What are the parking arrangements?

This should be fairly be obvious, but sometimes there's a separate garage or some longstanding unofficial arrangement. If there is no off-street parking you may have to pay for resident parking permits.

Have any improvements been carried out?

This is important, as extensions and structural works normally require planning or building regulations consent. There may be guarantees for timber, damp & beetle treatment works, and for double glazing or refitted kitchens and bathrooms. Mention these to your solicitor, so they can request the relevant warranties.

Below: Big improvement: New en-suite bathroom means fewer trips to outside loo.

Is the property on mains drainage?
In rural areas you may have a private drainage system shared with neighbours, which will have cost and access implications. Ask when any cesspits or septic tanks were last emptied.

Does anyone else have rights over the property?
Rights of way across gardens and through shared passageways aren't as unusual as you might think, and are not always obvious on site.

Does anyone else live here?
In other words, does anyone have a legal right to remain in occupation after you've moved in?

Is there any history of flooding, or are you on a flood plain?
If, in response to a direct question, the sellers mumble something vague and stare at their Wellingtons, or you notice that your feet are starting to feel a trifle damp, be sure to check online at the environment agency as well as via your solicitor.

Has the property been underpinned?
Subsidence is the property world's equivalent of syphilis. The ailment may have been cured but it can leave a stigma. Insurers and mortgage lenders usually worry if there is any history of underpinning, and may raise last-minute problems, so tackle this early.

How much are utility bills and what is the Council Tax band?
You can check Council Tax on the local authority's website.

For flats it's worth asking how long the remaining lease term is, and whether the seller has a copy of the most recent service charge and ground rent invoice.

Who are you dealing with?

By now you may have a shortlist of two or three suitable properties, although there is probably one that you like best. But before plunging in and making an offer it helps to figure out what sort of person you'll be dealing with. It's almost as important to suss out the people selling as it is to weigh up the pros and cons of the property. Should your offer be accepted, then over the next few weeks and months these people will come to dominate your life. This is where a large helping of luck enters the equation. Dealing with an honest, reliable seller can save months of tearing your hair out, and is probably worth a few grand on the purchase price. So you need to consider whether you trust them, and whether their plans and timescales are likely fit with yours.

The chain

Sadly, whether your sellers turn out to be paragons of virtue or not, they will still be at the mercy of everyone else in the chain. So it's important to ask them or their agent about the length of the chain before making an offer. The longer it is, the more chance there is that someone totally unknown to you could subsequently torpedo not just your purchase but also your sale (usually just when you're about to exchange).

One thing you need to be very wary of is sellers who are divorcing. If they're each moving to a separate new property, the chance of the chain collapsing can be multiplied by two (unless they're renting). And the bitterness of divorce means that every decision they make may be challenged and contested as each seeks to sabotage the other. Not the perfect backdrop for a swift and painless move.

The big decision

You've done your homework. You've physically walked around, measured and checked everything until you're blue in the face. But don't disregard your 'intuition' – it's just as important to be able to imagine yourself happily living there. If you strongly feel a place is right, it probably is. On the other hand, falling instantly in love with a property, can make it hard to keep the good news to yourself. However, it's best to contain your glee if at all possible. This is where being on good terms with the agent can lull you into a false sense of security. If you reveal your hand by showing them how thrilled you are, they and their client will feel better placed to drive a hard bargain. So by curbing your enthusiasm you should be able to save some serious money with some well judged haggling. By adopting a friendly approach, sellers are more likely to accept a lower offer because you've built a rapport with them.

19 | MAKING AN OFFER

You've found the property you want. Now all that remains is to have your offer accepted and put the wheels in motion to buy it. But should you start by offering the full asking price? If not, how hard should you negotiate? There is one factor above all that will dictate how best to play your hand – the current state of the housing market. This will normally determine whether you should haggle hard and grab a bargain, or whether by hesitating you're likely to blow it and miss out on the house of your dreams.

Estate agents are not necessarily the best source of impartial advice on this subject. In the optimistic world of the estate agent the sun is always shining and properties on their books are perpetually in great demand.

Valuation in progress

Sizing up the market

As we saw in Chapter 1, the housing market is notoriously cyclical. In a fast-moving *sellers' market* houses are often snapped up. In boom years, such as 2000, 2002 and 2007, there could be as many as many as ten potential buyers for every available property in some geographical hot spots. With rival buyers eyeing up the same property and ready to pay what the seller wanted, offering less than the asking price would be a waste of time.

Conversely, in a slow *buyers' market* properties take longer to sell as sellers struggle to attract interest. So in stagnant or falling markets, such as 1989 to 1995 and 2008–9, sellers may be willing to accept 'cheeky' offers just to offload their house, knowing they could save a similar sum on the property they're buying.

Even within the space of a single year, spring and autumn are traditionally the busiest times, so pitching an offer during the relatively quiet dark depths of winter may reward buyers with a better deal.

So what's it really worth?

You want to be sure that you're paying a fair price before committing yourself to spending squillions of pounds. As a buyer it's obviously important to justify the price in your own mind, a process made considerably easier where you, or your partner, have 'fallen in love' with the property. But in the cold light of day how can you tell what a property's really worth? The old adage that 'a property's worth whatever someone is prepared to pay for it' isn't a great deal of help when the 'someone' in question happens to be you.

Agents know that, psychologically, if we believe a product is in great demand by others it makes us lust after it all the more – this is the principle behind 'auction fever' and group viewings – so they may be tempted to help things along a bit by suggesting that other potential buyers are circling overhead eager to pounce with wads of ready cash. This may, or may not, actually be true. But even if it is an outrageous attempt at price manipulation, the best advice is to trust your own experience. Having spent the last few months slogging around numerous properties you should by now have a pretty shrewd idea whether a place is truly worth the money, compared to what else is on the market. On the other hand there is no keener buyer than someone who has just been outbid and lost out on a previous purchase.

When it comes to professional valuations, houses are normally valued by methodically comparing them with sale prices recently achieved for similar properties nearby. Values are then adjusting up or down to reflect the relative pros and cons of each property in terms of their condition, location and size. Obviously this is going to be more difficult for quirky one-off properties, such as a converted water tower, or anything featured on *Grand Designs*.

Comparing valuations

Before you finalise your offer, it's worth asking the estate agent who's selling the property what supporting sales evidence they originally used to justify their asking price. A good agent will have no trouble quoting other similar properties they've sold. An unprofessional agent, on the other hand, will either be totally flummoxed and get shirty, or will make up a pack of lies on the spot.

Like surveyors, estate agents base their valuations on what they know has sold locally. So you might well ask, how come three different agents sometimes give you three often wildly different values? One reason is that agents are under pressure from sellers to value optimistically, which is compounded by a terror of losing out to a rival agent who wins the business by valuing even higher.

The temptation to impress potential sellers with ambitious asking prices will be greater for negotiators who are new to the job or to the area. Some lazy operators just look at other agents' asking prices and add a bit. But as home owners we can also sometimes be guilty of harbouring unrealistic expectations of our property's value, especially where big money has been lavished on home improvements.

Quite reasonably, agent's valuations normally assume that properties are in decent structural condition. So unless

the building is visibly subsiding, the asking price won't take account of any hidden defects. A dated kitchen and decor will be noted, but a defective roof structure or leaning chimney stack probably won't be. This is worth bearing in mind should your surveyor later spot something awful lurking under the floorboards that justifies a price-reduction.

When it comes to valuing, surveyors have something of a reputation for being downright party-poopers. This pessimistic mind-set couldn't be further removed from that of irrepressibly optimistic agents, and is probably largely down to their liability for being sued by client's banks for 'over-valuing'. The true value of a property often lies somewhere between these two extremes.

Fortunately it has become a lot easier to do your own valuation by getting hold of comparable sales evidence on the Internet. Land Registry sales records showing what the houses in your street sold for are now widely accessible from numerous websites. These reveal the actual completion prices achieved, as opposed to inflated asking prices, although they don't tell you anything about a property's size or condition. You also need to allow for the fact that prices can be months or years out of date, and will need to be adjusted up or down to reflect the current market. This can be done using the Nationwide or Halifax online price calculators (see website).

Finally, there's a handy rule of thumb that's sometimes used by professional valuers. The 'square foot test' is a way

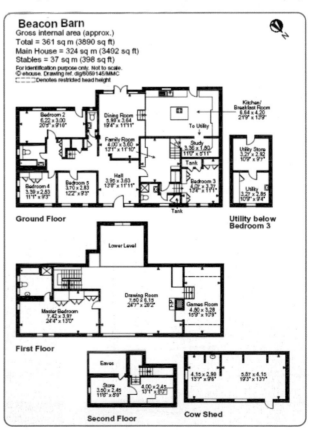

Photo: Ian MacMilan FRICS

Can you justify paying a higher price?

A higher sale price is sometimes justified by sellers who make a point of telling you how much they've spent on various improvements. But as we saw in Part 2, what's been spent doesn't necessarily translate directly to a higher property price:

Photo: wikimedia

■ **High value improvements** (up to 100 per cent of the cost recovered)
Adding a good-sized extra bedroom
Loft conversion
Extension

■ **Medium value improvements** (up to 50 per cent of the cost recovered)
New fitted kitchen
Refitted bathrooms
Off-street parking

■ **Low value improvements** (less than 25 per cent of the cost recovered)
Double glazing
Swimming pools

Of course, the precise addition to value will depend very much on the type of property and the extent to which the improvements overcome a big drawback with it. It also depends on the quality of the work. Some 'improvements' can actually reduce the value, such as period properties with inappropriate replacement windows and doors, stone cladding and polystyrene ceiling tiles, or extensions that eat up most of the garden.

Other factors that affect value include:

■ **Area**
In any given area there are some roads that traditionally command higher prices than similar roads nearby. Local agents and surveyors tend to know this, buyers from further away may not. Research may reveal such local quirks.

■ **Location**
Busy roads, noisy railways, Chinese takeaways, dry cleaners, petrol stations, knackers yards, drinking establishments…the list of potentially undesirable neighbouring uses is a long one. And it gets longer as you get older and fussier.

■ **State of repair**
In a boom market, buyers are sometimes willing to pay over the odds for tatty properties 'in need of modernisation', spurred on by the reckless rantings of TV property celebs. But it's very easy to underestimate the cost of refurbishing, and there's a skill in spotting houses that actually look in worse condition than they really are.

■ **Newbuild**
Many buyers are prepared to pay a premium for the privilege of moving into a brand spanking new house. But if you need to sell within a year or two of moving in, expect to lose money in a static market, as it won't command the same top price once 'lived in'. At the other end of the spectrum, charming period cottages also often command premium prices.

■ **Floor area**
In France, and much of the rest of the world, agents' details sensibly inform buyers of a crucial piece of information – the property's internal floor area. In the UK we instead tend to count the number of bedrooms as an approximate size guide, but this can be misleading. A bedroom can mean anything from a tiny boxroom to an enormous open-plan loft room. Agents do, of course, quote individual room sizes (in feet and inches), whereas surveyors measure the outside walls to calculate 'gross external' floor area (in square metres), including the walls, for each floor. This can provide a fairly scientific way of comparing values by so much per square metre or square foot.

of comparing similar properties you're interested in buying to work out if you're getting a fair deal. Here you calculate the price of a property per square foot (or square metre) of floor area.

Start by working out the property's total floor area, either by measuring the main walls, or from a layout plan or the room dimensions. Take the total upstairs and downstairs floor areas added together, including all the internal and external walls. Then divide the purchase price by the total floor area to get a cost per square foot/metre. So suppose, for example, you're paying £300,000 for a house with a floor area of 120 square metres, this would equate to a price of £2,500 per square metre. Of course, you've got to be sure that you're comparing like with like, in terms of the quality of the location and the condition of different properties.

Photo: wikimedia

Negotiating skills – 'A wing at the White House for a dome at the Kremlin?'

Working up an offer

Buying a property is a nerve-wracking business at the best of times. But now we come to the crunch – pitching your offer. By now, after weeks or months of gruelling house-hunting, you probably have a pretty shrewd idea how much you're prepared to pay.

But the process of agreeing a sale price requires participation in a strange ritual – the negotiation game. British people, who as a rule dislike haggling over prices, generally expect to offer a bit below the stated asking price when buying property. Everyone knows this game, not least estate agents, who will normally quote the seller two different prices – an *asking price* that's pitched 'to achieve' a lower *sale price*. What this boils down to is that buyers can normally expect to negotiate a reduction of anything up to about ten per cent off the asking price, depending on the market. The exception is in a booming sellers' market, where demand and strong competition amongst buyers can sometimes push offers way above the asking prices.

Unless you're buying from a private seller, it's normally the estate agent's job to negotiate the price, acting as a go-between, relaying the details of your offer to their client. The golden rule at this point is to remember that, however nice the estate agent is, they are acting in the interests of the other side. So if they volunteer any advice about how much you should offer, it sometimes needs to be treated with a degree of scepticism.

Negotiating tactics

Negotiation is a skill. Some are born with it, some acquire it, but we all at some point have a go at it. The main objective is to achieve the best price, but the real skill is for both parties to come away feeling good about the deal. A seller who is left feeling browned off, smouldering away

resentfully, is very likely to mess you about later or change their mind during the long weeks up to exchange.

It's always possible that the price being asked is already very reasonable, perhaps pitched to achieve a 'quick sale', or has already been reduced. By checking other sold prices for similar properties in the area you can get a pretty good idea of whether this one is already fairly priced. In which case the negotiations may need to focus more on issues other than the price – such as how fast both sides can realistically move.

Many of those employed in the estate agency business seem to have job titles that in some capacity include the word 'negotiator'. Indeed, some individuals are highly skilled in the art of negotiation, and many naturally radiate charm – an important attribute for successful negotiation. But others are simply full of wide-boy hot air banter that can actually hinder a deal, in which case it may sometimes be better to deal direct with the seller, on a straight one-to-one basis, especially if you're reasonably businesslike, confident and friendly.

Bargaining signs

In some cases sellers may be willing to accept a 'cheeky' offer. So, before making your opening gambit, see if you can spot any 'bargaining signs' such as::

- ■ Properties that have been on the market without attracting much interest, probably because they're overpriced.
- ■ A seller who needs to move quickly, having already found another property, and may be prepared to accept less for a quick sale.
- ■ Properties that needs a lot of work, which isn't reflected in the price. If you've had a survey, getting estimates for the works can help justify a lower offer. Remember that when the agent valued the property they wouldn't have been aware of anything more than the most obvious defects.

But as a rule, having a professional negotiator acting as intermediary between buyer and seller can help take the edge off any provocative issues, soothing and sympathising with each party in turn. Negotiation is, by nature, a confrontational process, and if done badly can spark profound hatred between fellow human beings.

Making your offer

Offers are normally made by phoning the estate agent, unless the property's being sold privately. If there's stiff competition to buy, you may decide not to beat about the bush and to offer the full asking price. But bear in mind it will be impossible to later reduce such a generous offer without causing immense ill-feeling.

More likely your first shot will be pitched a few per cent below the asking price. The psychology of haggling suggests that by disappointing the seller with a low initial offer, you will manage their expectations downwards. This should have the effect of making subsequent, slightly higher, offers more appealing. On the other hand, if you go in with a wildly low offer the seller could think you're having a laugh and duly take umbrage. The correct approach in any given situation will very much depend on whose side the market is on, and how keen the seller is to sell.

Of course, it's the agent's job to get the best price for their client. So when you express an interest in buying they may, as we saw earlier, encourage you to 'raise your game' by alluding to other interested buyers (who may, or may not, actually exist). This illustrates one possible benefit for buyers where they deal directly with the seller: it's generally believed that when approached on a one-to-one basis, sellers are less likely to come out with brazen lies.

If you offer below the asking price there may be some delay before you get a response. This could be a negotiating tactic – sellers do not want to appear too desperate. If you don't hear anything, chasing the agent or seller can make you appear to be the desperate one, playing into their hands.

If the seller rejects your offer, the estate agent should come back with a suggestion as to what price the seller may be prepared to accept. You may then go a little higher, and they may come down. The extent of negotiation will depend on how flexible both parties are prepared to be.

When making subsequent offers, you need to justify the figure by stressing all the benefits of your buying position – such as having no chain, being able to exchange with six weeks, being cash buyers or already having your mortgage offer approved.

One useful negotiation technique is to turn the tables and ask the other party to justify their position, by asking 'Why this amount?' or 'How do you justify this figure?' This is a fair tactic that can, of course, be used by either side, so you might want to have a few answers handy. Its effectiveness as a buyer largely depends on who you're

Photo: JNP.co.uk

dealing with, but introducing a degree of logic in what can be a highly emotional process can't be a bad thing. The reason sellers sometimes stick like limpets to a particular price may simply be down to blind faith in the estate agent who originally valued it at that level (as well as good old-fashioned greed).

A typical negotiation process might go something like this:

- Asking price £315,000
- *Buyer offers £290,000*
- Seller rejects this, but would accept £310,000 for a 'quick sale'
- *Buyer then offers £300,000*
- Seller says £307,500 is final
- *Both end up agreeing on £305,00 for an exchange within six weeks*

In some cases an impasse is reached. One party holds out for a few hundred quid, only for the other side to dig their heels in and eventually lose interest and go off the boil. A good agent may be able to break the deadlock with some helpful deal-making suggestion. A small compromise may be all that's required to reach a win–win outcome. Of course, it's essential to first weigh up the other side's negotiating position – *ie* how badly they want to sell, and whose side the market favours – before judging what level to pitch it.

Having reached agreement on price, or come close, the haggling then often moves on to peripheral items. So the final agreed figure is often subject to a list of conditions, such as 'carpets and curtains to be included'. If you can't get exactly what you wanted on price, pride can sometimes be salvaged by the small consolation of winning some extras that will indirectly save you a few thousand pounds.

But of course it's only too easy to make solemn promises in the heat of battle, such as committing yourself to exchange contracts within six weeks, which can just as easily be broken later when it comes to the crunch. Matters such as the dates of exchange or completion may not be entirely within your control anyway, especially if there's a chain involved.

Competition to buy

If you enjoy a hand of poker, then being one of several buyers interested in the same property can prove a stimulating experience. In a fast-moving sellers' market, when demand is greater than supply, it's not unknown for a bidding war to break out, bumping up the price.

Having made your offer, the estate agent may come back and ask whether you want to increase it to beat a rival buyer – who may then increase his offer, and so on.

To encourage such naked competition, agents sometimes market properties with an irresistibly competitive headline price, requesting 'offers in excess of' this guide figure. The agent then stands well back and watches gleefully as market forces ignite 'bidding fever', swelling the price.

Needless to say, buyers need to keep a cool head amidst such fireworks. Essentially you're in an auction, and the best advice is to stick to your maximum figure (unless you're only going over by a few hundred quid). Know when to stop. Stretching yourself too far can lead to funding problems, throwing your mortgage deal out of kilter. It also means you've fallen squarely into the agent's trap, and perhaps end up paying too much.

As the last ones standing fight it out to the bitter end, it's worth bearing in mind that it isn't always the person who offers the highest price who wins. It's common for agents to advise their client not to accept the highest offer, but rather the highest bid from the person best place to proceed (ie cash buyers with no chain). Winning bidders also have a habit of sobering up and later withdrawing, in which case the agent will phone around the runners-up to offer the property afresh.

It's generally best to avoid getting embroiled in a bidding war, unless you happen to have spotted something that makes the property especially valuable to you. Development potential can add value, but these days everyone's wise to this and, of course, it nearly always depends on getting planning permission. It's worth remembering that many buyers who beat off rivals and willingly paid over the odds in the 2007 boom celebrated prematurely. They were nursing big losses a year later.

Sealed bids

Agents have another trick up their sleeves that's guaranteed to boost prices when several buyers are after the same property. Going to 'sealed bids' involves asking all the hopeful purchasers to formally submit their 'best and final offer' confidentially in writing by a specified deadline. Similarly, properties are sometimes formally marketed 'For Sale by Tender', with an auction-style guide price to encourage prospective buyers to submit competing written offers. This is par for the course in Scotland and can dramatically speed up the process. The problem from the buyer's perspective is not knowing what others are bidding, so the temptation is to go a fair bit higher than the guide price, which may, of course, be cunningly pitched on the low side to stimulate demand.

In reality, bids tend to be submitted in rather odd sums, for fear of being pipped at the post by a rival offer that's a only measly 2p higher. Along with your bid always be sure to stress the strengths of your position in writing ('we are proceedable cash buyers' etc).

'Bidding fever' can see two determined rivals slugging it out, pushing up the price astronomically. But a crazy bid may later be retracted (as it's 'subject to contract'), and may invite mortgage problems later when the lender's surveyor downvalues it. Unlike the Scottish system, where the offer is legally binding, even if you win and the seller accepts your bid it's not guaranteed that you'll get the property. Someone else could still offer more at a later date, and agents are legally required to pass on all offers to their clients.

Most agents will manage this process in an honest and reputable fashion. But, perhaps unsurprisingly, suspicions of malpractice occasionally surface. After all, discovering that you've lost out by a mere 2p could understandably make you feel a touch bitter and twisted. So it's not unknown for estate agents – often unfairly cast as the wicked villains – to subsequently be bombarded with deranged allegations from failed bidders. Some may suspect, for example, that an agent's palms have been generously greased by property developers. But such allegations are notoriously hard to prove.

Offer accepted

Once the seller has accepted your offer it should immediately be confirmed in writing to both parties. This is normally done by the estate agent. Both sides should then provide their solicitors' details so that your conveyancer can make a prompt start. Unless you're buying at auction, offers are subject to contract ('STC') as well as subject to survey and to a hundred other things that could potentially rain on your parade over the coming weeks.

20 | THE WAITING GAME

Progress

Your solicitor/conveyancer can now spring into action, sending 'preliminary enquiries' to the seller's solicitor and obtaining a copy of the HIP already paid for by the seller. Their job is to safeguard your interests so that you don't end up buying a lemon. The various enquiries and searches that are about to be made on your behalf should uncover any serious concerns. For all you know the charming seller may be concealing whole tribes of skeletons in the closet. Perhaps their former partner still retains a legal right to live in the house and to remain in occupation after you've bought it. Or you may not have spotted any visual clues to the overgrown public footpath that runs across the garden, or the shared rights of way that are the owner's responsibility to maintain.

The solicitors should also sniff out potential dangers in the locality, such as any history of flooding. Matters such as illegal extensions and alterations or any recorded 'dangerous structures' (unstable chimneys etc) should also be flagged up, along with any history of disputes with nasty neighbours and whether the local council has scheduled the property for demolition. In most cases the buyer's solicitor will be simultaneously acting for the mortgage lender, who will be interested in anything of this nature that could detrimentally affect the value of their security.

As we saw earlier, over the next few weeks progress will be measured to a large extent against the legal framework. So let's remind ourselves just what your conveyancer will be doing:

- Sending 'preliminary enquiries' to the seller's solicitor
- Receiving and checking the draft contract
- Sending a local search to the Council (if the searches in the HIP are not acceptable)
- Checking the title with the Land Registry and raising additional searches
- Checking the mortgage offer received from the lender
- Agreeing the final contract and arranging for the buyer to sign the contracts
- Exchanging contracts

Whilst the various searches being pursued and the draft contract passing and re-passing between solicitors, there will be other matters closer to home to keep an eye on.

Your offer has been accepted and the property you want is now officially 'under offer', or, as many agents prefer to describe it, 'SOLD' – though this is slightly misleading as the deal is still very much 'subject to contract'. Nothing is legally binding until exchange of contracts, which typically won't take place for another 8 to 12 weeks. In the meantime prepare for the white-knuckle ride of your life. During this extended 'cooling-off period' buyers and sellers are highly sensitive to all kinds of distracting influences. A good estate agent will know the importance of correctly managing this all-important waiting game.

Photo: wikimedia

The long and winding road to exchange of contracts

Surveys and valuations

The mortgage valuation is one of the key stages in a purchase, unless, of course, you're rolling in cash and don't require mortgage funding. But even then you'd probably still want to arrange a private survey to make sure the building isn't going to crumble to the ground the first time you slam a door. This is an important stage that needs to be carefully managed – but in reality rarely is. The survey and valuation process is covered in detail in the next chapter.

Speeding up your purchase

You now have one single overriding objective: to exchange contracts as quickly as possible.

Once you've exchanged you're pretty much legally home and dry, and can afford to relax a little, but until then every extra day of unnecessary delay means a greater risk of losing the property. There is a direct link between the time taken to reach exchange and the chance of the deal falling through. Fortunately there are a number of things you can do to make the best of a bad system and

drastically reduce the chances of failure. Here are some tips for a successful purchase.

Being there

The next few weeks are probably the most critical stage in the entire process, so it's best to avoid spending too much time away from the action. It's sod's law that if you disappear off on holiday, then as soon as you've left the country there'll be a major last-minute hitch, typically a key document that's gone missing. This could delay exchange and hold up completion, adding considerable expense. While you're relaxing on the beach planning your new decor, back home the whole deal might be about to fall through. And as if the process of buying and selling property wasn't stressful enough, it's surprising how often a house move seems to coincide with the scheduled arrival of a new baby – something best not combined with undertaking a major house renovation project.

Confirm it in writing

By the time you finally reach exchange of contracts everyone involved is normally emotionally exhausted, with minimal reserves of patience. After weeks or months enduring buttock-clenching tension it's sometimes hard to remember precisely who said what to whom, so it's not unusual for silly misunderstandings to occur over incredibly unimportant things, such as whether you said you'd leave the dining room light fittings. When nerves are frayed, such trifles can all too easily blow up into major disputes. It can then become a matter of pride to make a point or stand up for a principle, even at the expense of the whole deal collapsing. Human nature strikes again. The best advice is to prevent destructive squabbles occurring in the first place by putting everything clearly in writing from the word go. This way, the chance of daft disputes arising is considerably lessened.

Good relationships

Until your offer's been accepted, there is always the potential for things to get a bit antagonistic. People can be surprisingly sensitive about the value of their property, even to the extent of feeling insulted at being offered a lower price for their pride and joy. But a good estate agent playing the role of middleman can help smooth the path to a mutually rewarding transaction.

However, now that your offer's been accepted, there's a lot to be said for developing your personal relationship with the sellers. Experience shows that by forging a direct link, the chances of skulduggery and dirty tricks later ruining your purchase can be significantly reduced. So once the deal's been agreed and the dust has settled, it's normally a good idea to arrange another visit, face to face on more cordial terms. Any pretext will do, such as measuring up windows for curtains. This gives both sides a chance to chill out and perhaps bond a little. A touch of diplomacy at this stage can relieve any lingering ill-feeling and help smooth ruffled feathers. If you're gifted in the PR department, some shameless schmoozing laced with complimentary comments, eye contact and sympathetic shoulder touching (of the appropriate variety) could pay handsome dividends in weeks to come.

You can also create goodwill by being flexible in peripheral areas, such as agreeing to fit in with the sellers' preferred completion date, or being willing to leave your bookcases or shrubs if they've really taken a fancy to them. This all helps lock them in to the deal.

Of course, it may be that you just can't stand the sight of them, in which case it's probably sensible not to risk making matters worse and to stay apart. But, as in business, building a good relationship should mean you're better placed to overcome problems that arise later on.

Communication

This is only the beginning. Far from being a done deal, over the coming weeks a neglected purchase could all too easily shrivel and die. This is because once the initial euphoria has worn off, things often go quiet for weeks on end. After a while, your mind starts to regard this silence with the utmost suspicion. Positive feelings turn to conspiracy theories. Both sides are sitting there thinking 'Why haven't we heard anything – are they actually serious about the property or just messing us about?'

Before you know it you've convinced yourself that the sellers are abusing your trust. Perhaps they're up to no good, cheating on you and flirting outrageously in an attempt to solicit higher bids. So much for the sacred vows of faithfulness uttered so glibly when accepting your offer.

The solution to such worries is to take the initiative and make regular contact. It's a mistake to assume the estate agent is diligently beavering away, assiduously attending to every last detail. Although the more professional agent will take pride in managing this stage, others may be asleep at the wheel, or occupied with other transactions. So you may need to step into the driving seat and keep the sellers informed at all the key stages – the date of the mortgage valuation or survey, the survey result, receiving

Photo: wikimedia

your mortgage offer, progress with the draft contract etc.

Ideally, keep in touch once a week. Email is a particularly useful medium for this purpose, being non-intrusive while inviting a corresponding reply to keep you updated. But even the occasional phone call will help maintain the bonding process and therefore reduce the prospect of foul play. It helps to create a feeling that both parties are working together towards a satisfactory outcome, which makes solving obstacles considerably easier. If you prefer not to liaise directly, communicating via the agents is still preferable to doing nothing and leaving it to chance.

Statistically there are two major culprits when it comes to deals falling through – mortgage problems and legal delays. Here are some tips to improve your chances of success.

Getting a quicker mortgage offer

Unless you're a cash buyer, you can't exchange contracts without having received a formal mortgage offer – because if you just went ahead and then couldn't lay your hands on the money to pay for the house, you'd be liable to pay out considerable sums in damages (as well as looking a bit of a plonker). So it's essential to receive your mortgage offer in good time. There are a number of ways you can speed this along:

■ Pick an efficient mortgage lender

A really switched-on bank can produce your mortgage offer within a couple of weeks. A dozy one could take a month or more. So it pays to choose your lender carefully, and ask them what their average turn-around time is. Brokers know which ones are hot and which are not, plus they can help chase things when the going gets slow. It's also worth making it clear to your lender from the outset that yours is an urgent case.

■ Apply early for your mortgage

With some lenders you can apply in principle for a mortgage even before you've found a property to buy. This means they can make an early start writing for employment references and doing credit scoring. Applying early can also buy time should the lender insist that you need to arrange a new life assurance policy as a condition of giving you a mortgage. In such cases a bank's underwriters sometimes require medical reports, which can take weeks to resolve – better to know this now than the week before exchange. It's also important to be very clear at the outset what costs are involved in your purchase so that you have sufficient funds available in time – double check legal fees, stamp duty and all those sneaky hidden mortgage charges.

■ Get the mortgage valuation done early

Lenders normally wait until they've received income references and completed credit checks before instructing the mortgage valuation. This is a sensible precaution because, were there to be a serious income or credit problem and the mortgage refused, you wouldn't have wasted money paying unnecessarily for the bank's mortgage valuation. But if you're confident that your financial standing in the community is bullet-proof, ask the bank to instruct their valuer asap – obviously this will be at your risk.

■ Alert your employer

One common reason for hold-ups is employers being unbelievably slow replying to income reference requests. Most banks will not accept a simple letter alone, and need their forms correctly completed. So if your employer fails to read the form properly and does it wrong, it will have to be resubmitted. It can therefore pay to pre-empt such tomfoolery by finding out in advance who it is in your organisation that will be dealing with your income reference. Then give them a call to keep tabs on progress.

■ Get chasing

If you don't hear anything, never assume that everything's going smoothly. Pick up the phone to your lender and regularly check progress of each stage as if your life depended on it. Keep phoning, faxing and emailing until you're officially known as Pain In The Arse Number One. This gets results.

Other things you can do to smooth the path of your all-important mortgage offer include making sure the property you're buying is acceptable to your lender. This is relevant when it's of unusual construction or a quirky design, such as a flat in a tower block, or a property with concrete walls. It also helps to choose a surveyor who can turn reports around super-quick.

Speeding up the legal work

A good, experienced solicitor/conveyancer can make all the difference to achieving a swift purchase. In Part 1 we looked at how to choose the right solicitor. If there's one thing that's essential to get right it's this. Other players, such as surveyors, perform an important role but they're only

Photo: wikimedia

involved for a relatively short period of time. The solicitor is with you all the way and has the potential to hamper or enhance each and every stage. But there are some areas where you, the client, can help speed things along:

■ Instruct early

Until your offer's been accepted there's not a great deal the buyer's solicitor can do, but having your 'legal team' already appointed and raring to go when you do find the right property can save a week or so in wasted time, which could prove crucial later on.

■ Local authority searches

As we saw back in Chapter 13, obtaining the local authority search (or the 'local land search' as it is officially known) is a key stage in the house-purchase process. So it may come as something of a surprise to learn that local searches aren't comprehensive. They only relate to the actual piece of land you searched, covering the property itself and roads within 200m. They don't check the surrounding area. So if your neighbour has just been granted planning consent for an enormous extension or is selling his garden for development, you may be none the wiser. Even if a waste-disposal plant is planned on adjoining land, you may not get to hear about it. Nor do all councils keep detailed records showing whether your house was built on contaminated land. So as a precaution it's always worth checking the Council's website to see if any planning applications have been made in the vicinity. If you have particular suspicions about scheduled development in the area, if you ask your solicitor they can make additional specific searches of nearby buildings, adjoining land or vacant plots close to the property.

Local searches have an unenviable reputation for being a major bottleneck that holds everything up. In a busy market, fingers are frequently pointed at councils for the time taken to turn round searches. A late search could be especially galling when potential concerns are uncovered, such as proposed road-widening schemes, or illegally built extensions. Such unwelcome revelations could result in a last-minute panic, in some cases becoming a deal-breaker. But the blame for delays can't always be laid at the Council's door. Submitting and paying for searches was traditionally sometimes left until fairly late in the process so that fees wouldn't be wasted should the purchase fall through.

Fortunately, local searches are now included in HIPs, and should be ready and waiting by the time your solicitor needs to see them. However, problems sometime arise where a purchase drags on for a long time and the searches become out of date. Searches are generally accepted where they will be no more than six months old at the date of completion, although some firms will consider them invalid if more than three months old when read. Should your solicitor or mortgage lender for whatever reason insist on a fresh search it's likely to set you back around £150–£200. Depending on which council you're dealing with and how busy they are, this can take anything from just over a week to almost a month. To prevent unnecessary delays it's essential that the correct forms are submitted, as incomplete applications occasionally have to be returned and then resubmitted, wasting valuable time. The local search is submitted in two parts, each with their own standard form. Form 'LLC1' covers the search of the 'local land charges register', showing any financial charges and restrictions affecting the property. This should turn up any improvement or renovation grants secured on the property (which may need to be partially repaid), as well as any tree preservation orders, conservation orders, smoke control restrictions and planning conditions. Form 'Con 29' covers enquiries of a broader nature relating to local planning, highways and environmental services.

■ Other searches
As well as a local authority search, the HIP should also include a drainage search provided by the Water Authority. Amongst other things, this will reveal whether the building's waste water goes into a public sewer or a private sewer or simply into a septic tank or cesspit in the garden. Environmental searches are becoming more common (but may only provide inconclusive results). As well as searches about the property you're buying, you need to know that the person you've just agreed to buy from is actually the true owner and isn't bankrupt. But perhaps most revealing of all is the Land Registry search (see below).

More on the law

Buying and selling property depends on digging out information from official records or registers. The first thing to note is that property is legally referred to as 'land', which means land including any buildings constructed upon it.

Title deeds
If you had always visualised your title deeds as ancient parchments adorned with immaculate copperplate handwriting executed with a quill pen, you will be disappointed. In a bid to move towards the holy grail of e-conveyancing, the Land Registry have now done away with traditional title deeds, which are no longer recognised. Even if you found your old deeds stuffed under the mattress and dutifully sent

them in, they would just be torn up. From October 2003, all the relevant information about ownership of registered properties has been transferred on to the Land Registry computer in London – the world's largest property database. So unless your property is one of the few that still remain unregistered (see below) your title deeds will consist, like everything else today, of documents stored on computer.

Many of us, of course, still like to physically grasp important documents in hard copy. So to keep us sweet, the Government introduced 'Title Information Documents'. These incorporate the same information as Land Certificates but take the form of a few sheets of printed A4 paper listing all the important matters that affect ownership together with a plan. But unlike the old Land Certificate in the title deeds, these documents are for information only, and do not provide legal proof of ownership. Traditionally, if you had a mortgage the lender would hold the deeds locked away down in their vaults as conclusive proof of their security. But mortgage lenders now rarely hold title deeds, for the very good reason that in most cases there aren't any. Your mortgage lender will also no longer need other once-important documents such as leases, guarantees and copies of planning permission.

So don't look too disappointed when the solicitor hands you a rather insignificant looking 'Title Information Document', which is really all your title deeds now consist of.

Unregistered properties
The vast majority of UK property is 'registered'. This means that ownership is officially recorded at the Land Registry in London and guaranteed by the State. But on very rare occasions it may turn out that a property only has 'unregistered title'. This occasionally arises where a house hasn't changed hands for the last 20 years or more, and means there may be little satisfactory record of ownership. So how can you buy such a property in confidence? The answer is, your solicitor has to turn detective and carry out additional legal work to prove ownership or 'title' by searching through old records.

In practice, this involves delving through a bundle of old title deeds known as an 'Epitome of Title' to prove a continuous link in ownership going back at least 15 years. Conveyances of earlier sales provide evidence of past changes of ownership, which in the case of some period properties could span several centuries. It should also unearth details of old mortgages and may show the result of any land charge searches made against previous sellers. References to ancient dust-encrusted deeds may provide further clues to how and when old legal obligations (such as hidden rights of way) were originally brought into being, and will need to be carefully checked. Hunting through elderly documents may also unearth old plans, which are sometimes of dubious accuracy.

Needless to say, all this burrowing around through a lot of crumbling old papers can add considerably to the time and expense involved in the conveyancing process, which is why when you get a conveyancing quote it is assumed the property is registered.

Some key additional records are kept at the Land Charges Department based in Plymouth. These include details of the following charges and interests:

- 'Second charge' mortgages or loans secured against it (see boxout).
- The dates when any restrictive covenants were first registered against the property.
- Matrimonial claims or notices of a spouse's right to occupy the property (usually registered where divorce proceedings are anticipated).

Crucially, some of the above information is registered against people's names, rather than against the address of the property as you might imagine. So when your solicitor makes the final pre-completion searches they search against the names of people contained in the title as well as against the sellers' names.

With unregistered properties, there is one important additional check that's required. This is the search of the Index Map, the only check that needs to be made with the Land Registry (see below). This is to ensure that no one has beaten you to it and already registered the title to any part of the land (it also reveals any 'cautions' where the land has been registered without a formal reference to them).

Registered property

Registration of title became compulsory for properties sold from as early as 1898 in London. This gradually spread throughout the rest of the country until finally Plymouth was included in January 1974. However, it didn't actually become law that all property titles had to be registered until around 1990. Details of registered properties are kept at the Land Registry.

The Land Registry

Your solicitor will apply to the Land Registry in London for a certified copy of the property's 'title information documents' (for a small fee). These certified copies are known as 'office copy entries', the meat of which is contained within three registers – the Property Register, the Proprietorship Register and the Charges Register (see below). The information recorded in each of these registers comprises what used to be known as the property's deeds. In total they may only extend to four or so pages.

Checking mortgages

There may be more than one mortgage secured as charges against a property, and not all of these will be shown in the deeds. Should a buyer fail to spot the existence of these loans, they could become personally responsible for paying them off. So how can you be sure that the property you're buying is completely mortgage-free?

In unregistered conveyances the main mortgage lender with the 'first charge' will normally hang on to the title deeds as security. This will prevent anyone selling the property without first having to pay off their mortgage. Potential buyers will be aware of this by looking at the deeds (as well as checking with the Land Charges department).

But how can you tell if the owner has subsequently taken out any additional loans that are secured against the property? Other lenders of second or third mortgages (aka *puisne* mortgages) obviously cannot also hold the deeds as security. Instead, they protect their interests by registering what is known as a 'c (i)' entry with the Land Charges department. Anyone buying the property will make a search of this registry before they complete. If there are any such charges they will have to be paid off on completion.

Missing persons

Regardless of whether a property is registered or unregistered, problems occasionally arise tracing owners. Suppose many years ago a house was bequeathed to several people under the terms of a will, but one of the present owners has since disappeared. If the property has an unregistered title, extra work will be involved ploughing through a series of documents. If there's still any uncertainty, an indemnity insurance policy can usually be arranged, although such 'defects in title' sometimes scare off mortgage lenders, unless they consider the risk is acceptable. Clearly having to make extra enquiries in such cases can delay the purchase.

With registered properties things are a lot easier because only one set of documents needs to be checked – the land registers – and the title is guaranteed to be accurate. Despite this, indemnity insurance is still sometimes needed in registered conveyancing, *eg* where a key document is missing because it was somehow never lodged with the Land Registry.

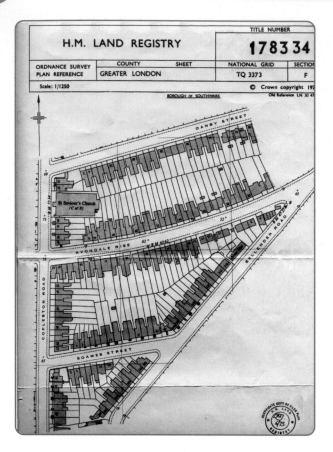

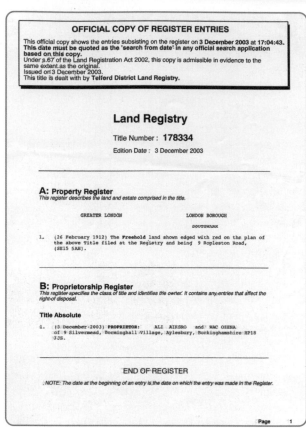

These title information documents provide conclusive proof of the property's ownership, backed by a watertight guarantee that the stated owner is the true owner. This obviously makes discovering who owns the title to a registered property a pretty simple matter. Because the 'office copy entries' are only copies (albeit official ones) it may sometimes appear that pages are missing where in fact blank pages in the original document have simply not been copied.

The key to tracing files at the Land Registry is the title number, a reference number that every registered property has, which appears at the top of each page of the 'office copy entries'.

A: The Property Register describes the land by reference to the title plan and postal address. Any rights that other people have over the property, such as footpaths and rights of way, can be found here under 'matters excepted and reserved'. Any rights of way that benefit the owner are also recorded. Leasehold properties have details of the lease (eg the remaining term, the parties, the ground rent etc).

B: The Proprietorship Register shows the present owners, and until recently also showed previous owners, a matter of some interest for house-history geniologists. Owners of freehold property usually have what is known as 'Title Absolute' (ie ownership is guaranteed). This also

applies to most leasehold owners, although in some cases 'Good Leasehold Title' may be shown instead, which is normally acceptable to lenders subject to confirmation that it complies with CML (Council of Mortgage Lenders) requirements. The weakest form of ownership is 'Possessory Title', which sometimes applies where the original deeds have been lost, or where a claim to ownership is only supported by 'adverse possession' or 'squatter's title'. As well as ownership, prices paid for the properties have been recorded since 1 April 2000 and are available online – see website.

C: The Charges Register alerts you to restrictions on a property such as any mortgages or other loans secured on it. It will also flag up any restrictive covenants (see below). Sometimes these are simply referred to in the form of a note, cross-referenced to an old conveyance document that can be traced back to a time before the property was registered. In such cases a little detective work may be required to unearth a list of restrictions, which are normally referred to by the seller's solicitor in the draft contract as 'incumbrances'.

More rarely you might come across 'cautions' declaring a wife or a partner's right to remain in occupation when the property is sold. Clearly this is not something most buyers would particularly relish, so the seller may need to apply to have these removed ('warned off'). Similarly a legal 'restriction' may appear in the register giving notice of other people's legal interests in the property.

Fortunately it's most unusual to encounter such complexities for the average property being conveyed, but should something of this type come to light there's obviously considerable potential for serious delays. If charges have to be removed or cancelled it may mean that a third party has to be officially notified, or that the sale be 'authorised by the court' – so you can wave goodbye to a swift conclusion.

Restrictive covenants

Restrictive covenants are 'promises not to do something' contained in the original deeds. Usually dreamed up by the original developers in an attempt to 'preserve the tone of the area', the general idea was to prevent future residents from partaking in unsavoury activities that could reduce values and take the area downmarket. Should your search

Photo wikimedia

Beware gifts
Where the present owner of the property was given it as a gift within the last five years, it could turn out to be legally unsaleable – at least until further checks are carried out. This is because, if the person who made the gift was made bankrupt, that gift can later be cancelled, because a creditor can apply for a court order to 'reverse the gift'.

But how do you know if the property you're buying was given as a gift unless the owner tells you?

One clue is where no price was recorded for the transaction at the Land Registry. Also, carrying out solvency and bankruptcy searches against the donor of the gift should also alert you to any potential risks.

Property given as a gift can still be reclaimed within two years where the person who originally donated it was solvent at the time. But where the gift was between husband and wife (*eg* where an owner transfers the house into his partner's name or into joint names for tax purposes) the law may presume the husband was insolvent at the time.

This is something of a 'grey area' for which specialist legal advice should be sought. However, to reclaim a property it must generally be established that the intent to get rid of it originally was to avoid creditors.

As with many other awkward and obscure legal issues, the simplest immediate solution is for the seller to arrange (and pay for) indemnity insurance. Otherwise it will be impossible for the buyer to raise a mortgage on the property.

The most common restrictive covenants
- Not to use the house for trade or business
- 'No building or extension' on the plot without the permission of the original developer
- Any house you build on the plot must be of a certain minimum value
- Not to do anything to cause a nuisance

of the Charges Register turn up such a restriction, it may very well not matter. If, for example, it's a restriction against 'bone boiling and leather making', commonly found in Victorian deeds, the chances are it won't cramp your intended lifestyle too much. Restrictions against running a business for the 'sale of intoxicating liquors' is another old favourite (but you couldn't do this without planning consent in any case). But restrictions on building extensions are also fairly common and can be more of an issue.

But surely the chances of an old bone-dry restriction being enforced today are virtually zero, so why all the fuss? The builder who made it is probably long dead, or the company concerned may no longer exist. Even if they are still alive and kicking, it would require them to spend money to enforce it, with no obvious benefit. If the grandson of the original builder has inherited the right to enforce it, he probably doesn't know anything about it and couldn't care less anyway. But if the relevant person has disappeared or has ceased to exist, the law says that the requirement to get their consent before you break the restriction no longer applies.

Unfortunately there's another scenario that's potentially more problematic. If your house is located on an estate, then all the other houses will probably have the same

Photo: Velux.co.uk

restriction, and it's sometimes possible that a neighbour could legally enforce the restriction. Of course there's only a very slim chance that this could actually happen, but it's still a risk, and your solicitors and mortgage lender won't be inclined to turn a blind eye.

One possible solution is to trace the 'covenantee' who inherited the right to enforce, and persuade them (with a fistful of pounds) to get the legal restriction removed. Alternatively, once you've bought the land you can then apply to the Land Tribunal to have the restriction overturned, although this can sometimes be costly and difficult. The usual solution is for the seller to pay a one-off premium to insure you and future owners against any risk of enforcement. Lenders will require such indemnity insurance to cover any possibility of a claim for breach of covenant. The estate agent or solicitor will know which firms can insure against such risks. The snag is, sellers may not be exactly overjoyed at the prospect of having to cough up several hundred pounds to pay for this, and may dig their heels in.

Sometimes it turns out that a property is already in breach of a restrictive covenant, because the owners simply weren't aware of any such limitations in the deeds. Perhaps there's a 'no building or extending' restriction, but the property has been extended. In such a situation, the first task is to discover how long the extension or building has been there. If it's more than 12 years then the covenant should no longer be enforceable. Despite this, ever cautious mortgage lenders will still require indemnity insurance if it's less than 20 years old. The subject of enforceability of covenants is notoriously tricky, so legal advice is needed if you plan to do something that might infringe such a restriction.

Matrimonial homes

There is one other nasty little trap that the buyer's solicitor has to watch out for. Where a married couple are selling a house, but the paperwork for the transaction only refers to

Photo: wikimedia

the name of one person, then there's always the possibility that their partner could have a claim for the property to be treated as a 'matrimonial home'. Where, for example, a husband is selling the property in his name, his wife may have already registered her right as a spouse to occupy the matrimonial home. Such rights are recorded at the Land Registry. Should your search unearth such a matrimonial right, then before proceeding with the purchase both you and your mortgage lender will need formal written assurance that the spouse has agreed to withdraw their charge from the register.

This can still be an issue even if the couple selling were divorced long ago. A judge could have make a 'continuation order' maintaining the spouse's right to occupy, and giving them priority over you, the purchaser. This is basically a way of ensuring that the house won't be sold or mortgaged without the spouse's consent or a court order. However, where the property is already in joint names this shouldn't arise (unless, of course, they're married to multiple wives or husbands). One argument against DIY conveyancing is the potentially dire consequences should you, through inexperience, fail to spot this kind of obscure trap.

Whilst on the thorny subject of people enjoying the right to stay in occupation of the place you're buying, what exactly should you do if the house of your dreams turns out to be subject to a tenancy? In the vast majority of cases tenancies should be apparent when you (or your surveyor) inspect the property. But just in case you failed to spot the gang of Bolivian asylum seekers hanging out in the loft, there are other ways of getting to the truth. First, the seller has to provide details of all occupants right at the start in their answers to pre-contract enquiries. Second, the contract should provide for 'vacant possession'. In other words, your purchase is subject to all present occupants, including any tenants, moving out prior to completion, so that you're free to move in immediately upon completion. If a tenancy is indicated then it's up to the seller to take the necessary action to rid the property of the tenant. However, before exchanging contracts you may justifiably want some reassurance that the tenant has departed for good, and hasn't just disappeared off on a week's shopping trip, to prevent potential problems delaying completion. Depending on the type of tenancy, a court order may be required before an occupant can be evicted, and your purchase can proceed – which can obviously consume a lot of precious time, hence the need for your sharp-eyed legal team to check such matters as early as possible.

The Charges Register at the Land Registry will reveal any 'long leases' originally granted for more than 21 years. This would be the case, for example, where a freehold property has been split into a number of leasehold flats sold on long leases. If the property you're buying is held on a registered long lease then it means you're actually buying the leasehold – not the freehold. Anything shorter would be classed as a 'short tenancy', with tenants renting the property.

21 | SURVEYS AND VALUATIONS

If you buy a cereal bar and it turns out to be stale or mouldy, the full force of the law will be on your side. You can demand your money back, or even sue for compensation. If, on the other hand, you purchase a house that turns out to be a damp, beetle-infested, asbestos-ridden hovel – tough. *Caveat emptor.* So it obviously makes sense to root out any such horrors before you buy.

Whether you decide to arrange a survey or not will depend to some extent on your knowledge of building. There's nothing to stop you doing your own survey. Or perhaps you're planning to demolish and rebuild the place, so why bother?

As with cars, there is a general rule that the older a building is, the more trouble you can expect. But even in relatively modern properties defects often exist, for example where dodgy conservatories and porches have been added. Even new houses aren't immune. Indeed, the majority of buyers of newly-built homes find faults after moving in.

However, in many properties, even though the fittings and services are getting on a bit, the chances are the building itself will be structurally sound. What you see is pretty much what you get. On the other hand, appearances can sometimes be deceptive. All manner of gruesome DIY botches and illegal structural alterations may have been carried out. And what if the original builders skimped on the parts that you can't see, such as the foundations or the drains?

What superficially appears to be a nicely refurbished Victorian terraced cottage may look very different upon closer inspection. Botched alterations and dangerous electrics may be quietly festering beneath the neatly polished exterior. And to judge just how bad a defect really is takes a trained eye.

What exactly is a survey?

Most buyers require a mortgage. So before handing over shed loads of cash, the mortgage lender will want to be sure that the property you're buying with their money really is worth the squillions you've agreed to pay. They will sleep easier at night knowing that they would get their money back if they had to repossess your home (*ie* their *security*).

So a qualified surveyor is normally instructed by the lender to take a brief mooch around the property and complete a simple mortgage valuation form, declaring an independent opinion of the property's market value. This figure will often, but not always, concur with the agreed purchase price. To pay for this, lenders usually charge the applicant a valuation fee (not all of which is passed to the surveying firm doing the job).

Most lenders send the buyer a courtesy copy of their valuation report, and this is where confusion sometimes arises, because buyers may assume that a survey has been

done. Part of the problem is that staff in banks routinely refer to mortgage valuation inspections as 'surveys'. But valuation reports are nothing like a proper survey. Many simply inform buyers that: '*The property appeared in a general condition consistent with its age and type although parts of the property are ageing and likely to require attention.*' Which basically tells you very little. To qualify for a mention in valuation reports, defects usually have to be quite extreme as well as fairly obvious.

This may explain why eight out of ten buyers traditionally haven't bothered with a survey. But times are changing. Ever keen to find ways of boosting their profits, many banks are instead instructing external 'drive-by' valuations, which at best are an educated guess. Worse, some lenders are relying on computer-generated valuations known as 'AVMs' (Automatic Valuation Models), a recent US import implicated as being open to manipulation, and fuelling the sub-prime lending crisis.

So it's increasingly likely that no qualified surveyor will be setting foot in the house that you're buying unless you instruct one yourself. However, the property in question will most likely have already received the attentions of a Domestic Energy Assessor for the purpose of producing an Energy Performance Certificate, which contains advice about a building's energy efficiency as part of the HIP. So never mind if the property is visibly subsiding and riddled with rot and beetle, at least you'll know its carbon footprint.

Instructing a 'proper' private survey is therefore becoming more important. Although money will inevitably be tight, the justification for spending a few hundred quid on a survey is that it could well save you thousands later. Any significant defects that come to light can provide useful ammunition to renegotiate the price, or have the sellers pay for any urgent works that would otherwise have been down to you. See website for a guide to survey prices.

Mortgage valuations

Until the mortgage valuation has been done, the lender can't issue your mortgage offer. And without that, you can't exchange contracts. So this is a crucial stage. But it isn't always plain sailing because it's not unknown for surveyors to value properties at less than the agreed purchase price.

Why does this matter? For one thing it suggests that you're paying too much, and reopening negotiations at this stage is never going to be easy. But the real worry is the possible effect on the mortgage loan. Banks look at mortgages as a proportion to the value of the property – a loan-to-value ratio (LTV) – and if the 'true value' turns out to be lower than the agreed price, they will lend against the lower figure, not the purchase price. If your mortgage is relatively high in relation to the value of the property, then a 'downvaluation' could push you into a higher, more

expensive loan-to-value band (say, above 75 per cent). Or it could totally scupper your funding. If this does muck up your finances, it may be possible to take evasive action and challenge the valuation (see Chapter 22).

In recent years, mortgage valuations on new properties have caused enormous problems. Although newly-built dwellings generally command a premium price, many developers have shown a certain fondness for vastly inflating headline sales prices by including generous incentives – sometimes totalling more than ten per cent of the property's value. This technique was designed to boost the amount of money purchasers could borrow and the existence of such incentives was often brushed under the carpet. Such deals would typically offer large cash-backs, stamp duty paid and free legal fees. In boom years, some individual valuation surveyors were placed under considerable pressure to take a benign view of the huge incentives concealed and 'value up'. So long as the market continued to boom, this wasn't a problem. But when values plummeted as the market cooled, lenders who burnt their fingers sought to recoup losses, in some cases by suing surveyors for 'overvaluing'. The net result is a wariness of new developments, especially large blocks of flats in areas burdened with oversupply. One positive outcome, however, has been the requirement for developers to formally declare all related incentives.

Even in the same road, properties can vary considerably

Checking for damp

What type of survey?

There are basically two types of survey – the RICS Homebuyer survey and the full Building Survey. In both cases a qualified chartered surveyor will inspect the building from top to bottom, from the loft down to the drains (where visible). Each part of the building is reported on in turn, both inside and out, and any concerns flagged up.

For the vast majority of properties the less expensive Homebuyer survey (which includes a valuation and is known as an 'HBR') is perfectly adequate. The surveyor should spot all significant defects, including structural problems, and advise you accordingly.

But for older period properties (*ie* those built before about 1880), or rambling residences with impressive price tags, a Building Survey offers more scope for the surveyor to customise the report and dwell in detail on their encounters with defects.

In the past, confusion sometimes arose because Building Surveys used to be known as 'structural surveys' or 'full surveys'. Perhaps not realising that less expensive Homebuyer surveys also report on a building's structural condition, customers sometimes opted for the more expensive survey when not strictly necessary.

The downside of both reports is that they do not physically test services, such as the electrics and drainage (although they will give a visual opinion of condition). The reports conclude with a summary of urgent or significant defects and may advise further investigation. In other words, the surveyor inspects the whole building and distils it down to a few areas of concern, providing an educated opinion as to whether these are typical for the type of property. The next step is get some idea of the likely costs involved in remedying the highlighted defects, by obtaining specialist tests and reports, commonly on such matters as electrics, timber and damp, or cracking. (See 'Specialist reports' below.)

	Homebuyer Survey	Building Survey
Suitable for	Most properties built since about 1880	Older, complex or very expensive properties
		Properties of non-standard construction
		Properties for development
Checks structural condition?	Yes	Yes
'Top to bottom' inspection?	Yes	Yes
Includes very minor defects?	No	Yes
Includes a valuation?	Yes	No
Typical price	About 50 to 70 per cent of the price of a Building Survey	£700–£1,000 (for an average property, depending on the purchase price)

For survey prices see **www.rightsurvey.co.uk**

A 'single survey' system was launched in Scotland in December 2008. Here the seller pays for a three-tier home report, similar in style to a Homebuyer survey, which includes a surveyor's analysis, an energy efficiency report and a property questionnaire.

Choosing a surveyor

Surveyors come in assorted shapes and sizes. Anyone can call themselves a 'surveyor', a title that is sometimes adopted by double-glazing salesmen for enhanced credibility. Qualified surveyors, however, are always the *chartered* variety and are members of RICS (the Royal Institution of Chartered Surveyors) and bear the qualification MRICS or FRICS after their names (denoting either a Member or a Fellow – there's little practical difference).

You will need a residential specialist (as opposed to those whose expertise lies in the fields of shops or offices, agricultural land, auctioneering, rating, quantity surveying or architectural design). You also want someone with bags of local experience.

The Internet has, of course, made finding good

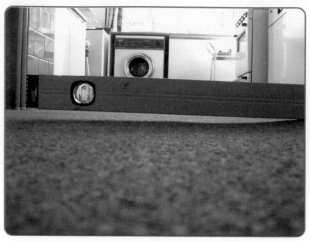

property professionals a lot easier – see 'Search for a surveyor' on the website. As always, it's worth asking friends if they can recommend anyone, but be aware that estate agents may be under commercial pressure to recommend firms with business links to their company, and may not always be the best source of impartial advice.

Banks and building societies are often very keen to arrange your survey, mainly because they get to keep a sizeable chuck of the fee. They will probably already need to instruct a mortgage valuation on the house you're buying, and may suggest that there is a saving to be made by having the same 'panel surveyor' undertake your Homebuyer or Building Survey at the same time. But in actual practice you should get a better deal by arranging the survey yourself. Another concern about letting the lender arrange your survey is that you have no control over the quality and experience of the surveyor they appoint. These are often panel surveyors working for large corporate firms, who may be under pressure to cram as many 'points' into the day as possible and consequently have less time to spend doing a quality job or to take the trouble to discuss the report with you afterwards. So when picking a surveyor there are a number of issues to consider:

■ Turnaround
Assuming that getting access to the property isn't a problem, a good surveyor should normally be able to carry out the inspection and have a Homebuyer report posted out to you within three or four days. Building Surveys take a little longer, often about a week or so.

■ Talk talk
A good surveyor should be willing to take your phone calls before and after the survey. Within reason clients should also be able to make requests in advance, such as 'Would the loft be suitable for conversion?' or 'Could you take a close look at the damp patch on the bedroom wall.'

At this stage in the process, everyone involved wants the purchase to go through as soon as possible. So news of defects that could hold things up is rarely welcome. But

surveyors know that buyers sometimes change their tune a few months after moving in. Suddenly every dripping tap will be blamed on them, and there will be cries of 'I wouldn't have bought this property if I'd known it needed a new boiler!' So there is a fine line to tread when writing reports, alerting buyers to the potential risk of defects without scaring everyone's pants off and derailing the purchase by overreacting to minor issues. If it does turn out that there are some significant defects it's important that your surveyor is willing to discuss them with you afterwards in plain English, and can clearly advise on the next course of action.

■ Local knowledge and experience
Surveyors should operate within a maximum radius of about 25 miles from their office, but it is not unknown for corporate firms to send surveyors twice this distance. It is always advisable to appoint someone who has lived and worked locally for several years and knows the area inside out. This means they will be aware of local risks such as those from subsidence, radon, mines and asbestos. They will also be better equipped to judge property values.

■ Insurance
All surveyors offering services to the public must carry suitable professional indemnity insurance. This covers them and their clients in the event of a claim should they miss a serious defect. So if you move in and promptly disappear down a hole in a rotten floor that the surveyor didn't spot, you should be able to claim compensation (see page 167).

Having selected your surveyor, the normal procedure is for the surveying firm to send out a *terms and conditions* form, which you need to sign and return together with payment up front. The terms are standard RICS-approved wording that brings to your attention the various limitations found in occupied properties, such as fitted carpets and furniture, and inform you about restrictions, such as the fact that the services won't be tested.

Interpreting the report

It's important to bear in mind that the surveyor's job is to point out defects, not to tell you what a lovely sunny outlook the property has. As a result, survey reports tend to read a trifle gloomily, even for the most delightful residences.

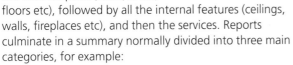

Survey reports are written in logical sequence, methodically describing all the external parts (walls, roofs, floors etc), followed by all the internal features (ceilings, walls, fireplaces etc), and then the services. Reports culminate in a summary normally divided into three main categories, for example:

■ Urgent matters
These are the killer items – ones that need to be rectified immediately. They include any 'actual or developing threats' to the fabric of the building, such as a wall that is bowing out dangerously. They also include risks to personal safety, such as dodgy electrical alterations, or loose roof tiles or chimney pots that are about to hurtle down to earth.

■ Significant matters
These are defects that may not be urgent, but if not attended to could detrimentally affect the fabric of the building. Such items, for example deteriorating external timbers, could affect the price you are prepared to pay for the property.

■ Observations
These include things that you may have noticed yourself, such as the avocado bathroom suite, tired decor and decrepit boiler. Therefore it's unlikely you could use these as ammunition to renegotiate the price.

Specialist reports

Where urgent or significant defects are reported, the next step is normally to get an idea about what it's going to cost to fix them. You can also get a rough idea of costs for routine works online – see website.

Occasionally mortgage lenders get involved at this stage. Banks usually insist that mortgage surveyors faithfully employ the lender's own 'standard phrases' in valuation reports when describing certain defects. This normally applies where there is any hint of structural movement or even minor damp or timber problems. The use of such standard phrases, sometimes drafted by lawyers with little experience of property, may automatically trigger a follow-up 'white van man' inspection, whether or not the surveyor in truth believes this to be necessary. This often results in unnecessary expense and hassle.

The same 'sledgehammer to crack a nut' lending mentality applies to shrubs or trees within 'influencing distance' of buildings, for fear they could potentially contribute to structural damage. Once again, lenders may stipulate that standard phrases are routinely trotted out, with the result that homeowners reading such comments can be terrified into a 'slash and burn' frenzy, ripping out perfectly innocent trees, shrubs and bushes, which in turn can cause other problems. This is another reason why commissioning a Homebuyer or Building Survey is advisable, since the surveyor has the scope to actually explain what they really think.

Experienced estate agents will only too familiar with the scenario as downhearted buyers stall progress upon hearing the news that their dream home may not be in as healthy condition as they'd imagined. Agents should normally be able keep things on track and organise specialist reports for common ailments such as suspected damp and timber decay, electrical faults and cracking. Most estimates should be free, because the contractor has a vested interest in winning some business. Structural

Left: Cavity wall insulation
Right: Trees close to old buildings can cause movement
Below: Are the beams structural or decorative?

Left: Re-roofing in progress

Right: Old movement remedied with steel restraint

engineers, however, will charge for their report, so there's often a debate as to whether the seller or buyer should foot the bill. Splitting 50/50 with the seller is sometimes an acceptable compromise.

Builders' quotes

Surveys don't normally include estimated costs for fixing the defects that have been highlighted. This is where builders should be able to provide estimates based on the survey report after a quick look at the house. For more serious works, some surveyors will write a detailed specification or schedule of works, for an additional fee. This is a detailed list of the work required, which can be used to accurately price the job by obtaining builders' quotes.

Structural engineer's report

All properties move and most show some signs of minor cracking, which in the vast majority of cases will not be significant. However, some mortgage valuation forms pose questions such as 'Are there any signs of movement?' and then insist on a standard phrase being used, which may then trigger the requirement for an engineer's report, even

Left: Subsidence cracking

for relatively minor problems. From a lending point of view, there are basically two kinds of movement – 'progressive' and 'historic'. The former is of concern because it is 'live' and ongoing, as opposed to something that happened in the past and is no longer a threat.

However, the cause of cracking isn't always simple to diagnose, so even if you pay for a full Building Surveys, the surveyor may recommend that a second opinion is sought from a structural engineer, especially where a property has been underpinned or has a history of subsidence. The engineer will then visit the property to inspect the problem and will write a brief report, usually concluding by stating whether the movement is significant or not, and advising what (if any) remedial works are required. More often than not, cracking will turn out not to be serious. But in some cases – notably those linked to insurance claims for subsidence – it is fairly common for 'monitoring' of cracking to be required over a period over six months or more. This traditionally requires the fitting of a small 'tell-tale' measuring device across the crack, to record any ongoing movement. Which isn't much help when you're due to exchange next week. So in such cases the solicitors normally advise that the buyer takes over the existing buildings insurance policy, perhaps after some limited renegotiation of the purchase price.

Timber and damp reports

Over the years, many timber and damp contractors have done good business carrying out totally unnecessary treatments, because mortgage lenders made such works a condition of their loans. To add insult to injury, a lot of injected damp-proof courses and timber treatment works have been carried out incompetently, causing more damage to the building than they remedy. But mortgage lenders weren't bothered as long as the contractor provided a 'guarantee'.

A mortgage valuation is only a very quick look round, so specialist reports are sometimes recommended as a precautionary measure. The problem is that the 'specialists' who carry out the subsequent inspection have a vested interest in confirming problems that, surprise, surprise,

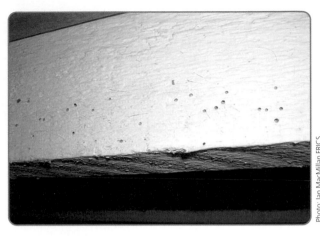

Photo: Ian MacMillan FRICS

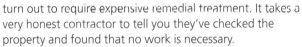

Above left: It's damp - but not necessarily rising

Above: Wood beetle, but is it active?

Left: A nasty case of wet rot under the floorboards

the floor is made of solid concrete it's obviously not going to be at risk from rot. Advice on dealing with damp, wet rot, dry rot and woodworm can be found in the Haynes *Victorian House Manual*.

Claims

Finally, what do you do if you move in and your roof starts leaking and the windows fall out the first time you slam the front door? If you didn't instruct a survey, then there's not much you can do. If you did have a survey, such defects should have been spotted and flagged up.

In the unlikely event that you have to submit a claim, the original survey firm or their insurers will appoint a qualified impartial expert to come and inspect the defect to assess whether you have the basis of a successful professional indemnity claim. The usual measure of damages is the difference between the amount the surveyor valued the house at, and what it would actually have been worth with the defects. This may not always cover the cost of repairs, depending on the state of the property market when the property was purchased. In a booming market buyers will pay over the odds even for properties with significant defects. Alternatively the RICS operate a dispute resolution service, which could save you time and legal fees – see website.

turn out to require expensive remedial treatment. It takes a very honest contractor to tell you they've checked the property and found that no work is necessary.

Damp-proofing and timber treatments for rot and beetle (woodworm) are normally carried out by the same 'timber and damp contractor'. The industry has a trade body, the BWPDA. By all means obtain quotes for treatment, but if the problem is not serious try living with it for a while before paying good money for unnecessary work.

The main reason for such consternation about rising damp in walls is that timber floor joists in contact with them are prone to rot, which over time can ultimately lead to collapse. That said, true rising damp or active beetle infestation is extremely rare, and a good surveyor should be able to explain the likely level of risk. In many period properties it is quite normal to find a certain amount of damp and some old beetle boreholes. What may *appear* to be rising damp is often caused by something completely different – such as condensation, leaking gutters, defective windowsills or high ground levels. To check whether it's really a problem, it's worth lifting floorboards adjacent to a damp wall to see if the timber floor joists are OK. A good flow of air under timber ground floors is important to prevent rot, so check that there are sufficient airbricks in the walls near ground level, and that they aren't blocked. If

22 | WHEN THINGS GO WRONG

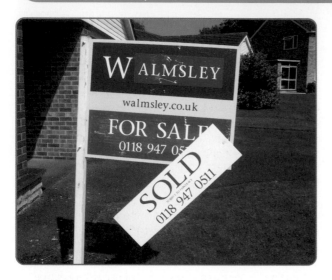

This would be a much shorter book if we only concentrated on the things that *can't* go wrong. In truth, no matter how experienced you are at dealing in property, there's always something nasty that can jump out and bite you. The trick is to see it coming and deal with it promptly (after having a bit of a rant at anyone within shouting distance, obviously). A lot of problems are simply down to poor communication. Which is why, when disaster strikes, you often find yourself shouting 'Why didn't they tell about us this *weeks* ago?'

If you have to blame anything, blame the system. Getting safely to exchange of contracts is rather like crossing a bridge in a storm. Many countries have robust modern structures designed to achieve a smooth and successful transaction. We, on the other hand, have to

make do with an ancient rope bridge sagging precariously above the rapids. Despite this, the odds of reaching the other side without plunging to your doom are still in your favour. But should you slip en route, the chances of success can be boosted by applying the following tried and tested remedies. Often a small amount of compromise and some skilful renegotiation is all that's required to save the day.

Renegotiating

Most problems ultimately boil down to money. But trying to renegotiate an already done deal is never easy. The only genuine justification is where important new evidence has come to light since the offer was agreed. Perhaps you have belatedly discovered that a particularly gruesome murder took place at the property some years ago (prior to redecoration). More likely the need to renegotiate would be down to the extra expense of fixing defects spotted by your surveyor. Or perhaps the mortgage valuation has come in lower than the agreed purchase price. The surveyor or solicitor may also have pointed out drawbacks with the location that you weren't aware of, such as flight paths, electrical substations, or vandalism.

Either way, the first course of action is to have a chat with your surveyor or solicitor to get the facts straight. If you still want to proceed, the problem will need to be quantified by being translated into a sum of money, for example by obtaining estimates for the cost of repairs (although some things are obviously harder to put a price on than others). It's then a question of negotiating a revised price to reflect the cost and hassle of sorting things out.

There is, of course, an art to negotiating. This might boil down to the fact that when you originally made the offer, you weren't aware of whatever the problem is – let's say the plague of gerbils inhabiting the soil pipe. This will involve you in considerable unforeseen extra expense estimated at £5,000, which now needs to be factored into the purchase price.

It helps to be polite and to calmly justify your position. Of course you're really making an implied threat that you'll pull out unless a suitable compromise can be reached. This could come as something of a shock to the sellers, who may need time to consider the changed situation. It might be best to broach the subject via their agent so that an overly defensive first reaction on their part doesn't muddy the waters. An important tactic when negotiating is to always leave the door open, so that it's easy for the other side to call you back later and co-operate without losing face.

Deciding whether to proceed

If the sellers simply refuse to budge, or will only accept a small reduction in price, you then need to consider whether you still want to proceed. This will depend on how easy it would be for you to start over – to find, and then buy, an equivalent property for less money. Your calculations should take into account all the expense and hassle of pulling out. When you consider the potential loss of your time, the wasted fees and especially the risk of losing the people who are buying your property, the better option is normally to stay the course and stick with the devil you know. After all, there's no guarantee that your next purchase will go any more smoothly. If you can get at least some degree of compromise to reflect your concerns, through a partially renegotiated price, it may be better to see things through to the bitter end, (albeit through gritted teeth).

What can go wrong?

The aim of this chapter is to identify the things that can go wrong, and show what can often be done to save the day. The most common ills that afflict the house-purchase process are:

- The seller changing their mind and pulling out
- Problems with the chain
- Gazumping and gazundering
- Mortgage and survey problems
- Legal problems

The seller pulls out
The single most common reason for sales falling through is a simple change

of mind by one side or the other. If you're on the receiving end of such a reversal of fortune all you can reasonably do is find out what motive lies behind their decision – which may not actually be as simple as it sounds. If their estate agent doesn't know, or pretends not to, contact the sellers direct.

Of course, there are a million reasons why we humans change our minds – not all of them entirely rational. One common reason for sellers pulling out is that they've hit problems with the property that they're buying. Perhaps they couldn't get the mortgage they'd anticipated (see 'Mortgage problems' below), or maybe their survey has frightened the life out of them with the careless use of killer words such as 'asbestos' or ' beetle infestation'.

So to stand any chance of solving the problem, you first need to get to the bottom of things and ascertain their true reason for withdrawing. In order to elicit a more fulsome response and avoid 'yes'/'no' answers, it can help to ask 'open questions' – ie ones that begin with 'what', 'how', 'who', 'when' or 'why'.

To see through superficial excuses and ultimately ascertain the truth, it may help to employ 'digging techniques', a method hailing from the world of advertising sales. For example, suppose the sellers initially say the reason they changed their mind is because they now won't be able to move out in time to meet the agreed completion date. This can be tested to see if it's true or just an excuse by replying 'I quite understand, but if this wasn't a problem and you *could* move out in time, would you still want to proceed?' If they then come up with another possible excuse, try the same technique: '...but suppose this wasn't a problem, what then?' Ultimately it should be possible to identify their real reason for pulling out. Hopefully this can then be addressed and it may be possible to work out a solution. If the moving date really is the big issue, then you could perhaps offer to go into a hotel for a few days perhaps sharing the cost 50/50, or move in with friends or relatives. A good estate agent can be invaluable in holding deals together in these circumstances.

A break in the chain
Of all the things that can go wrong, a break in the chain is the one you have least control over. The chain comprises a string of individual deals, downwards from the person who's buying your house and upwards from the person that you're buying from. The longer this chain is, the greater the chance of trouble occurring with one of these deals somewhere along the line.

A typical chain might comprise about three or four linked transactions, but in some cases there could be as many as ten. At the bottom there will often be a first-time buyer or a buy-to-let investor, perhaps purchasing a flat.

First-time buyers commonly require very large mortgages as they may have relatively low incomes and minimal savings to cover deposits and fees. So there's a greater risk of problems with funding. For example, mortgage calculations can be totally wrecked in the event of the surveyor 'downvaluing' the property. On the plus side, the person buying at the bottom of your chain isn't, by definition, dependent on selling a property.

Estate agents know that the chance of things going wrong is far greater where buyers haven't yet sold their own properties, and will be wary of advising their clients to accept offers from such buyers.

Obviously, it's very much in the interest of all the estate agents involved to nurture all the individual transactions along the chain, since a fracture in any individual link could cause the whole thing to fall apart, with their commission sucked down the plughole. Of course, some agents are better than others at 'sales progressing' and if things go wrong should be able to help pinpoint where the problem lies. As with your own transaction, fixing a problem elsewhere in the chain is often a matter of negotiating financial compromises. In an ideal world everyone in the chain would be willing to club together to help pay to fix a breakage further down – because it's ultimately cheaper to do this than having to start all over again.

In slow market conditions there is more chance of your move being jeopardised because of problems at the bottom of the chain. Some sellers have solved the problem by taking direct action – stepping in and actually buying the property that's causing the problem. Once the logjam is busted, it should allow the sale of your house to proceed as planned, which in turn should leave you free to buy. But taking such heroic action would probably mean having to arrange a buy-to-let mortgage with a 25 per cent or larger cash deposit. And becoming a landlord will mean taking a long-term view on owning property as an investment (see Chapter 24). Of course, your noble act will also benefit everyone else in the chain by preventing the whole thing collapsing. So if time permits, the various estate agents involved may be willing to show their appreciation by drumming up contributions to alleviate your financial pain. But naturally the more people involved the more complex and slow this process becomes.

Gazumping and gazundering

As we have seen, the big problem with the home-buying system is that it's such a long, drawn-out process with no binding commitment until exchange of contracts. This is bad enough when the property market is reasonably stable. But when house prices are wildly accelerating or, alternatively, dropping like a stone, one side or the other can eventually be tempted to go back on an agreed deal and 'renegotiate'. Adding fuel to the flames, of course, will be the usual frenzied media speculation, either hyping the market with stories of rocketing prices and unbridled greed, or spreading doom and gloom with predictions of imminent house price crash Armageddon.

Such antics may not be illegal, but they're widely regarded as dirty tricks and can easily cause a deal to collapse. One obvious way to minimise risk on both counts is to speed up progress and swiftly reach exchange.

■ In a falling market

The strength or weakness of the market will dictate which side has the upper hand. As we saw in Part 1, in a slow property market where house prices are falling buyers sometimes worry that the value of the property has diminished in the weeks since their offer was originally accepted. This can lead to them later attempting to reduce their offer, an act known as 'gazundering'.

As a buyer, you may feel that the prospect of gazundering is really the seller's problem. But it's still best avoided because it can create such bad feeling that it ultimately derails the purchase, as well as being unethical and highly stressful.

The obvious solution is to take future market conditions into account at the time when you negotiate your offer. Although this is easier said than done, covering yourself for any likely short-term fall in prices over the coming eight to ten weeks should put your mind at rest. So if the market's dropping at, say, roughly one per cent a month, on a £250,000 house you'd be looking at negotiating around £5,000 off the price to cover you during this period.

To gauge likely market performance over coming months check the Halifax, Nationwide or Land Registry websites. Negotiating a lower price when making an offer can be justified to the seller as a kind of insurance policy against future gazundering, a guarantee against last-minute stunts.

■ In a rising market

When house prices are rising, the property market favours sellers. In some cases there may be several buyers competing to secure a single property. 'Gazumping' is the disease of booming property markets, and the curse of honest purchasers. So how does this come about?

Under the Estate Agency Act, agents are legally obliged to pass on all offers they receive to their clients, even if a property's already under offer. If prices have risen strongly in the weeks since your offer was accepted, the seller could be tempted to accept another higher offer. If this happens to you, you've been gazumped.

To reduce the risk of rival offers materialising later, it's common for buyers to insist that the property in question is taken off the market as a condition of their offer.

However, there's still a risk that someone who's already viewed it before you made your offer could come back with a late bid. Plus there's nothing to stop a private purchaser bypassing the agent and approaching the seller direct.

The prospect of a higher offer can be extremely tempting for a seller, particularly if negotiations to this point have been aggressive and you've somehow riled them in the process. One person who may be on your side, however, is the estate agent, who may know from bitter experience that a bird in the hand is often worth two in the bush. They may therefore be keen for the current deal to go through in order to secure their commission sooner rather than later. Plus this higher, rival offer could be from a deranged speculator, a man of straw who turns out not to have two pennies to rub together. So if you're approaching exchange of contracts, the agent will most likely caution their client against accepting the rival offer, unless the other person can prove they are proceedable.

You normally discover that you've been gazumped when, the agent phones you one fine day and casually announces that the seller will sell to another purchaser unless you stump up an extra ten grand. You may not even be given the option if you're informed point blank that they've suddenly decided to sell to someone else for a higher price. Even the Sopranos would blush at such a blatant blackmail attempts.

Part of the problem here is good old-fashioned human psychology. For example, when a property sells for its full asking price directly it's put on the market, there's a good chance the sellers will at some point start to think that they should have asked a higher price. 'We must be selling it too cheap, it's obviously worth a lot more because it was snapped up so quickly.'

So what can you do? One wise precaution is to bite the bullet and plan for the worst by setting aside some emergency funds, such as the money you'd earmarked for furnishings or building an extension. In the heat of the moment, it's easy to forget that in a strongly rising market the property may indeed have significantly increased in value.

If you play ball and agree to raise your offer, albeit reluctantly, you will have to absorb the increase, unless of course you pull the same stunt with your buyers. Like a bizarre pyramid selling scam, this would put you in the unfortunate position of passing on the blackmailing virus. Logically, however, in such a situation there is scope for financial creativity. Suppose you refused to raise your offer and instead pulled out, the entire chain would probably collapse, and everyone else in the chain would suffer a loss. To prevent such a catastrophe, it's not impossible that all the other buyers and sellers would be willing to stump up a couple of grand each, saving the day by sharing your pain. But it is rather unlikely. In reality, such last-minute tricks often backfire as people often refuse on principle to consent to blackmail.

■ Tips to avoid being gazumped

There are a number of practical steps you can take to protect yourself:

☐ Don't make an offer to buy until your own property's under offer.

☐ Exchange contracts as soon as possible by getting your funding sorted early and chasing progress.

☐ Get schmoozing – build a good personal relationship with the seller and keep them regularly informed of progress.

☐ When making your offer, confirm that the agreed price includes any likely market price increases up to exchange.

☐ As a condition of your offer, formally request that the agent withdraws the property from the market, to discourage other offers being submitted. It should even be removed from websites for those who search under 'sold' properties, and For Sale or SOLD boards should be removed. Only where a purchaser hasn't yet sold their own home is it reasonable for sellers to keep a property on the market once under offer.

☐ Ask the agents if they have a policy on gazumping and whether their clients have confirmed they will not accept later offers.

☐ Insurance can be arranged that pays out if the deal falls through after your offer has been accepted.

■ Lock-outs

A lock-out agreement may sound like something from 1970s trade union folklore, but is actually a very useful device enabling both parties to inject some certainty into the process.

A lock-out (aka an exclusivity agreement) essentially asks the seller to take their property off the market after you have agreed the price for a certain number of weeks, and not to accept offers from anyone else during this period. Such a deal requires both parties to stick to a strict timetable.

If the property is being marketed by more than one agent, make sure they are fully aware that it's been withdrawn and is no longer on the market. Other agent(s) employed on a joint or multiple agency basis could be tempted to undermine the successful agent's deal to scoop up the commission, and so may take some persuading.

In practice, lock-outs are not always quite the panacea they seem to be. For one thing, it can take a surprisingly long time for both parties to agree all the terms. Some sellers may not always have sufficient spare funds to commit as a deposit (if most of their money is tied up in the house they're selling). And as a buyer you need to consider what would happen if your own sale fell through and you were locked-in to your purchase.

■ Pre-contract deposits

An alternative to a lock-out agreement is for both parties to put some money on the table as a deposit. The way this works is that the buyer and seller each fork out a few thousand pounds (typically 1.5 per cent of the agreed price) to an independent solicitor. If either party subsequently pulls out without good reason they lose their deposit. Of course, the devil is in the detail and a lot will depend on how you define 'good reason' – for anyone wanting to pull out their reason is always good! Acceptable reasons should therefore be defined in the agreement, such as where the mortgage valuation values the property at a lower price, or a survey unearths a previously unknown serious defect. The beauty of this arrangement is that the seller knows the buyer won't change their mind at the last minute or pull a stunt; and the buyer, having spent hundreds of pounds on legal and survey fees, knows the seller won't walk away and accept a higher offer. Perhaps this should be compulsory for all transactions.

Mortgage problems

The most commonly encountered problems for home buyers relate to mortgage funding. There are two main areas where problems can arise and seriously hamper a house purchase – those relating to personal credit or income references, and those relating to the property you're buying.

■ Income and credit references

Employment references

As we saw in Chapters 14 and 20, delayed income references can sometimes hold up your mortgage offer. So it's worth chasing your employer and checking with your lender that the forms have been filled in correctly. Problems also sometimes arise where your income includes bonuses, overtime and commission, because lenders may only take half their value into consideration. The solution may be to persuade your employer to guarantee this income, or to find a lender with more generous lending criteria.

Credit problems

To make sure that you are a good risk and do not have a history of running up debts and not repaying loans, one of the first thing lenders do is to check your status with a credit reference agency. The problem is, that the information they hold isn't always 100 per cent accurate. For example, your credit reference could also be negatively

---

Buttering up

Achieving a successful purchase isn't just about money and lawyers. Applying a little psychology can make a huge difference to whether a transaction succeeds or stumbles at one of the many hurdles along the way. So it's smart to get the seller on your side. This is the cheapest and easiest way of inoculating yourself from the gazumping virus. Your strategy should cover the following:

- Offer the full asking price – and prove you have your mortgage funding already arranged.
- Don't fuss over details – forget quibbling over curtains and lightshades.
- Plan your schedule to fit with the sellers' timeframe for moving out.
- Establish a friendly relationship – use the power of guilt so that the seller would feel bad by considering another offer.
- Keep in regular contact so that they know you're 100 per cent committed throughout. Good communication will also help detect early warning signs of trouble after your offer's been accepted.

affected if someone else living at your address or a previous occupant has run up debts. By applying to see your file and proving you have no connection with the other party, you can request that a 'correction statement' is placed on your file. If you have a recent CCJ (*ie* within six years), mainstream lenders will normally automatically decline a mortgage unless it's been 'satisfied' (fully paid). In some cases you can appeal against a CCJ and apply to have it removed. At worst you could apply to a lender specialising in 'impaired credit', but this will inevitably mean paying higher fees and a more expensive interest rate (see Chapter 14).

Even if your references are OK, a loan can still be refused should you not achieve a high enough 'credit score'. This is the second major check that lenders make and the longer you have been resident at your current address or with your present employer the more brownie points you should score. They will also take into account your occupation, your age, whether you have a home telephone and how long you have been with your bank. Self-employed people or those on short-term contracts may score fewer points as they are not such an attractive risk. You will either pass or fail depending on the total points scored.

If a lender does turn you down for credit they should explain whether it's due to credit scoring or as a result of information obtained from a credit reference agency. Brokers normally know why applications are declined. If your application is refused without giving any reason, it's probably down to the credit score. Fortunately different lenders operate different systems, so the fact that you have been turned down by one will not necessarily mean that you will be declined by others.

Electoral register
Another common reason for being turned down for credit is where the applicant's name recorded on the Electoral Roll doesn't match the address they've given. Because councils make money by selling our personal electoral details to bothersome junk mail organisations, it can be tempting to avoid registering. But nothing rings alarm bells at Banking

HQ quite like missing names or addresses. If you know this to be the case, perhaps because you only recently moved to your present address from outside the area, it's important to make it known before applying. A lender may instead be placated with a mix of sworn statements, passports and utility bills. It's worth checking with a credit reference agency that your name actually appears on the electoral register/voters' roll at your current address.

■ The property

Lending criteria
Back in Chapter 16 it was mentioned that some types of property are not acceptable to certain mortgage lenders. This should only be an issue in rare cases where buildings are of non-conventional construction. Different banks have their own particular hang-ups, and most prefer properties with walls traditionally built from masonry – *ie* brick, stone or blockwork (which could be rendered or clad with tiles etc). Modern timber-framed properties are also acceptable

Photos: wikimedia

Left: 'Cornish' PRC semis
Above left: 'Unity' PRC Council houses, now mostly re-clad
Above right: Mortgage lenders often decline flats in blocks higher than 5 stories

since they have a masonry outer skin to the main walls. Lenders also favour buildings with traditional pitched roofs clad with tiles or slates – which covers the vast majority of UK properties.

Concrete wonders

Problems sometimes arise with ex-Council houses built in the late 1940s and 1950s where their main walls are constructed from pre-manufactured concrete slabs (known as 'PRC' or pre-reinforced concrete). There are several weird and wonderful varieties of terraced and semi-detached houses built during this era, with crazy names like Airey, Cornish, Woolaway, Unity, Hawksely, Howland and Reema Hollow Panel. Designed as a short-term solution, these houses were effectively the bigger brothers of the 'prefab' bungalows of the same era.

By the 1980s it was discovered that in some buildings the concrete was becoming chemically eroded, and the final nail in the coffin came with the Housing Defects Act 1984 which classified 20 types of PRC houses as defective (although many continued to be let to council tenants). Today, unless suitably upgraded, banks will normally refuse to lend on these buildings, making them 'unmortgageable', which is the kiss of death when it comes to selling.

The good news is that such properties are normally acceptable once they've been 'suitably upgraded to PRC standards' – which generally means being re-clad with a brick outer wall. However, with a pair of semi-detached houses normally both will need to have been upgraded for either one to form acceptable security.

But PRC wasn't the only type of post-war construction to challenge convention. Estates of prefabricated steel-framed 'BISF' (British Iron & Steel Federation) properties sprang up, their thin walls clad with metal sheathing and render, and their steel-framed roofs clad with asbestos sheeting. These too are unmortgageable today unless suitably upgraded. A more robust type of construction appeared in the form of houses with thick 'poured concrete' walls. Tough as old boots, there were two main types. 'Wimpey No Fines', which are generally acceptable to mortgage lenders, and 'Laing Easiform', which are acceptable to some lenders but not all.

Other problem properties that may not be mortgageable include older timber-framed houses (built prior to circa 1960). It may also include homes of 'scout hut' construction, *ie* where timber-frame walls are clad externally with a non-masonry finish, such as timber clapboarding. Despite being very common in North America, some consider such houses to be potentially vulnerable to the damp British climate. Other objects of lenders' scorn include flats in blocks higher than five storeys, houses where the entire roof is flat (such as some 1930s classics), properties devoid of mains services, and anything located in areas that are seriously at risk of subsidence, landslip, mining collapse or flooding.

If it looks like your chosen type of property could be contentious for your lender, be sure to notify them before they instruct the mortgage valuation. Be aware, however, that staff working for banks are sometimes unaware of such details in their own company's lending policies, and may need to check with their valuation department to save wasting your time and money paying for unnecessary valuation fees.

If you're buying a house with an exotic form of construction, a good broker should know which lenders will find it acceptable. If a bank does decline a mortgage on this basis, there may well be other lenders who will happily accept it.

But even if you succeed in getting a mortgage on an unconventional property, consider this: if more lenders

Steel framed BISF house being re-clad

decide to blacklist these types of houses in years to come, it may become virtually impossible for buyers to raise a mortgage on it by the time you come to sell, drastically narrowing the property's appeal to only cash buyers (thereby massively slashing the value).

Late mortgage valuation

When the mortgage surveyor duly arrives at the seller's door one fine day to carry out the valuation inspection, it should provide some welcome reassurance. It confirms that the sale is proceeding satisfactorily and reminds them that you're a serious buyer, and not just stringing them along. The valuation should normally be instructed within a couple of weeks of submitting your mortgage application, but can sometimes be delayed when employment or credit references are slow or require clarification.

Surveyors acting for lenders have strict turnaround targets, so the bank should receive their (electronic) copy of the valuation report within a mere 24 hours of the visit.

However, this very much depends on bank staff providing accurate access information in the first place – it is not unusual for mistyped contact names, erroneous phone numbers and even wrong addresses to be issued. It also depends on the surveyor being able to gain access to the property. So where sellers have disappeared on a fortnight's holiday without leaving a key, or are just plain awkward, things will temporarily grind to a halt.

Late mortgage offer

One of the main reasons for hold-ups is a delay in receiving the formal mortgage offer. You should receive it within about five to ten days of the mortgage valuation being done, unless any significant problems were highlighted (the majority of mortgage valuations are plain sailing). So after about a week, phone the lender or broker and push whoever is responsible for processing your application until it's received. Actively chase each stage of the process. You may be a little unlucky and have applied during a busy period (although this, of course, is the banking world's universal excuse for incompetence).

The property is downvalued

As we saw in previous chapters the size of mortgage that a bank is prepared to lend is expressed as a percentage of the purchase price *or* the valuation, whichever is the *lower*. So if the property is valued lower than the agreed price, this 'loan-to-value' (LTV) ratio will effectively increase in relation to this lower value. Once LTV ratios rise above about 75 per cent they are regarded by lenders as higher risk, and you may get stung with a higher mortgage rate or an expensive 'higher lending charge'. Should this happen to you, there are a number of options to consider.

First, it's entirely possible that a 'downvaluation' is correct. The price you've agreed to pay may be way over the odds, given the location or condition of the property. The surveyor may have spotted expensive defects of which the estate agent and seller are blissfully unaware. So this could turn out to be a blessing in disguise, justifying a reduction in price and saving you money. But this can spark acrimonious attempts at price renegotiation between buyers and sellers that ultimately cause the deal to fall apart.

Alternatively you could bring the LTV ratio back into balance by reducing the amount being borrowed, but that could mean having to find more money for the deposit. For example, if you're buying a house for £250,000 with a 90 per cent loan of £225,000, you will have to finance a deposit of £25,000. But if the surveyor values it at £230,000, a 90 per cent loan will only provide £207,000, so to make up the balance of the £250,000 purchase price you will need a larger deposit of £43,000 – a substantial increase (unless you renegotiate the price).

The other alternative is to take the bull by the horns and challenge the valuation. But bear in mind that surveyors don't just pluck figures out of thin air. They need to justify valuations with supporting evidence of at least three recent comparable sales, adjusted to reflect the subject property's condition, location and size as well as current market trends. Valuing, however, is not an exact science, and surveyors operate within a margin of error, generally not downvaluing within five per cent of the agreed sale price. So suppose you've agreed to pay £200,000, and the surveyor actually thinks the place is only worth £194,000 (*ie* three per cent less); they would normally give it the benefit of the doubt and round it up.

Coming up with an accurate valuation is clearly a lot easier where the adjoining streets are stocked with dozens of virtually identical houses. Problems are more likely to arise with unusual 'one-off' properties, or where an especially high price has been agreed, and a lack of good sales evidence may encourage the surveyor to adopt a cautious approach resulting in a lower valuation.

To challenge a valuation retrospectively, you normally need to come up with some compelling sales evidence that supports a higher value.

In most cases the surveyor should be willing to reopen the case and consider fresh evidence, revising the valuation if necessary. The seller's estate agent should be able to assist.

At worst you might be able to persuade the mortgage

lender to instruct another valuation from a different locally-based surveyor in the hope that they may come up with a more optimistic figure – but there's no guarantee this would actually achieve a different result.

The mortgage lender keeps a retention

A typical bank's mortgage report form will include a box labelled 'Essential Repairs' that the surveyor has to fill in. Depending on the condition of the property, and the attitude of the surveyor writing the report, this may include one or two expensive-sounding repairs along with a recommendation to keep a hefty retention of a few thousand pounds. The extent to which such issues are flagged up will also very much depend on which mortgage lender you're using – some intensely dislike retentions, others positively encourage them. As a rule, the bigger High Street names tend to be more relaxed in their approach than small 'daytime TV lenders'.

At the end of the day it's up to the bank's underwriters whether they keep a retention, by 'holding back' part of your loan. If they decide to impose this on you, a sum of between £1,000 and £5,000 is normally retained until repairs identified in the report have been done or specialist reports obtained, whereupon a re-inspection by the surveyor may be instructed. In practice lenders rarely bother to check, and may release the funds upon receipt of an estimate for repair works.

This is rather a strange way of doing business, since by keeping back a few thousand pounds for the cost of repairing a flat roof the lender is withholding the money that you may well need to pay for the works! Some more enlightened lenders will simply require an 'undertaking' – a written promise that you will sort out the listed repairs. Otherwise you could perhaps bridge the cost by paying for the repairs on your credit card and then immediately apply for the retention to be released before the card payment is due – although obviously this depends on getting the timing right.

Your survey finds significant defects

As per the previous chapter, any major defects noted in

your survey will need to be translated into hard cash. This means arranging builders' quotes or obtaining specialist reports, typically for things like drains, heating systems and electrics. Structural engineer's report are occasionally requested to confirm whether movement such as cracking is 'progressive'. Based on the total cost of these works, you may have grounds to renegotiate the price.

However, not every minor blemish gives buyers the right to demand a price reduction. Some defects are fairly obvious. Things like seriously off-putting decorations and prehistoric plumbing, would have already been factored into the asking price. So if you later try to renegotiate on the basis that 'the windows need replacing', the seller will quite reasonably point out that this should have been clear when you made your original offer.

Buildings insurance problems

As we saw earlier, properties that have been underpinned often carry an indelible stigma that can lead to possible insurance problems. Insurers rate postcode areas according to the likely risk of subsidence – which includes most of southern England with its shrinkable clay subsoils. Subsidence became the *bête noire* of the insurance industry after a tsunami of insurance claims as buildings cracked and subsided following the long hot summers of the mid-1970s.

But this was before something even scarier became a major issue. For insurers, flooding is the new subsidence. Postcode areas are now also weighted to reflect the risk of flooding, and properties built on flood plains can be more expensive to insure. See links for flood maps on website.

The normal advice in such situations is to take over the current buildings policy from the current owner. However, you could try asking for a reduction in purchase price as compensation for paying more expensive insurance premiums over future years.

Medical reports

Lenders sometimes insist on you taking out life insurance cover as a condition of the mortgage. This may apply in cases where applicants are of a certain age or have an exciting medical history. Or it may simply be a back-door way of subsidising a competitive headline interest rate. Either way, the cover may depend on obtaining a medical report, which should take up to about ten days to arrange.

Even if your health is poor, most risks can be insured at a price. A specialist insurance broker's advice will be needed.

Legal problems

After blaming the banks, it's customary for solicitors to be put in the dock for the inexplicably long delays that seem to afflict anyone buying or selling property. Back in Chapter 4 we stressed the importance of selecting the right conveyancer. This is because a good solicitor can apply sound professional judgement, allowing matters to proceed where a pedantic colleague would make a mountain out of a molehill. Once stuck with a quill-wielding doom merchant, however your options are limited. Changing solicitors halfway through is not normally realistic because of long delays in getting documents transferred.

Solicitors do get very busy and may need chasing up, so it can help to regularly communicate by phone, fax or email so that your case hopefully stays somewhere near the top of the pile. It often helps to form a good relationship with the secretary – who may not be used to clients being friendly and polite! On the other hand you may be confronted with frosty receptionists who can kill with a single glance from 200 yards. However, from the solicitor's point of view, constant chasing can be counter-productive. If they took calls from all their numerous clients on a daily basis, they'd never get any work done!

Even as the winds of e-conveyancing blast away the cobwebs, some lawyers can still be guilty of unnecessary tardiness and unapproachability. Many clients simply want to know why things are taking so long. But they may not have bargained for the profession's well-proven defences against any customers impertinent enough to expect swift results. Quaint legal terminology may be employed to flummox and deter the clients. For example, the response 'we are still pursuing our enquiries on title' is not tremendously enlightening for most of us wrestling with an urgent sale or purchase.

Listed below are a number of the more common legal problems that can arise and cause delays, together with possible solutions:

■ Delays in obtaining 'office copy entries'

Before preparing the draft contract, the seller's solicitors will need to obtain 'office copy entries' by applying to the Land Registry (except in rare cases where properties are unregistered). These should be included in the HIP, and be readily available. Otherwise delays may occur when solicitors wait before applying in order to avoid paying fees should the sale fall through.

■ Delays investigating title

'We're investigating title' is another potential cause of delay. Here again the ownership of the property should be confirmed in the HIP, and is only likely to be a serious concern if the property you're buying is one of the very few that is not registered.

■ Delays in receiving the draft contract

The purchaser's solicitors should receive the draft contract from the seller's solicitor within a week or so of the purchase being agreed. Delays could be due to difficulties obtaining documents, as described above, or simply due to good old-fashioned incompetence, and should be chased via the seller or agent. Sellers have a key role to play here too. The process is greatly assisted if they swiftly return the answers to the pre-contract enquiries to their solicitor, and make sure they provide payment as early as possible for initial costs such as fees for obtaining 'office copy entries'.

■ Unregistered title

As described in Chapter 20, there are still some rare cases where the title, or ownership, of a property is still 'unregistered'. This might be the case for example where the house in question has been in the same family for donkeys' years. Unlike with registered properties, ownership is not guaranteed by the state, so your solicitor must embark on an in-depth trawl through ancient conveyances to prove title. In actual practice, your solicitor needn't put on their archaeological hat for too long because the legal requirement is simply to find a good 'root of title' of not less than 15 years (which usually means having a 'good root' back in time). However, should a dispute arise over the seller's title, it could drag on for months, or even years, in which case you may be well advised to find another property.

■ Delays in obtaining the title deeds

For unregistered properties, the seller's solicitor will need to obtain the title deeds before they can prepare the draft contract. Traditionally these were held by the seller's mortgage lender, or where the mortgage had been paid off lodged with a bank or a solicitor or simply stashed under the floorboards. Normally mortgage lenders could provide these within about a week. But if the deeds have been lost, there could be serious delays whilst the sellers have to prove their title to the property.

■ Disputes over the terms of the contract

Draft contracts are normally based on standard templates with standard clauses. Nothing too exciting normally occurs, unless the seller's solicitor decides to introduce non-standard clauses. Suggested amendments are then ping-ponged back and forth from one side to the other for weeks on end, sometimes with a degree of personal antagonism developing between the 'learned friends' on either side. It's important to be kept aware of delays resulting from difficulties in 'agreeing terms of the contract'. As the customer you have the right to have a clear explanation. Problems often relate to simple issues concerning completion dates or fixtures and fittings, and matters can sometimes be resolved with a quick phone call to the seller or their agent.

■ Delays in obtaining local searches

'We haven't completed the searches' has become a stock response from solicitors questioned about delays. However, now that searches form part of the HIP the risk of delays has been substantially reduced. Where your solicitor or mortgage lender insists on an independent search a lot of time can be saved by applying for it as soon as possible, preferably within the first week (although should the purchase fall through this means your search fee will be lost).

In the event of a last-minute crisis, there is a short cut. A super-quick 'personal search' can be undertaken. This normally means paying a specialist search agent to urgently traipse around the various council departments, rather than leaving it to an overworked council employee. In such cases an insurance policy is also normally required to protect you and your lender should something important have been omitted from the personal search. Note, however, that your mortgage lender must have agreed to this type of search, otherwise there's no option but to stick with the traditional plain vanilla variety. (See Chapter 20.)

Who pays for the upkeep of a shared driveway?

■ Delays in answering preliminary enquiries

One of the first jobs for the buyer's solicitor is to submit a long list of questions to the seller's solicitor. These are standard questions printed on a form and include availability of mains services; responsibility for boundaries and any associated disputes; guarantees for work; NHBC warranties; planning and building regs consents; and details of fixtures and fittings. There may be some extra questions added below the standard ones.

Traditionally these are met with blame-deflecting answers such as 'Not known' or 'Please rely on your own enquiries'. But a seller who makes a false declaration can be liable to being sued for damages. The most problematic questions often centre around the following:

Boundary disputes

Minor disagreements between neighbours about boundaries have a habit of flaring up into open warfare, and may even be the reason your seller is selling. Sellers are legally obliged to declare any such disputes, although they will obviously want to downplay the significance.

If any problems come to light it's best to arrange a

True story

Josh was selling a recently built mews house, 2a Soames Street (right), in a Victorian suburb. A week before exchange the buyer's solicitor discovered that a £5,000 charge for an 'improvement grant' was registered against the property, as shown in the Council search documents. This required repayment of the grant in full to the Council upon completion of the sale.

But Josh had no knowledge of any improvement grant. How could this apply to a three-year-old property? After some detective work it transpired that the search had been carried out against the wrong property – the neighbouring Victorian house, number 2 Soames Street, which had recently benefited from grant-assisted roof works. With only a week to go until exchange the buyers had to hastily commission a last-minute personal search, this time of the correct property.

meeting with the neighbours in question to ascertain whether this is a deal-breaker. Perhaps the issue will be of no consequence to you, or maybe a compromise can be reached. Sometimes personal chemistry and pride has a lot to do with such disputes. Any agreement to resolve the problem should be confirmed in writing and witnessed.

Restrictive covenants

Suppose you're buying a property on a small housing development. It may be that the original developer put a restriction on the deeds of all the houses preventing them being extended, for fear that ugly extensions would later disfigure the estate. If you're thinking of building even a small conservatory in future this needs to be resolved. Normally an indemnity insurance policy can be arranged within a couple of weeks to swiftly resolve such problems. (See chapter 20).

Planning and Building Regulations

When planning consent is granted for new housing developments it is quite common for 'permitted development rights' to be removed. So if the house you're buying has such a restriction, it could hinder your plans to

But did they get Planning and Building Regs consent?

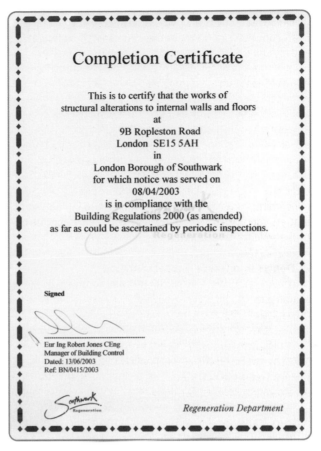

Completion Certificate

This is to certify that the works of
structural alterations to internal walls and floors
at
9B Ropleston Road
London SE15 5AH
in
London Borough of Southwark
for which notice was served on
08/04/2003
is in compliance with the
Building Regulations 2000 (as amended)
as far as could be ascertained by periodic inspections.

Signed

Eur Ing Robert Jones CEng
Manager of Building Control
Dated: 13/06/2003
Ref: BN/0415/2003

Regeneration Department

TP(Permit)

SOUTHWARK COUNCIL

TOWN AND COUNTRY PLANNING ACT 1990 (as amended)

Council

PLANNING PERMISSION

Applicant Mr Ian Roples	LBS Registered Number 03-AP-0525
Date of Issue of this decision 29/04/2003	Case Number TP/2118-79

Planning Permission was GRANTED for the following development:
    Conversion of single dwellinghouse into 2 self-contained flats.

At: 9 Ropleston Road SE15

In accordance with application received on 06/03/2003

and Applicant's Drawing Nos. 001E, 002E, A1.0E, B2.0E, B3.0E, A1.0P, B2.0P, B3.0P & Site Plan

Subject to the following two conditions:
1   The development hereby permitted shall be begun before the end of five years from the date of this permission.

    Reason
    As required by Section 91 of the Town and Country Planning Act 1990.

2   The dwellings hereby permitted shall not be occupied before details of the arrangements for the storing of domestic refuse have been submitted to (2 copies) and approved by the local planning authority and the facilities approved have been provided and are available for use by the occupiers of the dwellings. The facilities shall thereafter be retained for refuse storage and the space used for no other purpose without the prior written consent of the Council as local planning authority.

    Reason
    In order that the Council may be satisfied that suitable facilities for the storage of refuse will be provided and retained in the interest of protecting the amenity of the site and the area in general from litter, odour and potential vermin/pest nuisance in accordance with Policy E.3.1: Protection of Amenity and Policy T.1.3: Design of Development and Conformity with Council's Standards and Controls of Southwark's Unitary Development Plan.

Signed   Andrew Cook
                            Development and Building Control Manager

Your attention is drawn to the notes accompanying this document

Any correspondence regarding this document should quote the Case Number and LBS Registered Number and be addressed to: Head of Development and Building Control, Council Offices, Chiltern, Portland Street, London SE17 2ES. Tel. No. 020 7525 5000

                                checked by

build a porch, conservatory, loft conversion or an extension. More commonly problems arise when existing extensions and alterations have been carried out without consent. Such omissions sometimes only come to light just before exchange, because no one bothered to check earlier. Surveyors normally flag up any potential concerns with statements such as 'The valuation assumes that all necessary local authority consents were obtained.' This should tip off the solicitor to check. If consents weren't obtained, it's normally possible to apply retrospectively. But this can take several weeks, and consent could still be refused or the unauthorised building works demolished. Which would be a bit of a bummer. However, the Council's right to take enforcement action lapses where four or more years have passed since construction (ten years for a breach of a planning condition) and two years after a breach of the Building Regs.

In such cases there are some possible solutions:

☐ Ask the sellers as early as possible whether written approval was granted for any extensions or structural works, or whether the works were small enough to be classed as 'permitted development'.

☐ Instruct a survey and ask the surveyor to comment on the quality of workmanship, and point out any defects or inadequacies. Hidden things like foundation depths can only be checked if you pay to have trial holes dug.

☐ To save time, an indemnity insurance policy can sometimes be arranged to compensate you should retrospective consent not be forthcoming. Compensation actually covers you against action by the local Building Consent Department for breach of building regulations. It does not cover or guarantee the quality of the work. So such policies don't actually solve the problem, but they can be a handy 'sticking plaster'.

Occupancy restrictions

Properties are sometimes subject to 'occupancy restrictions' imposed by the Council when they originally granted planning permission. If you come across a rural property at a bargain price, it may be because it's subject to an agricultural occupancy condition (AOC). This will normally be mentioned in the estate agent's details. As the name suggests, at least one adult occupier must be in agricultural employment (or their widow/er), but the details may be open to some interpretation. As a result the market appeal, and hence the value of such properties, will be considerably reduced. However, it is sometimes possible to make a successful planning application to lift such restrictions where you can prove that they are no longer relevant, dramatically boosting the value of the property.

Fixtures and fittings

As has already been mentioned back in Chapter 11, many a potential purchase has hit the rocks over the most trivial issues, with arguments raging over such things as

ownership of coat hooks and light fittings. But no matter how annoying the other side are, don't let this happen to you. Keep your eye on the big picture and be prepared to compromise on minor bits and pieces. Fortunately, in most cases such details should be clear from the outset because one of the first tasks when selling is to complete a detailed list of what's included and what isn't.

■ Insufficient funds to exchange

Your solicitor will not exchange contracts until they are in receipt of funds for the deposit. This is typically five or ten per cent of the purchase price, which means you now have to come up with the readies. They will also want proof of the existence of the full funds required at completion, hence the importance of the mortgage offer being received before exchange.

Problems sometimes arise where buyers suddenly realise their building society savings account is subject to a nasty penalty unless three weeks' notice is provided.

Paying by cheque is too slow and unpredictable, especially when insufficient time has been allowed for your cheque to clear into the solicitor's bank account. Transferring funds yourself via Internet banking can fall foul of daily maximum payment limits and still requires time for funds to clear. Payment can be made with a banker's draft, for which the bank charges a sizeable fee, or by telegraphic transfer of funds (TTF), for which there is also a fee. When you take the potential loss of interest into account, an instant TTF is often the cheaper option. If you need the money the same day try using CHAPS (Clearing House Automated Payments System) – again, paying a fee of about £25 may work out cheaper than losing interest over several days on a large amount of money.

■ Deposit sharing

Normally you find yourself as part of a chain of property deals. All these linked transactions need careful co-ordination so that, when the time comes, contracts can be exchanged simultaneously – which, given all the obstacles to success, is something of a minor miracle.

In most cases it should be possible to utilise the deposit money due from your purchaser towards the deposit that you're due to pay on the property you're buying. However some solicitors are not keen on such arrangements, so it should be verified in advance in case an alternative source of funds is needed at the critical moment.

■ Agreeing completion dates

Chains sometimes collapse because somehow a mutually acceptable completion date just cannot be agreed. There are some things you can do to help prevent such a problem arising:

☐ Provisionally agree your completion date as early as possible (but at the same time you need maintain some flexibility in case of delays with mortgages etc, so this is not 'set in stone', and you shouldn't book removals and time off work).

☐ Although completion often takes place a couple of weeks after exchange, it can be any time you agree. It can even be done simultaneously at the time of exchange, although this is not usually advisable unless you're 'chain free' (because there's nothing to stop the other side pulling out at the last minute, which can cause immense problems with aborted removals and mortgages). Sometimes a longer period of a month or more will suit everyone better.

☐ Consider moving into rented 'holiday accommodation'. It may mean moving home twice but that's still cheaper than paying abortive fees and starting all over again. You may even be able to get a contribution towards the costs if it makes the whole chain work.

Problems with leasehold properties

Though we looked at some of the complexities with flats and leasehold properties in Chapter 17 it's worth reiterating some of the issues that commonly cause problems:

Short lease

Unlike freeholds, leases slowly become less valuable over time, eventually reverting to the freeholder (or, more likely, their grandchildren) after the full original term has expired (commonly 99 or 125 years or 999 years). If the remaining lease term is now only 70 years or less it can cause problems when you come to sell some years later, so it's important to enquire as early as possible about the cost of

extending the lease (which could be £10,000 or more). The mortgage valuer will have assumed 'a reasonable remaining lease term' (ie more than 70 years). Otherwise the sale price may have to be renegotiated to reflect the cost, risk and hassle involved. If a leaseholder and freeholder can't agree on a reasonable price to renew or extend the lease, the leaseholder should be able to appeal to the Land Tribunal, who will decide the fair price that the freeholder must grant the lease extension. Professional advice is required as the rules can be quite complex.

Defective lease

Some older leases were badly drafted, which could cause problems for you as the new owner. Responsibility for the maintenance of communal areas in blocks of flats, shared gardens and garages etc should be clearly defined, but sometime isn't. If no one is officially responsible for maintenance it tends not to get done. The net result is that blocks of flats become unkempt and unpleasant to live in, and lose value. Your solicitor might suggest obtaining a 'deed of variation', which means getting the freeholder's permission to change the original terms of the lease. Needless to say, this can easily get bogged down over several months, so unless you're prepared to accept a degree of risk (hopefully in exchange for a reduced purchase price) it may be better to find somewhere else to buy.

Unpaid service charges

It's not unknown for freeholders to exploit their power by implementing hefty 'service charges' but fail to carry out much maintenance work. But should you, on the other hand, fail to pay the ground rent of service charges the freeholder can implement draconian powers and notify your mortgage lender. This is one reason why jointly owning the freehold and managing the block with the other leaseholders is a better option.

Before purchasing a leasehold property, the seller must pay all charges due. Your solicitor will therefore demand that the seller's solicitor pays all arrears up to completion from the proceeds of sale. But because landlord/ management companies are often slow to prepare the accounts and detailed estimates for the current year, it means that at completion no one may be truly sure how to fairly apportion these costs between the seller and the buyer. So where there's an obvious backlog of maintenance evident on a property you may want to negotiate a reduced price to reflect the likely future liabilities, expense and inconvenience.

23 | EXCHANGE AND COMPLETION

Photo: www.pickfords.co.uk

not unknown for typing mistakes or the wrong information to appear in the text. Although wading through a contract can be a bit heavy going, before signing check that any 'extras' you've negotiated with the sellers are actually included – things like additional parking spaces or perhaps the use of a garage sited on a separate plot. If the property is being purchased jointly, for example with your partner, you will both need to sign.

Buildings insurance

There is only one type of insurance that's compulsory when you're buying a property, and that's buildings insurance. All mortgage lenders stipulate that the property must be fully insured in the buyer's name from exchange of contracts. This may appear to be a slightly odd requirement given that the sellers will normally be occupying their home until completion, plus you haven't even finished paying for the property yet. The question is, what would happen if the house burned down in the period between exchange and completion? The answer is that legally a buyer may still be required to proceed with the purchase of the burnt-out ruin. So it's essential that you're covered.

Your new home needs to be insured for what it would cost to rebuild it – which is not the same as the purchase price (which is higher because it includes the value of the land the house is built on). The official rebuild cost for your property can be found in most mortgage valuation reports and all Homebuyer surveys. This is calculated in accordance with the price per square metre for the type of property in the official BCIS reinstatement cost tables.

To work out the total gross external floor area of the building, surveyors measure the outer surface of the main walls for each floor of living accommodation. Outbuildings such as garages will then be added. The precise rebuild cost will obviously depend on the quality of the building, as well as its size, age and location. So a Listed period house will clearly be a lot dearer than a bog-standard 1950s semi. As a rule of thumb, rebuild costs commonly fall within the price range of £1,000 to £2,000 per square metre.

Given the care taken to accurately calculate rebuild costs, it's a little surprising that you can simply pick up the phone and arrange buildings insurance cover just by

It's been a long time coming, but when your solicitor at last confirms that the final version of the contract is ready for your signature it's a sure sign that exchange of contracts is imminent. However, you can't afford to relax just yet.

By now your solicitor should have double-checked that everything is in order – most importantly the searches, the terms of the contract, the title and the funding. This is where a dozy conveyancer will suddenly discover some killer problem that should have been identified and neutralised yonks ago. And there only needs to be one dozy conveyancer in the entire chain to hold everyone up whilst desperate last-minute enquiries are made.

It's worth casting an eye over the contract yourself when it duly arrives for signing, or when you pop down to your solicitors' office to sign it. It's

"Did they say the keys were under the pot?"

stating the property's age and the number of bedrooms. The problem with such shortcuts is that you risk either paying too much or else ending up with insufficient cover. This may not sound too worrying, but if it turns out that you're underinsured, and you have to make a claim, your insurer could then refuse to meet the full cost of the works, no matter how small.

If you're buying a flat or maisonette, the freeholder of the block will normally be responsible for arranging cover, for which you will be invoiced to reimburse your share of the cost.

Getting removal quotes

Unless you're seriously considering taking the DIY route and doing all the heavy lifting yourself (not normally advisable), now is the time to obtain quotes for removals. In most cases this needs to be done before exchange, because by leaving it any later there's a risk that all the decent firms will be booked up. Quotes from three removal firms should be sufficient. The booking can be firmed up directly after exchange.

The best way to choose removal firms is by personal recommendation from friends and colleagues. Otherwise, a good local estate agent should be able to point you in the right direction. To avoid cowboys, it

helps to pick a member of the British Association of Removers, because should anything go seriously wrong you have the reassurance of knowing that you could lodge a complaint or even seek compensation. Other industry organisations whose members follow approved codes of practice include the Removals Industry Ombudsman Scheme and the National Guild of Removers and Storers.

A representative from each firm will duly pay you a visit to try and comprehend exactly how much stuff they'll be dealing with. This may take anything from a brief ten minutes to over half an hour. They will ask whether you're opting for the 'removals only service' or the 'full packing service' (described below). At this stage you may want to keep your options open and get quotes for both services.

Careful planning ahead should ensure a smooth move on the day. For example, any really large, awkward pieces of furniture should be flagged up. Sometimes the only way to accommodate giant four-piece sofas and monster wardrobes is by temporarily removing windows (including upstairs ones). An experienced eye should spot potential obstacles.

If you want them to quote for packing, mention any items likely to require special treatment, such as valuable antiques and paintings. Point out any awkwardly shaped objects, and any exceptionally heavy or bulky items that will need prior dismantling.

Tell them whether you intend to move any items yourself, otherwise you'll be charged for moving anything that isn't bolted down. Ideally write out a list of everything to be moved and give them a copy, not forgetting to include the contents of your garage, loft and garden shed. Make a note of any carpets or curtains that you're taking with you – and who's job it is to prepare them for transportation. The quotes should arrive within about a week.

Removals only

Most people do their own packing, paying only for a removal firm to shift their stuff from A to B. This is a sensible choice that allows you to save money , whilst professional removal staff take the effort out of all the lifting and carrying. Some removal firms will even be happy to loan you dozens of cardboard boxes free of charge a couple of weeks in advance,

Photos: www.pickfords.co.uk

Photo: www.pickfords.co.uk

"It's on the top floor …."

on the condition that they're returned within a few weeks of moving in. Other firms make a small charge per box. Thankfully the use of traditional wooden 'tea chests' with razor-sharp edges is now a thing of the past.

But doing all the packing yourself is an incredibly tiresome and unbelievably time-consuming process, so you may actually be better off opting for the 'full packing service', leaving you free to concentrate on other important tasks.

Full packing service

There's an art to packing correctly so that your stuff doesn't get damaged, smashed or leak all the way to your new home. So if packing isn't your strong point, or you simply haven't got the time, consider paying the extra and opting for the full packing service. Trained staff have the skill to pack your goods safely and get the job done in a fraction of the time that it would take you to do it. On the other hand, some folk would regard sifting through their stuff as too intimate a business to entrust to complete strangers. There's an urban myth that removal men working for some less reputable firms routinely place bets as to whether or not the lady of the house owns a battery-powered 'marital aid'. So you may want to pack any sensitive or especially valuable items yourself.

Comparing quotes

To help assess competitive quotes on a like-for-like basis, it helps if the prices are itemised so that you can compare hourly rates, insurance and packing costs. But price is by no means the only factor. Without wishing to put a dampener on things, it's worth considering what would happen should problems arise. Occasionally, completion doesn't quite work to plan and you could be left stuck at the last minute with a lorry-load of possessions and nowhere to put them. So you want a firm that can provide emergency storage facilities.

One key factor to consider when picking your removal firm is what kind of insurance cover they have. What would happen if the van driver had to perform an emergency stop en route, scrambling your valuable goods and chattels beyond recognition? And are you covered in

the event that something inadvertently goes missing? Insurance is especially important if your goods are going to be left in their care overnight, or if you have high value items. Sometimes the cover that removal firms provide is woefully inadequate, so it might be worth taking personal responsibility for transporting precious possessions. Otherwise your existing contents insurance may provide some additional cover.

Bear in mind also that some removal companies charge more for moves on a Friday and there may be a surcharge for weekends.

With every last penny already allocated, it can be tempting to save money by picking the cheapest removal firm on God's earth. But on top of all the stress of the last few months the last thing you need now is to see your prize assets end up in shattered fragments or being redistributed on eBay. Of course, that doesn't mean you can't still negotiate a 'cracking' deal. But first it's important to consider what level of service you're likely to require.

Exchange of contracts

Before these three magic words can at last become reality there are some key points that must first be checked:

- That your mortgage offer has been received and is correct
- That your funds to pay the deposit have cleared into your solicitor's bank account
- That your survey and searches haven't raised any major worries
- That both sides' solicitors are satisfied with the contract
- That a mutually acceptable completion date has been agreed
- That you have arranged buildings insurance cover on the property

'Exchange' normally involves each side swapping identical copies of the contract documents, one signed by each

party. In practice, however, contracts are actually 'exchanged' verbally by one solicitor phoning the other, the documents following later. Your solicitor will forward the deposit funds to the seller's solicitor and the other side holds this money until completion. Normally you should receive a phone call confirming the good news directly exchange has taken place, at which point a celebration may be in order.

Once contracts have been exchanged you can breathe a sigh of relief, since the deal is binding on both sides. It is highly unlikely that anything will go wrong between exchange and completion. If you pull out now you can say goodbye to your deposit. Indeed, either side backing out could suffer draconian penalties, being open to legal action for all the abortive costs and legal fees.

However it's not entirely unknown for problems to arise at this stage, for example one of the parties could go bankrupt or decide to get divorced. But within the space of a week or two this is highly unlikely.

Insurance

Apart from buildings insurance, there are other types of cover that may, or may not, be worth considering. Banks know that when people are moving house they can be receptive to being sold all kinds of financial 'products'. A few extra quid spent here and there can seem like small beer when you're dealing in hundreds of thousands' worth of property. These are the most common types of additional cover:

■ Contents insurance
Contents cover is always advisable, but some policies have limitations, *eg* where you take in a lodger. Check also whether your possessions are covered during transit, and ask your removal firm for a copy of their policy.

■ Accident, sickness and unemployment (ASU or MPPI)
These policies have been heavily criticised for loopholes and severe limitations on payments, so check the small print. Some policies will not pay out just when you need them most, for example if you resign from your job or if you're sacked. It's possible that your employer may already cover you, making any new policy unnecessary.

■ Critical Illness
If you were unfortunate enough to contract a debilitating illness such as cancer, or have a stroke or a heart attack, so that you couldn't work, this insurance cover would pay off your mortgage. Again, check the small print for limitations and exemptions.

■ Permanent Health Insurance (PHI)
This should pay at least half your salary for a limited period, in the event that you become unable to work. But some employers automatically provide this, so you may already be covered.

Post-exchange

The period between exchange and completion provides a welcome interlude in which to recover your sanity and generally take stock. But after allowing yourself the indulgence of a few moments' peace, the looming enormity of the final ascent becomes only too apparent. In other words, there's suddenly a lot to get organised in a very short time. Once contracts have been exchanged, the agreed completion date is now set in stone, normally taking place between one and four weeks after exchange – a fortnight is fairly typical.

Removals

It's important to contact your chosen removal firm as soon as possible after exchange to confirm the booking. The paperwork should then be signed and promptly returned.

It's a good idea at this stage to agree an approximate timetable with your removal firm so that the people buying your house know your schedule on moving day. You will need to ensure that the removal company has easy access to both properties. Providing a layout plan showing the rooms in your new house will make it a lot easier to identify the correct destination for all the various items. Also check in advance that the massive removal lorry will have sufficient space to park as close to the front door as possible. If there's

no off-street parking, it might be an idea to arrange for cones to be placed to reserve a super-sized parking space.

If you're not moving directly into your new home, you may have to consider temporarily hiring storage facilities for your furniture etc. Obviously the more stuff you've got, the more this is likely to cost. As a rough guide, the contents of a typical two-bedroom house would probably fill up to four containers, whereas an average three-bedroom house can fill up to six containers.

DIY packing

Somehow we always imagine that packing all our stuff can be accomplished in the space of an afternoon, or perhaps even the night before the move (after a couple of fortifying beers down the pub). In reality this is a gruelling process that can drag on for days if not weeks, consuming phenomenal quantities of boxes, containers and sticky tape. Of course, it doesn't help if you're tempted to fondly examine ancient photo albums and browse through all your old books. What you *don't* want to find is that you're still desperately cramming things into boxes with the removal men downing their eighth cup of tea and your purchasers hammering at the door. So it's not a bad idea to give yourself extra time by starting the job of packing before exchange (at the risk of tempting providence).

It pays to start packing non-essential items as early as you can. However a few key things can be left until the day before you move, such as spare clothes, food and kitchen essentials. Make sure each box has plenty of protective padding and clearly mark any that contain fragile or hazardous items, indicating which way up they should go. Pack the heaviest objects at the bottom and the lightest on top and don't overfill boxes. The last thing you want is the bottom dropping out, or your dad suffering a slipped disc. Don't forget to mark on each box where it's supposed to go upon arrival at your new home. Make sure you clearly label boxes; ideally they could even be colour coded for quick reference.

DIY moving

Don't let anyone tell you that doing your own move is an easy option. There may be the small consolation that it's a

Packing materials

Doing your own packing means getting organised with all the necessary packing materials:

- Cardboard boxes (order more than you think you'll need!)
- Plastic storage boxes
- Brown parcel tape and plain sticky tape
- String
- Padding – bubble wrap, styrofoam 'beads', shredded paper, old newspapers etc
- Scissors/knife
- Labels
- Marker pens
- Trolley

Packing tip

Remember to pack all the essential 'hand luggage' items that you're likely to need together in one box. By the time you arrive at your new home it may be quite late, and you won't want to be searching round for kettles, toothbrushes and duvets.

sure-fire way to lose weight quickly, but the same is true of slave labour. This is when you begin to realise that removal firms really do earn every penny.

DIY moving probably isn't the ideal option for those who have amassed assorted junk over decades or an extensive collection of cumbersome Victorian wardrobes. However, there are some occasions when doing your own thing might just be worth a shot, saving you a very useful few hundred quid. Perhaps you're only moving up the road, or maybe you're a first-time buyer without much stuff and rather short on funds. But if you're hoping that it can all be done in a few car journeys, think again. It's more than likely that you'll need a van.

Of course, it's a good start if you've got some decent manpower at your disposal, such as a bunch of (preferably sober) mates willing to do some pushing and shoving. Many hands make light work, so ask the family to help as

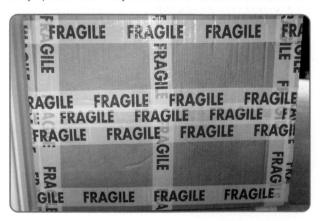

well. But before opting for the DIY route, it's important to do your sums. After accounting for all the costs of van hire, petrol and hiring of cartons and chests, then buying lunch and drinks for your mates, the net savings might not be so convincing.

If you do plump for this option, book your van directly your moving date has been agreed and is legally binding. Hire the largest vehicle you can, as everyone underestimates the sheer volume of stuff that needs to be transported. With a normal car licence the largest van you can hire is a 7.5-tonne box van. Larger vehicles require an HGV licence. Preferably opt for a model with a 'drop-down' tailboard, or ideally an electronic tail winch, to make lifting stuff in and out easier. When you go to collect the vehicle, you'll need to provide suitable ID and a clean driving licence. Some firms provide the Full Monty, including boxes and trolleys. On the day of your move, be sure to make a very early start – the job will inevitably take longer than you imagined.

Conveyancing

With so much going on preparing for the big move, and with exchange of contracts safely out of the way, the daily events at your solicitor's offices may no longer be of such riveting interest. However, in the short period of time between exchange and completion they will still have a number of important tasks to fulfil. The remaining legal stages up to completion are as follows:

1 Checking seller's title
Proof of ownership can be checked by referring to a copy of the title documents, or a summary known as an 'abstract title'. This information is provided by the seller's solicitor, to whom any further questions, known as 'requisitions on title', are now sent.

2 Arranging a bankruptcy search
Two final checks on the seller's financial status are now carried out. A bankruptcy search is necessary because should the seller be declared bankrupt the property could no longer be theirs to sell. It could instead be deemed to belong to a creditor, who might conceivably put a spanner in the works by refusing to agree to the sale going ahead. Also, a final land charges search is instructed to check that the seller hasn't sneakily raised a last-minute loan secured against the property you're buying.

3 Preparing the mortgage deed
Your solicitor will now write to your mortgage lender, notifying them of the completion date. This is to make sure that all the necessary funds will be available in time for completion.

The mortgage deed confirming the lender's interest in the property as security for the loan will therefore need to be checked so it's ready for signing. You will also be asked to provide your solicitor with the money for the balance of the purchase price that's not covered by the mortgage (*e.g.* by bankers draft or telegraphic transfer). Sufficient time must be left for funds to clear

4 Preparing the draft conveyance/transfer document
Your solicitor should receive a draft of the 'transfer document' from the seller's solicitor (for unregistered property this is known as the 'conveyance'). This is the document or 'deed' that will officially transfer ownership of the property from the present owner to you. When both sides are happy, this deed will be 'engrossed', which means a final version is printed ready for both the buyer and seller to sign.

5 Buyer signs the final mortgage deed and conveyance
As the buyer, you will now need to sign the mortgage deed. Both the buyer and seller will need to sign 'engrossed' final version of the transfer document (or conveyance)

6 Collecting stamp duty tax
Your solicitor must now send the transfer/conveyance document to the taxman at HMRC.

Where the purchase price falls within the relevant stamp duty thresholds, they will duly issue a large tax demand on behalf of HM Government, to be paid (on your behalf) by your solicitor upon completion of the purchase.

7 Completion
Transfer of funds is made to the seller's solicitor, who should then confirm that keys can be released to the buyers. Finally, the transfer and mortgage are registered at the Land Registry (see 'Post-completion' below).

Photo: www.pickfords.co.uk

Preparing for completion day

During the 'no man's land' period between exchange and completion there are a surprising number of practical matters that need to be sorted out before moving.

■ Moving date

The date of your move will normally be the same day as completion. However, if you're currently in rented accommodation it's sometimes easier to leave the physical move until the next day. This gives you a clear run, avoiding the risks of the sellers overrunning on time and holding you up, or last-minute delays with keys.

From a practical perspective it's generally better to move during the week rather than at the weekend, since if there are any last-minute hitches – such as with funds or keys not materialising – it helps if the solicitors and estate agents are contactable, which may be more difficult at weekends. Superstitious folk may prefer to avoid completing on Friday13th; but on a more practical note, if you move in late on a Friday and discover a leak its could be harder to get a plumber round without paying an extortionate emergency call-out fee.

■ Budgeting

There may be additional costs when you move in that need to be budgeted for in advance, such as new carpets and furnishings, or any urgent repairs. It's advisable to keep a decent wad of cash handy on the day to pay for snacks, tips and any last-minute emergencies.

■ Empty the freezer

Any frozen food stands a good chance of being ruined during the move, so in the weeks leading up to completion start munching your way through the stuff in the freezer. It's surprising what you find. Once empty, the freezer can be defrosted and cleaned.

■ Chucking it

The packing process will inevitably involve having to trawl through shed loads of old stuff, posing the occasional dilemma about whether to chuck out objects of dubious sentimental value. Then there are all those slightly odd things you've hung on to for years because 'they might come in useful one day' – old offcuts of 4x2, the tent with a hole in it, and that classic carburettor with a bit missing. Your partner will doubtless announce that many of your long-treasured artefacts are valueless tat that should be unceremoniously dumped. Which is a strange thing to say when it's so obviously their stuff that's a total waste of space and is crying out to be recycled. Either way, you'll be getting to know the route to the Council tip rather well over the next week or two.

The more you dispose of now, the less you'll have to pay to be transported so that it can clutter up your next home. If you simply can't bear to chuck it out, try selling it. But car boot sales and selling stuff online can be incredibly time consuming, so you may want to give it away via a local recycling website where people come and collect it.

■ Let people know you're moving

Compile a list of people and organisations that need to know your new address and moving date. Financial institutions like banks and insurers normally need a signed letter with as much notice as possible (even then there's a good chance at least one of them will bollix it up and keep sending confidential information to your old address). It is especially important to check that they have correctly processed this information, as there is a potential risk of identity theft should confidential documents be sent to your old address. Other organisations may accept notification by email or by phone. Likewise, friends can be informed once you've safely moved in.

■ Utilities

Unless you want to spend the first night in your new home huddled around a candle shivering in the dark, be sure to

Who to notify about your new address

- ☐ Banks and Building Societies
- ☐ Credit card / finance companies
- ☐ Pensions, private healthcare, life insurance providers
- ☐ Savings and investment companies
- ☐ Home insurance
- ☐ Suppliers: water and drainage, gas, electricity, oil, LPG, phone, mobile phone, broadband, digital suppliers and TV licensing
- ☐ Car: DVLA for driving licence and vehicle registration, car insurance, MOT, breakdown service
- ☐ Passport office
- ☐ Health: doctor, dentist, optician, gym
- ☐ Education: school, college, university
- ☐ Leisure: magazine subscriptions, gym and club membership, mailing lists, friends, loyalty schemes
- ☐ Services: window cleaner, gardener, online shopping services
- ☐ Government: HMRC, Council Tax, electoral roll
- ☐ Department of Work & Pensions
- ☐ Child Benefit Agency/HM Revenue & Customs

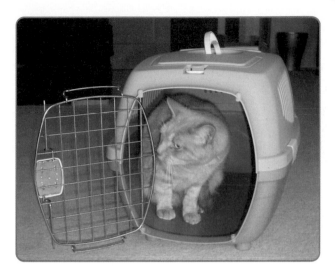

notify the utility companies in good time. Naturally this means being prepared to endure endless queuing systems to call centres scattered throughout the third world. But by preparing yourself for the worst, you could be pleasantly surprised when an occasional supplier actually does their job properly.

Explain that you'll be taking over the present owner's existing supply and that the service is not to be discontinued. Be sure to read the meters at the new property on the day of arrival.

■ Phones and IT

If you're moving to a house with the same exchange code it may be able be possible to transfer and keep your existing phone number. Otherwise it's a case of contacting your landline provider to arrange either to take over the seller's existing number or to request a new one, which will hopefully be ready on the day you move. Make sure you give BT (or whichever provider you use) plenty of warning, especially if you want to order extra new lines in advance;. Cancel your old landlines.

Broadband can take a few days to rearrange. Some rural areas my not have high-speed Internet, but if this is important – for example if you work from home – you will have checked this before buying the property. Similarly, non-urban areas may not have cable TV or Internet services.

■ Arranging care for pets and children

Since moving day is stressful enough without pets and children getting under your feet, it might be worth arranging day care (with friends, parents or relations) so that you can concentrate on the move itself.

■ Accommodation

If you've got a long way to travel you might need to book overnight accommodation.

■ Owner information

If you're still on speaking terms, ask the sellers to jot down the important bits and pieces of information that you'll need to know soon after arriving. This might include stuff like how the burglar alarm works, and where items like the meters and mains water stopcock are located. Ideally, keys should be labelled to save you fumbling around trying to work out which ones fit the garage, conservatory, window locks etc. Information about bin collection, recycling and local services will also be appreciated. Do the same for your own buyers.

Photo: www.pickfords.co.uk

Completion day

As you rise bleary-eyed at the crack of dawn on completion day, the enormity of the logistical nightmare confronting you swiftly becomes apparent. Despite many hours of preparation there will inevitably still be some last-minute packing jobs to complete. Still-warm beds will need dismantling, and, unless you're unnaturally well organised, sheds and garages may yet require a final clearance and sweep through.

The removal firm should have given notice of their scheduled arrival time, perhaps around 8:00am or a little earlier. Once the removal men descend, you may be assigned to tea-making duties and directing traffic. One thing's for sure, time will now fly by.

You should receive a call from your solicitor or from the estate agent during the morning confirming that funds have been successfully transferred and that the keys are ready for collection. Alternatively, the sellers or their agent may meet you at the property. With a bit of luck your old house will be fully cleared by lunchtime, before for the arrival of your purchasers, traditionally around 2:00pm. It's worth agreeing as late an arrival time with them as possible in advance in order to buy yourself some extra leeway. Eventually, the removal van will slowly lumber off down the road, loaded to the gunnels with all your worldly goods. The usual arrangement is to start unloading when you meet them shortly after arrival at their destination.

In the vast majority of cases the move will go smoothly. But before you're entirely home and dry there are two possible problems with the completion process that can occasionally mar a move – money and keys.

Money problems

On completion day, a remarkable thing should happen – the synchronised movement of money up the chain to fund all the purchases of everyone involved. Funds are normally transferred by TTF (telegraphic transfer). This is a slightly archaic system that can take several hours, so if there are any delays the outstanding funds may not actually arrive until the next day. As a result, on rare occasions, non-completion due to non-arrival of funds can happen. Such problems are compounded where completion takes place at the weekend, when banks' and solicitors' offices may be closed.

If someone in the chain doesn't receive the money for the sale of their house it will normally prevent them from completing their purchase, which in turn can hold up completion of the whole chain. This is a potential nightmare, not just because removal firms are booked and ready, but because as a purchaser you are legally obliged to complete on a certain date, and can be held liable for expenses incurred by sellers as a direct result. The inadequacies of the system mean everyone ends up blaming everyone else, until somehow they muddle through to the next day. To get some early warning of any such problems, keep in regular telephone contact with your solicitor or their 'completions department'.

Non-release of keys

If your sellers' solicitors haven't received your completion money, the seller and the agents will be legally prevented from handing over the keys. This won't be the kind of news you're hoping to hear, surrounded by removal men waiting patiently to get on with the job (although this won't be the first time they're experienced such a problem). No matter how nice the sellers are, their solicitors will have advised them of the serious consequences should they kindly allow you access and you

Photo: www.pickfords.co.uk

then fail to complete. If you are prevented from completing on the appointed day through no fault of your own, you may be able to claim compensation from the guilty party, for example where a blunder by a mortgage lender was the cause of the hold-up.

The arrival

Assuming the completion funds have been successfully transferred, upon arrival you should now be proudly grasping the keys to your new home. With a bit of luck the removal van's satnav will have directed them to the right county, and your arrival will synchronise neatly with the

Photo: www.pickfords.co.uk

Photo: www.pickfords.co.uk

sellers' departure, the whole house being clear and vacant by early afternoon at the latest. Clearly your arrival time will depend to a large extent on how far you need to travel.

One of the first tasks is to clearly label each room in the new house, to help the removal team identify where individual boxes and pieces of furniture need to go. This also reduces the chances of you subsequently having to shift a grand piano from the study to the dining room after they've departed.

If the unpacking can proceed without you permanently directing traffic, it's worth taking a few spare minutes to perform some essential tasks, such as meter readings, switching on fridge-freezers and checking that all the agreed fixtures and fittings have been left in place. You may also want to give some of the rooms a bit of clean before you start unpacking food and kitchen utensils, hanging curtains and making beds. But don't completely disappear, because the removals team may need guidance from time to time.

Once the cavernous removal lorry is finally emptied and everything's been brought into the house, the removal team's job is done. Check that nothing's been damaged or broken, in case you need to make a claim for compensation. If you're happy with the job, give them a decent tip – these are low-paid guys who have toiled extremely hard, saving you hours of backbreaking work.

Now you can breathe a sigh of relief. But before cracking open a celebratory bottle, there are a couple of quick checks to perform so that your first night isn't too uncomfortable.

Check the services and read the meters

One of the first things to check upon arrival is that the electricity, gas and the hot and cold water supplies are all doing what they're supposed to do. Does the heating work? Is there a dial tone on the phone line? Doing this as early as possible should give you time to contact the service providers should any have been inadvertently disconnected.

Keep a record of meter readings so that when you get the bill you know you're not being charged for the previous occupants' energy consumption. Meters in external boxes

have standard keys, which the sellers should have left for you, otherwise a pair of long-nosed pliers can come in useful. If you get stuck, duplicate standard keys are available from DIY stores or from service providers.

Fixtures and fittings

How we laugh at stories of miserly sellers unscrewing light bulbs and even removing door handles. In reality few people are that mean, but it's worth fishing out your list of the agreed fixtures and fittings, as some missing items may not be immediately obvious. If there's a gaping hole where the integrated oven used to be, or any other major item is missing, you are within your rights to take legal action to recover your loss (although it would have to be a large enough loss to make it worthwhile). More likely, you may find the sellers have failed to fully clear the house. Perhaps the loft or garage is full of old junk that should have been taken to the dump. In reality there's not much you can do except roll your sleeves up and deliver it into the capable hands of the militant recycling operatives at the Council tip.

Sorting out the paperwork

Once the mountain of unpacking has been whittled down to size and you've settled into your new home, there are some formalities to be dealt with. It's important to safely file away all the documents and correspondence relating to the move as it's easy to lose track of these amidst the general turbulence. The new house should already have buildings insurance that you arranged from exchange of contracts, but the firm providing your contents insurance nay need to be notified.

Post-completion

Your solicitor isn't done quite yet. Their remaining tasks include getting the transfer document stamped, so that the Land Registry can record your legal title to the property along with your lender's mortgage charge noted against

Below: Home sweet home
Right: Have the sellers left all the agreed items?

Legal stages: post-completion

1 Registration of the new title

Proof of ownership of your new home must be registered with the Land Registry, who will promptly publish the address and sale price of the property on the Internet, so everyone in the world can see exactly how much you paid for your house! The names of the new owner(s) will be recorded in the Proprietorship Register and details of mortgages secured against the property recorded in the Charges Register.

2 Land Registry charge certificate

The Land Registry will send a 'Charge Certificate' to your solicitor to confirm that they've recorded the above details, and a copy is then passed to your mortgage lender. If you bought in cash and there's no mortgage or loan secured against the property, the Land Registry will instead send your solicitor a 'Land Certificate'.

3 Completion statement

Now you can see where all the money's gone. The solicitor will send a completion statement listing all costs and fees.

the security. The solicitor will pay your stamp duty tax along with their own fees and charges before sending you a final completion statement showing a breakdown of all the fees and costs. Old mortgages are paid off and any redemption penalties paid. With flats, the solicitor will also notify the freeholder and pay any administration charges. After some weeks the solicitor's completions department will send you copies of all relevant documentation, including your freshly registered title to the property.

Finally, get the kettle on and start enjoying your new home. And don't forget to arrange that house warming party!

24 | BUYING FOR PROFIT

long period of time, or being a developer. As we know from TV schedules packed with property shows, refurbishing and developing, if done correctly, can reap generous rewards. But no matter how gifted an investor or developer you are, ultimately you're at the mercy of the market (see Chapter 1).

Buying opportunities in a downturn

As prices fall you hear a lot in the media about 'buying opportunities'. But demand doesn't decrease at the same rate for all types of property. Some tend to fall more steeply in a downturn than others. For example:

- Flats, especially studios
- Poorly presented properties
- Properties in fringe 'up and coming' areas

Once the green shoots of recovery become established, these types of property also tend to rebound more quickly, until ultimately, in a boom market, buyers will pay almost as much for a house in need of refurbishment as they would for the equivalent fully restored property.

Investment and renovation

For the majority of UK home owners, property has proved to be a goldmine over the years, providing significant wealth. In boom years, many people earned more money from house price rises than from salaries. Despite periodic market downturns, property has one overriding benefit that many other financial investments cannot offer: at the end of the day its value is derived from meeting a fundamental human need – accommodation. In comparison, share certificates or gold bars have little practical value.

Investing in property to make money normally means either becoming a landlord over a fairly

Buying to let

People have to live somewhere. When the sales market is in the doldrums, demand for rented accommodation usually takes off and rents start to rise.

Buy-to-let investors may take a hammering as the value of flats and houses fall during a downturn, but most have done very nicely over the years and know that property, like stocks and shares, is considered a sound long-term investment. At the peak of the market, as many as ten per cent of all mortgages taken out in the UK were buy-to-let. Although banks have reined in funds and tightened lending criteria since then, buy-to-let mortgages are still available to investors with a 25 per cent or larger deposit.

Continuing high demand for rental accommodation isn't only a result of a rise in the overall UK population. Long-term demographic changes, such as a high divorce rate and growing numbers of students, continue to boost demand. Investing in a second property should reap considerable financial rewards over time, with the mortgage paid by renting it out to tenants. As rents increase it may even provide an extra source of income. However, becoming a private landlord should not be seen as a way of getting rich quick. There are a number of risks and it can be very time-consuming, so it's important to first do your homework.

Getting a buy-to-let mortgage

There are some key differences between ordinary residential mortgages and those available to investors. Buy-to-let loans are pitched at a higher interest rate, although a choice of fixed, tracker, discounted and capped rate deals should be available, usually on an interest-only basis. Crucially you will need a bigger deposit on a buy-to-let mortgage because the risks are greater. Most lenders require a 25 per cent or larger deposit, funding only up to 75 per cent of the purchase price. There may also be age restrictions on who can borrow money – such mortgages

typically being the preserve of those aged 25 or over. Lenders will also be more picky about the types of security they're prepared to lend on. Properties must already be in a suitable condition to rent, so dilapidated examples will not normally be acceptable.

One of the big advantages of buy-to-let mortgages is that the amount you're allowed to borrow is primarily based on the property's rental income, rather than being calculated solely from your salary. So if you're self-employed or on a low income, this may allow you to borrow more than you could with a standard mortgage.

Rental cover

Although lenders will ask you how much you earn, what they're primarily interested in is the amount of 'rental cover' – the extent to which the rent exceeds the monthly mortgage payments. There needs to be a pretty sizeable surplus each month. As a guide, you should be aiming to achieve a gross rent of around 140 per cent of the monthly mortgage payments. So if the mortgage costs £600 a month, you would need to generate £840 in rent from your tenants. Different lenders have different requirements, some demanding as much as 150 per cent, others placing more reliance on your salary with less stringent rental cover targets.

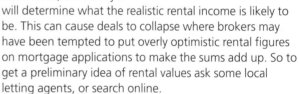

When the bank's mortgage valuation is carried out, the surveyor will determine what the realistic rental income is likely to be. This can cause deals to collapse where brokers may have been tempted to put overly optimistic rental figures on mortgage applications to make the sums add up. So to get a preliminary idea of rental values ask some local letting agents, or search online.

Void periods

If you're relying on the rent to pay your mortgage, what will happen if the property is empty? Obviously it's essential to minimise any such 'voids' between one tenant moving out and recruiting the next one. To cover yourself against shortfalls, try to save any surplus cash left over after paying the mortgage each month. Ideally you want to have enough in reserve to cover several months' worth of mortgage payments. Professional landlords budget for void periods of at least one month per year.

It's perfectly normal to lose a few days' rent through voids from time to time. But what if you just can't recruit a tenant and the void period drags on for ages? Perhaps the rent you're asking is too high, or maybe you're advertising in the wrong place. If the property's looking a bit tired it's likely to require decorating and updating to enhance its appeal (and rental value). If all else fails, you could consider moving in yourself, if it's easier to rent out your main home instead.

'It's important to do your homework'

Are you a potential landlord?

The popular image of landlords is not exactly flattering, being variously portrayed as greedy oafs salivating as the rent rolls in, creepy Rigsby types overcharging for damp, squalid hovels, or hardened criminals with a talent for harassing and evicting vulnerable tenants. In reality a successful lettings business requires the application of sound business skills to provide a professional and well-run service for your tenant customers.

So one of the first decisions that needs to be made is whether you've got what it takes to successfully manage your own properties, or whether to instead entrust it to a letting agent. Clearly, this will depend on how much time you can spare and whether you're personally cut out to play the landlord role. If by nature you're hostile, impatient or easily manipulated, managing tenants probably isn't for you.

Ideally you need to be a 'people person' with good negotiating skills. It's also important to be able to keep a lid on your emotions, so you can handle tenant problems or complaints in a positive manner. You also need to be well organised with basic accounting skills. Being able to turn your hand to the occasional spot of DIY maintenance or repair work can also be a godsend. And it helps to live locally so as to keep an eye on things and be able to dash over in an emergency. Employing a letting agent may make life easier, but it will come at a price, setting you back by as much as 15 to 20 per cent of the rent. By managing it yourself you can also keep a cap on charges for repairs and maintenance.

Do your homework

Before committing yourself, you need to work out your financial bottom line. Calculate what level of rental income you need to break even, once all the mortgage costs, maintenance and running costs have been absorbed. Hopefully there will be some surplus each month to cover voids and unexpected repairs. Try not to overestimate the potential income. Be realistic and assume you can charge 95 per cent of the rent quoted for comparable properties, and budget for at least one void month a year. If it turns out that you actually achieve a better return, that's a bonus.

Picking the right property

Local tenant demand will obviously determine what sort of properties are easiest to let in any given area. But as a rule, flats and small starter homes are popular (unless the local area is flooded with large blocks that developers have struggled to sell). Demand is greatest at this end of the market because there's an increasing demographic trend for people to live on their own. Proximity to local amenities is obviously key for attracting tenants, many of whom may not run cars. So the bus or railway station should be within ten minutes' walk.

In terms of making money, flats normally generate higher yields than larger properties simply because the rent you can charge is higher in relation to the cost of buying them. Of course, if you cram tenants into every room a standard three-bedroom house can be made to achieve an impressive 'headline rent', but this is curtailed by greater voids and management problems.

Being a landlord

Fixing the rent

To judge how much rent to charge for your property, take a look at what similar properties are letting for in the locality on a monthly basis. If you set the rent too low, it may not cover the mortgage payments, and you'll be losing money in unclaimed income. Pitch it too high, and you'll struggle to find tenants – an empty property will quickly lose money as you have to pay the mortgage out of your own pocket.

Picking the right tenants

The golden rule with letting is to make sure your property is generating income as much of the time as possible. This means getting it occupied on a long-term tenancy, or being able to recruit a consistent supply of incoming tenants ready to fill the shoes of those departing. The right tenant is someone who pays the rent every month like clockwork, looks after your property, and doesn't disrespect the neighbours.

Finding the right tenant means first considering what your target market is. In other words, what kind of people would want to live at your property? The answer will depend on several factors:

- **Size** – One-bedroom flats and studios are likely to appeal to singletons or couples on a budget. Larger flats and starter houses should attract young professionals. Families are obviously going to prefer larger houses with gardens.
- **Location** – The perfect location to buy rental property is in an area swarming with suitable tenants. Demand will normally be greater for properties with good proximity to transport links, offices, shops and factories. Universities, colleges and hospitals are all fertile sources of tenants (although some landlords prefer not to rent to students). Employees of certain businesses may be attracted to specific locations conveniently situated for their work. The postcode area can dictate whether a property would appeal to more upmarket tenants.

Convenient for station

Photo: wikimedia

Photo: wikimedia

Some landlords prefer not to let to students

- **Quality** – Dingy decorations and cheap fittings will deter more discerning, professional tenants.
- **Amenities** – You can broaden a property's appeal by stressing peripheral features such as gardens, garages and storage space, or by being willing to accept pets.

Attracting tenants

Even if you're not planning to employ a letting agent, most offer a one-off 'finding and signing' service, perhaps for the price of a month's rent. But that's a fair old chunk of money. The cheapest way to recruit tenants is via word of mouth, so ask work colleagues and friends if they know someone looking for a place to rent. Put a note on the notice board at work and email everyone in your address book. Normally, however, you will need to advertise. Start by placing a small classified ad in a local paper, or in a free sheet that covers your area. You don't need to spend a fortune advertising, so avoid national papers and glossy magazines unless you're aiming at the premium end of the market. Free online listings can be highly effective on sites such as **gumtree.co.uk**.

When you receive email enquiries or phone calls from prospective tenants, ask a few simple questions to weed out obvious fruitcakes, mad axemen and fraudsters. Ask them how far they have to travel to work, their occupation and whether the flat's for themselves or for a couple or group. Ask 'What sort of place are you ideally looking for?' because they may have the wrong end of the stick, and this helps save time by ruling out fruitless viewings.

Showing and vetting

If there's an avalanche of interest it can save time if you hold open-house viewings, where you show the property to several prospective tenants simultaneously over a couple of hours. This needs to be organised so that people aren't left completely to their own devices. To save having to answer the same question a hundred times, it's a good idea to issue would-be tenants with a basic information sheet covering things like the date it's available, the rent, the term, whether it's furnished, and any restrictions such as pets and smoking.

No matter how charming a prospective tenant may seem, there are plenty of cases of Jekyll and Hyde

characters who, once safely ensconced in their new home, then proceed to make their landlord's life a misery. So it's essential to take precautions so that you don't get taken for a complete mug. Someone who fails to pay the rent or damages your property will cause immense stress and expense, especially if you have to resort to eviction. So ask all prospective tenants to complete a form providing basic information – see the accompanying boxout.

You will need to contact their current or previous landlord and check whether they have a good track record paying their rent on time. But be aware that if a landlord is desperate to get rid of an abominable tenant they may try to conceal the shocking truth. Also ask for an employers' reference confirming their salary and how long they've worked there.

Some prospective tenants arrive already equipped with reference letters from landlords, or even a copy of their credit file from a credit reference agency. This may demonstrate a commendably businesslike approach, or it could be an attempt at deception, with the references written by a mate. Tenants who turn up armed with suitcases full of cash but no evident source of income should be treated with suspicion, as there's a fair probability of the funds emanating from illegal activities such as drugs, pimping or money laundering.

Once you're ready to confirm your choice of tenant ask for the name of a guarantor, such as a parent, who can agree to pay the rent should the tenant default. As a precaution, it's worth paying a small fee for a credit reference check revealing any history of debts or non-payment.

At this stage everything will be sweetness and light, so it's a good time to remind them of how and when the rent is to be paid (*eg* by monthly standing order) and that all the household bills, including Council Tax, are the tenant's responsibility. Explain in writing what the landlord is responsible for (*eg* keeping the flat in good repair, maintaining the heating system etc) and what the tenant's duties are (keeping the garden tidy, keeping windows clean, not causing damage etc). Provide a list of restrictions, such as no redecoration or alterations to be made without your written permission, and noise to be kept down between certain hours.

Once you've decided which tenant is the right one for you, a mutually convenient moving-in date will need to be agreed. Before signing the contract and handing over keys you will need to collect the deposit money and the first months' rent (paid directly into your bank account or by banker's draft). The tenant will need your bank details so that a direct debit for monthly rent payments into your account can be set up.

Contracts

All new residential lettings automatically become Assured Shorthold Tenancies (ASTs), unless specifically agreed otherwise. Each side's rights and responsibilities are set out in a tenancy agreement. This is a written contract which each tenant will need to sign, along with the landlord. You don't have to pay a solicitor to do this, as AST tenancy agreement forms can be purchased from a legal stationers.

You simply need to fill in the blanks in the contract, such as the rent and the date it's due to be paid (usually monthly), the deposit, and the term of the tenancy – *ie* how long it lasts.

Once you've completed two copies of a tenancy agreement, both landlord and tenant should sign each one in the presence of a witness who also signs, and should keep a single copy each.

Assured Shorthold Tenancies start with an initial fixed rental period, usually six or twelve months, although you can make this as long as both sides want. Most opt

Tenancy information form
- Tenant's full name and address
- Contact details: mobile, landline, email
- Current landlord: name, address, mobile, landline, email
- Work contact details and name of employer
- Suitable contact for a character reference (*eg* a friend of the family)

TENANCY AGREEMENT F301

(for a Furnished House or Flat on an Assured Shorthold Tenancy)

The PROPERTY   69 Eviction Street, Ocean Heights, Kent ME109

The LANDLORD   MR RIGSBY

of   Rackman Mews, Eviction City, Liverpool 8

The TENANT   A. Homewrecker

The GUARANTOR

of

The TERM   6   weeks/months* beginning on   12th Never 2012

The RENT   £ 550   per week/month* payable in advance on the   25th of each week/month*

The DEPOSIT   £   which will be registered with one of the Government authorised tenancy deposit schemes ("the Tenancy Deposit Scheme") in accordance with the Tenancy Deposit Scheme Rules.

The INVENTORY   means the list of the Landlord's possessions at the Property which has been signed by the Landlord and the Tenant

DATED   01 Jan 2011

Signed and executed as a Deed by the following parties

Landlord   MR RIGSBY   Tenant   A. Homewrecker   Guarantor*

Landlord(s)' name(s)

Rigsby   Tenant(s)' name(s)   *A. Homewrecker*   Guarantor's name

Landlord(s)' signature(s)   Tenant(s)' signature(s)   Guarantor's signature

In the presence of:

Witness signature   ConMan 1   Witness signature   ConMan 2   Witness signature

Full name   address   Full name   address   Full name

Address   address   Address   address   Address

address   address

THIS TENANCY AGREEMENT comprises the particulars detailed above and the terms and conditions printed overleaf whereby the Property is hereby let by the Landlord and taken by the Tenant for the Term at the Rent.

for six months. You can't repossess the property during the initial term unless the tenant violates the terms of the agreement (and even then it's not easy). You also can't increase the rent or revise the terms of the agreement. So it's often better to stick to a shorter initial term, which may also suit the tenant better because they are legally liable for paying the rent for the whole initial period, even if they move out after the first week.

When the initial fixed term comes to an end, you can then either renew it by signing another similar contract or just do nothing, in which case the tenancy will continue on a 'periodic' basis, normally running from month to month. The tenant has no security of tenure after the end of the term that you stipulate. As long as you give the necessary two months' written notice using the appropriate 'section 21 notice' (available from stationers) you are certain to gain possession and can move into the property yourself (but see 'Eviction and courts' below). When the tenant wants to leave they need only give the landlord one month's notice.

Inventories

To cover yourself in the event of a dispute arising later about the condition of the property, it's important to keep some kind of record before the tenant moves in. So take large numbers of photos and write out an inventory listing all the contents. Go through this list with the tenant before they move in, and agree the condition of fixtures and fittings – and also the furniture if you're letting on a furnished basis. Then get them to sign a copy to confirm their agreement. If, at the end of their tenancy, there's any

damage or something's missing, you've got proof to justify deducting the cost from the deposit.

Deposits

The purpose of a deposit is to cover the landlord against the cost of making good any damage, or for any excessive cleaning that's required when the tenant leaves. Departing tenants are supposed to return the property in the same condition as when they moved in (allowing for fair wear and tear). The tenant should be made aware that reasonable deductions can be made for damage such as

Deposit protection schemes

Landlords must ensure that tenants' deposits are legally protected. There are two types of scheme. 'Custodial schemes' are free to use but landlords must submit the deposit money for safekeeping. With 'insurance schemes' landlords keep the money along with any interest earned but pay a premium to insure the deposit. The three main service providers are:

- The Deposit Protection Service (custodial scheme)
- The Tenancy Deposit Scheme (insurance based)
- Tenancy Deposit Solutions Ltd (insurance based)

The landlords must give the tenant written details of the scheme used to protect their deposit within 14 days of taking the money. At the end of the tenancy, the agreed amount of deposit should be paid back to the tenant within ten days. When landlord and tenant disagree, the schemes will retain the disputed amount until an agreement is reached. Landlords not joining a scheme can be fined three times the value of the deposit, as well as having to refund the deposit to the tenant. They will also be restricted from evicting tenants using the normal 'notice only' procedure.

cigarette burns or bad stains. It also provides some reassurance in the event of the rent not being paid.

However, one of the main complaints from tenants over the years has been about unscrupulous landlords failing to return deposits. To remedy this injustice all deposits must now by law be covered by a protection scheme. These schemes ensure repayment of the deposit to tenants at the end of a tenancy after deducting any agreed amounts for damage or to cover any shortfall in the rent. They also offer a free dispute resolution service to sort out disagreements between landlords and tenants about how the deposit should be divided when the tenancy ends. Disputes will only go to court if the landlord and tenant agree not to use this service.

Rent collecting

Tenants will normally have completed a direct debit form when the contract was signed. Once their bank has processed this instruction, the rent should be paid automatically into your account on the agreed date each month. This is far better than messing about with cash or cheques, with the added hassle of having to chase late payments.

It's sometimes advisable to arrange the timing of monthly payments so that they come out of the tenant's bank account the day after their salary goes in. This gives you first call on their money, although it may not synchronise with your own monthly mortgage payment dates. It's also a good idea to include a clause in the tenancy agreement that stipulates there will be a charge for late payment of rent.

Maintaining the property

All that lovely rent money comes with price tag. If you're managing your own property rather than paying an agent there will inevitably be some routine maintenance to carry out from time to time.

If you're not much of a DIY genius, consider finding a local handyman who is. This is essentially all that lettings agencies do, passing the full cost to you plus an extra charge for their trouble. Landlords have a legal duty to maintain let properties in a safe and habitable condition, so you need to deal with maintenance requests from your tenants quickly and professionally, no matter how inconvenient. Happy tenants make good occupants (usually).

The good news is that you can claim repairs against rent for income tax. You can also claim back a sizeable chunk of the cost of installing insulation in let properties as part of the 'Landlord's Energy Saving Allowance'. However, home improvements such as refitted kitchens and bathrooms won't reduce your income tax bill, but can usually be offset against Capital Gains Tax when you later come to sell the property.

Getting the occasional urgent phone call at any time of the day or night goes with the territory of being a self managing landlord. You are your tenant's emergency

Photo: www.savrowstilts.co.uk

There will inevitably be some maintenance jobs to carry out – some more routine than others

199

service, for which you are earning the sizeable fee that would otherwise go to a letting agency. The first task when you pick up the phone is to assess how urgent a problem is, so it helps to have at least a rudimentary knowledge of plumbing, heating and electrics – the most common problem areas. If there's a water or gas leak, tell the tenant to turn off the supply at the stopcock or the meter. Then visit the property to fix the problem, or arrange a contractor to carry out urgent repairs. Boilers, heating and hot water systems should be covered by an annual maintenance contract. Systems that are regularly serviced should run smoother and last longer, plus there's an emergency number for the tenant to call. It's also essential as a landlord to comply with the law requiring a number of safety measures, otherwise you could end up being fined several thousand pounds or even imprisoned – see the boxout.

Landlords' safety measures

- **Smoke detectors** must be installed on every floor. Although this technically applies only to properties built after June 1992, smoke alarms should be provided in all properties as a matter of course. Anything that potentially saves lives and prevents your property from becoming a burnt-out wreck has got to be money well spent.
- **Gas appliances** must have an annual safety check by a CORGI-registered engineer, and a gas safety certificate handed to your tenant.
- **Furniture** provided by landlords must be fire-resistant in compliance with the 1988 Fire & Safety Regulations. Second-hand furniture that predates 1988 should be avoided. If in doubt, chuck it out.
- **Houses In Multiple Occupation** – an HMO is a property shared by a number of unrelated people. Generally this would comprise an entire house or flat which is let to *three or more tenants* who form *two or more households* and who share a kitchen, bathroom or toilet. A typical example would be a shared student house or a property split into bedsits or flats. Where an HMO is three or more storeys high (including basements), and is occupied by five or more unrelated tenants, by law the landlord must apply for a licence from the local council before letting. This requires properties to meet special standards in terms of their size, amenities, fire precautions, and escape from fire, as well as in their overall state of repair. The cost of a licence itself is typically around £500, although some authorities charge up to £2,000.

Problem tenants

Despite taking sensible precautions, you could be unlucky and get stuck with a rogue tenant. This is most unlikely to involve blatantly obvious anti-social behaviour such as openly dealing drugs or running a brothel from your cherished abode. It's also unlikely that tenants will persistently fail to pay the rent, deliberately damage the property or continually annoy the neighbours. You're more likely to encounter less brazen, yet immensely irritating problems, such as always being a few days late with the rent, or doing something in breach of the tenancy agreement, like smoking or keeping pets. This may not warrant eviction, but even if it's a minor concern you should keep a record of it.

Eviction is normally a last resort because it can be emotionally stressful for all concerned, as well as costing a fortune in lost rent and legal fees. But if rent is consistently paid late, action will be required. Write to inform the tenant that late payment is a breach of their tenancy agreement. If it continues, instruct a solicitor to write to them, making the same point. If you included a clause in the tenancy agreement imposing a fine for late payments, inform them that an amount will accordingly be deducted from their deposit.

It's not unknown for tenants to invite their boyfriend or girlfriend to move in with them, strictly in breach of contract. Should this become apparent, you need to talk to them to find out what's really going on. A temporary guest may be acceptable for a couple of days, otherwise the newcomer will need to move out, or be formally added to a new tenancy agreement and start paying rent. Noisy tenants should be spoken to in a formal but non-aggressive manner, and if the problem continues, issued with a written warning.

Because tenants are liable to pay the rent for the full initial term, they may be tempted to do a midnight flit still owing you some rent. However, this shouldn't be a major problem as regaining possession and renting out the property to new tenants can be achieved fairly swiftly, and their deposit should cover a minimum of a month's rent. But before taking drastic action, be sure to check that they haven't just gone on holiday!

Where you have several housemates sharing your

Photo: wikimedia

property, one may wish to move out early. In such cases you are within your rights to retain the full deposit until all the occupants (*ie* the signatories to the tenancy agreement) have completed their term and all moved out. The person leaving early will need to sort out their deposit with the other tenants. If the remaining tenants can't find someone else to move in, they will be responsible for paying the full amount of the rent, as per the tenancy agreement.

Eviction and courts

Evicting a non-paying or disruptive tenant can be a long and expensive process and cannot be done without a court order. The first step is for the landlord to instruct a  solicitor to serve an eviction notice claiming possession (at the landlord's expense). Providing the correct notice is served, the court must make a possession order, assuming the tenant is at least two months in arrears with their rent (on the date the notice is served as well as on the date of the court hearing), or has been doing something in breach of their agreement for at least eight weeks. The court will then normally grant an order for possession in 14 days, although the tenant can extend this for up to a total 6 weeks on the grounds of hardship. Even when the date for possession has arrived, you can only enforce it by instructing the county court bailiff – which can take another month.

In cases where the tenant owes rent, most tenants will be keen to avoid being taken to court because they'll end up with a CCJ (County Court Judgment) against their credit record. So the threat alone may do the trick, magically eliciting the rent that's due. Otherwise the aggrieved landlord has to complete a form (provided by the court) explaining the amount of rent owed, and any losses incurred such as any possessions that have been stolen or any damage caused. If you win, you should be entitled to recover the court costs from the tenant, who can either choose to pay up or alternatively counterclaim against you. Often it is the judge who decides the outcome. But if the tenant simply can't afford to pay, you may be advised not to proceed further.

If the case does go to court and a CCJ is made against the tenant, for the rent owed, the judge will decide how much should be paid over what period of time, perhaps being deducted from the tenant's wages. If the tenant then refuses to pay in breach of the CCJ, a bailiff can remove goods to sell and pay the debt.

Letting agents

If reading the above has put you off the idea of being a hands-on landlord, you might prefer to sacrifice some of your hard-earned rent and pay a letting agent to deal with all the hassle instead. The advantage of appointing an agent to manage things is that they're already geared up for recruiting, vetting, signing up and managing tenants, as well as collecting rent and handling out-of-hours emergencies.

The disadvantage is that not all letting agents do a particularly professional job. There's rarely any guarantee that tenants will pay the rent, and void periods can still occur. When emergencies happen, they will probably pick up the phone to you, which is not much different from being bothered directly by the tenant, although the agent should be able to appoint a contractor to fix things (at your expense). The main disadvantage, of course, is that the fees will eat substantially into your profits. Before appointing an agent it's worth bearing in mind that most let properties require very little management and, on the whole, things run pretty smoothly. Which may explain why cynics sometimes claim that running a lettings business is money for old rope.

One point of concern is that lettings agents are even less regulated than the Wild West world of estate agency and there are few barriers to prevent cowboys and crooks setting up in business. A lot of estate agents dabble in lettings as a subsidiary service to boost profits when the sales market is struggling, and some may have

Before you sign the contract

Not all letting agents are the same. The following points should be considered:

- Is the agent fully insured? They should be a member of the Client Money Protection Scheme, which provides indemnity insurance that safeguards your rent and your tenants' deposits.
- Check that you can cancel the contract by giving no more than 30 days' notice.
- Confirm exactly how and when the rent will be paid to you.
- Check how often the agent reports to you – which should be at least on a monthly basis – and check who is responsible for paying expenses such as mortgages and insurance.
- Obtain a clear written list of the services they provide, not just vague promises.
- Have your solicitor check the contract, which will be written in their interests, not yours.

What's included in the full management service?

These are the services that an agent should provide as part of a full management service:

- advertising, recruiting and conducting tenant viewings
- vetting and selecting tenants
- preparing the tenancy agreement
- writing inventories
- collecting rent and paying the net balance to the owner
- providing regular accounts
- regular condition checks of the property
- organising repairs and maintenance, liaising with and invoicing the owner
- enforcing the terms of the tenancy agreement
- dealing with tenants' complaints
- checking out departing tenants, returning deposits and collecting keys

no qualifications and little experience. So if you do decide to employ a letting agent be sure to carefully check their credentials. Pick a member of ARLA (the Association of Residential Letting Agents), or the government-backed NALS (National Approved Lettings Scheme). If the partners in the firm are members of the RICS (Royal Institution of Chartered Surveyors) so much the better, since it means rigorous standards should apply.

Levels of service

You can select the level of service that suits you best – you don't have to opt for the full management service. The options are as follows:

Service	Typical charge
Full management service	15% of the monthly rent
Rental collection only	12.5% of monthly rent
Finding and signing tenants	One month's rent or 10% of monthly rent

However, charges vary widely. Some agents charge a lower percentage but have fixed fees for things like filling in contracts. Some charge a one-off 'finding fee'. Most agents operate on a 'no let no fee' basis, receiving a percentage of the collected rental income for managing the property. So it may be worth appointing more than one agent to increase the chance of letting your property quickly. A few firms charge a flat fee per month, but normally the best option is for the management fee to be charged as a percentage of the rent actually collected each month, since this motivates the agent to collect it on time.

Property development: buying to renovate

Whereas becoming a landlord investor is a long-term business, making money from property renovation or development can achieve far quicker results. Instead of simply riding the currents of the sales and rental markets, here you're adding real value and aiming for as swift a turnaround as possible.

The thing both businesses have in common is, as we saw earlier, the influence of the market. You need a stable or rising market as a backdrop to property development, unless you're wealthy enough to sit on a land-bank for years waiting for things to pick up. Although it obviously helps greatly if the market is pointing in the right direction, if you're serious about making money from property you must outperform the market, not just ride it. This depends on getting three things right:

- Buying the right property
- Adding value with the right improvements
- Minimising your overheads

Buying the right property

Buying a suitable property to 'do up' and sell at a profit means being able to assess its potential to make money. This will depend on its location, its condition and whether there's any development potential. Auctions can sometimes be a fertile source of refurbishment projects, as can specialist websites like **www.pickupaproperty.com**.

LOCATION

In a nervous market the quality of location becomes more significant. While opportunities can arise to buy in good-quality areas that were previously unaffordable, it also becomes more important to avoid properties with obvious negatives – like busy roads, or flats above chip shops and dry cleaners.

If you're looking to speculate over the medium to long term, proposed infrastructure changes such as new rail or road links can cause a sea change in the perception of an entire area. If you spot this early enough, you may reap big rewards.

CONDITION

To make money, you need to focus on improvements that add value in the eyes of a buyer. Buying a property that is structurally sound and watertight will leave you more money in the bank to spend on the visible improvements that matter to buyers, and therefore justify a higher price tag. The trick is to pick properties that aren't too hopeless. Reject those that are likely to need expensive structural work, especially to walls and roofs. You want to refurbish, not rebuild. There are two types of property to avoid in particular:

- Houses that were originally built to a cheap, sub-standard quality
- Buildings that have suffered from incompetent DIY 'improvements'

Poorly-built older properties may have missing party walls in lofts, rear additions built from wafer thin brickwork, and weak under-structured timber floors. As if that wasn't bad enough, incompetent DIY alterations are sometimes found where chimney breasts and load-bearing internal walls have been illegally removed without Building Regs consent.

What you really want is a shabby specimen that 'looks worse than it is', perhaps simply in need of a thorough decorative makeover and updating to kitchens and bathrooms. But appearances can be deceptive. Sometimes expensive well-decorated properties conceal serious problems, such as potentially dangerous structural defects or hidden damp and timber decay. A roof that needs replacement can deter even the most determined of renovators, but don't be put off by a minor leak at a flashing or a slipped tile or two. Such defects can look fairly off-putting and scare away rival buyers, but can justify a low price and are often reasonably cheap to fix.

In most properties suitable for refurbishment you're likely to find that the electrics, plumbing, hot water and heating systems are getting on a bit and will need updating, or at least partial replacement. Planning a successful refurbishment means being able to tell which bits are genuinely knackered and need replacing, and what merely looks scruffy but is actually salvageable. Even dire-sounding afflictions like asbestos, beetle infestation and structural movement are not unusual in older properties and in most cases probably aren't serious. Judging what's serious and what isn't is the skill of the surveyor. So if in doubt, take professional advice. See 'Find a surveyor' on website.

IS THERE POTENTIAL TO DEVELOP?

There is more to property development than simply 'retro-fitting' rundown old houses. To make serious money, it often helps to spot an opportunity for:

- Adding extra accommodation. Is there potential to extend or add loft accommodation? Redundant buildings can sometimes be converted into flats (subject to planning permission for 'change of use').
- Building a new dwelling. Is there potential for squeezing a new house onto an existing plot, for example by demolishing an old garage? Corner plots can sometimes offer such develoment opportunities. The major obstacle to adding value through development rather than refurbishment is gaining planning permission.

Corner plots may offer potential to extend or develop

BUDGETING

There are five key questions you need to answer when planning a development:

1. How much will the property realistically sell for once refurbished?
2. What's the lowest purchase price I can negotiate?
3. What will it cost to refurbish?
4. How much will the fees be for purchase, sale and professional advice?
5. How much will the loan interest cost for the duration of the works plus the time it takes to sell?

To get an idea of the price that you'll ultimately be able to achieve when selling the refurbished property, check the 'ceiling' prices that have actually been achieved in the same street as well as in the broader area – see website. Seek the opinion of local agents. You will then need to factor in market predictions over the next 6 to 12 months. The lower end of the price range should give some idea of prices paid for properties in need of updating.

To work out how much profit you can expect to make, you need to draw up a development budget. Of course, at this stage it's natural to be dead eager and want to crack on with the job. But the main reason for projects running over budget is, quite simply, badly drafted budgets. Get this wrong and you could end up slaving away for peanuts. So it's essential not to rush this. Be sure to include all those hidden buying and selling costs that eat away at profit margins – such as legal, mortgage and survey fees, most of which are geared to the value of the property.

Budgeting for refurbishment works will always be more difficult than for newbuild because you have to allow for the cost of any hidden defects. Prices of materials are easy to research online or by simply walking into your nearest DIY store. Labour rates, on the other hand, are more directly affected by supply and demand, and can vary significantly from area to area. It's not unknown for builders to stick on an extra 20 per cent for jobs in posh postcode areas – if they think the market will bear it.

At the end of the day, if the figures stack up and provide a profit margin of around 20 per cent you should be on to a winner. But just in case, always have a contingency up your sleeve (how much would it let for?).

Adding value

To develop successfully you need to understand what buyers in the local market really want – something estate agents usually know pretty well. By making the right improvements, *ie* the ones that add value in the eyes of a buyer, you should be able to demand a higher price when you come to sell.

■ What improvements add most value for buyers?

Consider who is likely to want to buy your property, *eg* young professionals or families? Then decide what features matter to these buyers.

Many buyers are strongly influenced by first impressions, especially decoration, lighting, kitchen and bathrooms. Smooth-plastered wall and ceiling finishes usually go down well, as do neutral plain off-white or cream decorations. They may be less overwhelmed by proud boasts of new drainage systems or damp proof courses since it's normally assumed that a house is already weathertight and structurally sound. Among the things that add to buyers' perception of value are:

- ☐ Kerb appeal: the front of a house makes a big first impression
- ☐ Quality of decorative presentation
- ☐ Kitchen and bathroom fittings
- ☐ Size of accommodation
- ☐ 'Liveability': space, layout and style
- ☐ Original period features
- ☐ Off-street parking and gardens

■ Original features

You can save yourself a lot of work and expense by avoiding unnecessary replacement work. In period

properties, try to retain original features. Don't replace, just overhaul and upgrade – it's cheaper as well as greener. Victorian materials such as naturally-seasoned timber, clay tiles and natural slate were of far higher quality than modern equivalents, and may be salvageable. Restoring original features like sash windows can add value, whereas 'modernising' a classic period house with UPVC double-glazed casements means you could spend thousands and actually reduce the value of the property. So go ahead and strip those original pine floorboards and by all means restore old tiling, cornices, fireplaces and architraves to their former glory.

■ What not to do

Make sure the price of the new fixtures and fittings is in line with the price bracket of the property itself. You can spend too much as well as too little. For instance, putting top-of-the-range fittings in a bog-standard house can look peculiar – and is a waste of money. In one house worth £200,000 the vendor had put in a £25,000 handmade kitchen – definitely a selling feature, but would it really add more than 10 per cent to the price? By spending so much money that a property becomes 'the best house on the worst street' does not normally pay. On the other hand, fitting the cheapest laminate flooring that you could find into a million-pound-plus property would put off discerning buyers, and would therefore be a false economy.

ADDING VALUE ON A BUDGET

The amount of value a particular improvement will add depends not only on what buyers want, but on the extent to which it overcomes a major drawback with the existing property. The good news is that you can still add value, whatever your budget.

■ Small budget: up to £10,000

Brighten the interior

In single-storey kitchen extensions as well as landings and bedrooms, it's often possible to open up ceilings into roof voids, or create a light and airy interior by fitting a skylight or solar tube.

Add parking

Apply for permission to lower the kerb and create off-street parking at the front. This can cost less than £1000, but can add more than £10,000 to the sale price if it overcomes a lack of parking.

Add space

If you've run out of space inside, how about building a good-quality home office or hobby room in the garden? Modern 'sheds' are smart and fantastically useful – and, in most cases, do not require planning permission. Fully insulated and wired models start at around £5,000.

Photo: Gardenlodges.co.uk

Improve the garden

Many a good house has been rejected because its garden wasn't up to scratch. Putting yours right can cost as little as £1,000 – and add ten times that to the price tag.

Get planning permission

An easy way to add value is by getting planning permission, without doing any building work yourself. Getting plans drawn up for an extension or loft conversion starts at about £1,000 plus about £150 to get them through planning, but could add £10,000 to your home's price tag

■ Medium budget: £10,000 to £25,000

Replace kitchen and bathrooms

It's no secret that good kitchens and bathrooms sell houses. A good-quality fitted kitchen can cost less than £10,000.

Alter the internal layout

Making the most of space you've already got can be done by opening up hallways, removing doorways or repositioning walls to create a more contemporary environment and better use of space. A set of architects' plans for a typical semi starts at about £2,000. But many buyers of period properties expect original layouts, so research this carefully. Structural alterations to spine walls etc must not be done without Building Regulations consent.

Photo: Keuco

Photo: Garageconversion.com

Left: Hedging your bets - part conversion of double garage.
Above: Probably the best ways to add value – converting your loft.

Convert the garage

Converting an integral or attached garage can cost less than £10,000, adding valuable extra space for a bargain price. But this doesn't always add much value. Buyers of starter homes may only expect a car space, buyers of larger properties often want a garage, so getting planning for a new replacement garage is advisable. Also consider converting outbuildings.

Add a conservatory

A conservatory can be a useful short-cut way of building a low price extension. If done well it can add value, *eg* by opening up a kitchen/diner. Otherwise conservatories are perhaps a little out of vogue, suffering from being unbearably hot in summer and chilly in winter.

Add a first-floor extension

Where you have an existing single-storey extension, it may be possible to extend out, building it up to first-floor level, subject to adequacy of foundations. A lot cheaper than building one from scratch, but subject to planning consent.

■ Big budget: £25,000 to £50,000

Convert the loft

Generally considered to be the best way of adding extra space and value, and usually cheaper than building an extension, An extra bedroom with en-suite bathroom is the most popular use of space.

Build an extension

When planning an extension, make sure you do not make the property too top-heavy or bottom-heavy (*eg* a five-bedroom house with only one reception or one bathroom would be top-heavy). Even the dearest extensions are likely to be a snip compared to the cost of excavating a basement. Creating a large kitchen/diner is a popular use of space, and adding extra bedrooms should significantly boosts the value. Permitted development planning rules have recently been relaxed – see website.

Minimising your costs

The third golden rule when it comes to making a profit is fairly obvious but is widely ignored, especially it would seem by TV property developers. You have to *Be mean!* Control your budget as if your life depended on it.

This is an area where smaller operators can beat the big boys by making savings and therefore boosting profits:

■ Living in the property

'Serial home renovators' often live in the properties being done up, before moving on to the next project. Apart from saving on accommodation costs there can be tax advantages.

■ Renting out rooms

Some developers earn extra income from renting out rooms at a discounted rate in properties awaiting renovation. Every little helps.

■ Do it yourself

Tackle some of the work yourself, if you have the skill. Otherwise it can be more profitable to stick to your day job, earning more money than it would cost to pay a professional builder.

■ Make savings on materials

At the outset, calculate the quantities of all the main materials that your project will require. Submit your list to two or three competing builders' merchants for quotes to supply the bulk of your materials.

■ Pick your builders carefully

As always go by recommendation, and check references and their track record on past projects.

■ Don't change your mind

Be clear at the outset exactly what work you want done. Explain it clearly, and then stick with it. Clients who keep changing their minds clock up lots of profitable 'extras' for builders.

Tax

It's essential to keep a lid on tax to minimise your overheads. Listed very briefly below are some of the key issues to consider:

■ Sole trader or limited company?

You have a choice whether to operate as a sole trader or a limited company. For small companies corporation tax is only half the 40 per cent higher rate tax you have to pay on your profit as a 'sole trader'. No further tax is incurred until funds are transferred out of the company into your pocket (*eg* via dividends, or into your pension). As a limited company it's easier to retain more of the profit to carry forward and use in the next development. However, if you are financing property acquisitions with mortgages, ownership through a company could affect your ability to raise loan finance.

■ Income tax or capital gains tax?

Are you are doing up a property with the objective of selling at a profit, or renting it out? In other words are you *trading* or *investing*? Building or refurbishing properties for sale is normally classed as a 'trading activity' subject to income tax. Investment activity, on the other hand, can be taxed under the more generous rules that apply to capital gains tax (CGT). CGT is preferable to income tax, but to qualify as 'investment activity' a property has to be let for the medium to long-term. The longer you've lived in the property as your main residence the better, since profits from the sale of 'main homes' are exempt.

The obvious way to minimise Window Tax, back in the 18th Century

Photo: wikimedia

VAT concessions

Developments that are VAT Free:

- New dwellings.
- Listed Buildings: 'approved alterations' or 'substantial reconstruction' qualify for zero rating (works that require Listed Building Consent).

A reduced five per cent rate applies for:

- Conversions of non-residential buildings to residential use, *eg* a barn, office or warehouse conversion.
- Conversions of houses into flats, or conversions of flats or bed-sits back into a single house.
- Conversions for a 'relevant residential purpose', such as an old people's home.
- Refurbishment of residential properties that have been left empty for two or more years.

Renovation work to properties empty for over ten years will be zero rated, so you can claim back the VAT paid.

■ VAT

Renovation of residential properties is still subject to VAT at the full whack, so you can't recover any of the VAT that you are charged. However, there are some concessions on certain projects – see boxout.

One way of legitimately avoiding paying VAT on all projects is to employ subcontractors who don't need to be VAT registered if their earnings are low enough.

And finally...

Congratulations on making it through to the bitter end. Hopefully this manual has succeeded in throwing some light into the darkest recesses of this country's unnecessarily complex and frustrating home buying system. Knowing how it's all supposed to work can only help avoid the numerous submerged icebergs when steering a course through such treacherous waters.

Talking of disasters, even in the space of time it took to write this book several well-known mortgage lenders were taken over or managed to go out of business – which underlines the fact that the property world is constantly changing. We therefore make a point of updating the Haynes house manuals each time they come up for reprinting. But just in case the Government has a change of heart in the meantime and suddenly decides to abolish stamp duty or waive VAT on property refurbishment, updates can be seen on **www.home-moving.co.uk**.

It only remains to wish you the very best of luck with your sale and/or purchase!

INDEX

Acronyms

ARLA	Association of Residential Letting Agents
AVM	Automatic Valuation Model
BACS	Banks Automated Clearance Service
BCIS	Building cost information service of the RICS
BISF	British Iron & Steel Federation
BMR	Base mortgage rate
BTL	Buy-to-let
BWPDA	British Wood Preserving and Damp Proofing Association
CAM	Current account mortgage
CCJ	County Court Judgment
CHAPS	Clearing House Automated Payments Service
CML	Council of Mortgage Lenders
EPC	Energy Performance Certificate
HA	Housing association
HAT	Housing Action Trust
HCR	Home Condition Report
HIP	Home Information Pack
HMO	House in Multiple Occupation
HSV	Homebuyer Survey
IFA	Independent Financial Advisor
LTV	Loan-to-value
MIG	Mortgage Indemnity Guarantee
NAEA	National Association of Estate Agents
NALS	National Approved Lettings Scheme
NHBC	National House-Building Council
OEA	Ombudsman for Estate Agents
PPI	Payment Protection Insurance
PRC	Pre-reinforced concrete
RICS	Royal Institution of Chartered Surveyors
RSL	Registered social landlord
RTB	Right to Buy
SAP	Standard Assessment Procedure
STC	Subject to contract
SVR	Standard variable rate
TTF	Telegraphic transfer of funds
VAT	Value Added Tax

LC   5/05/09